THE
BATTLE
OF
BARROSA
1811

THE
BATTLE
OF
BARROSA
1811

Forgotten Battle of the Peninsular War

JOHN GREHAN & MARTIN MACE
FOREWORD BY PETE JACKSON, MBE

Skyhorse Publishing

Visit our website at www.skyhorsepublishing.com.

Typeset in Ehrhardt by CHIC GRAPHICS

10 9 8 7 6 5 4 3 2 1

Library of Congress Cataloging-in-Publication Data

Grehan, John.
  The Battle of Barrosa : forgotten battle of the Peninsular War / John Grehan & Martin Mace. -- First North American edition.
    pages cm
  Includes bibliographical references and index.
  ISBN 978-1-62873-724-0 (hardcover : alk. paper) 1. Barrosa, Battle of, Spain, 1811. I. Mace, Martin. II. Title.
  DC233.B38G74 2014
  946'.06--dc23
                                2014011536

Jacket design by Jon Wilkinson
Cover painting by David Rowlands (www.davidrowlands.co.uk): *The Battle of Barrosa, 5 March 1811*, depicting the charge of the 28th (North Gloucestershire) Regiment against the 2nd Battalion, 54th Ligne
Printed in the United States of America

ISBN: JS: 978-1-62873-724-0
Ebook ISBN: 978-1-62914-073-5

Printed in the United States of America

Contents

Foreword

The Battle of Barrosa, 1811: Forgotten Battle of the Peninsular War is a fresh and thought-provoking take on a battle that some Peninsular War historians and authors, in my opinion, have not given the attention it deserves. John Grehan and Martin Mace, in producing this book, have embraced the opportunity to study the decisions taken by commanders from all sides and through applied reasoning they are able to offer sound understanding of those decisions.

Barrosa was a significant encounter for a number of reasons. It was, as one soldier put it, 'an inspiring fight for Englishmen', in that it was won against every possible disadvantage. Not only were the British troops outnumbered, they were also caught totally unprepared as they marched towards Cadiz, and, in part, the French held the high ground and compelled the British to attack uphill. That the British troops succeeded showed that they could beat the French under almost any circumstances, and that they could beat them in the absence of their inspirational leader, Wellington. Possibly even more significant is that defeat at the hands of the French might well have led to the occupation of Cadiz and the capture of the Spanish Government. The consequences of this are incalculable. John and Martin have stated that this makes the Battle of Barrosa the most important battle of the Peninsular War, and they have made their case well.

For the past eleven years I have spent many hours retracing the steps of those commanders and soldiers engaged in the defence of Cadiz and Tarifa during the Peninsular War. *The Battle of Barrosa, 1811*, provides everyone, from the mildly interested tourist to the fully fledged battlefield tour addict, with an all encompassing historical account and thorough understanding of the importance of the outcome of the Battle of Barrosa.

It has always surprised me how so few British people have any knowledge of the battles of the Peninsular War and I have always held the belief that those history books which were available through my school years were not easy reading and therefore discouraging. John's and Martin's writing style is exactly what was missing and I have found their work most engaging. I was compelled to continue turning the pages long after 'lights out'!

There is only one thing left to say. Sit back and enjoy this excellent book

Pete Jackson, MBE
General Manager
Siege Battlefield Tours

Introduction

'A few cannon shots'

It is sadly ironic that the attempted French conquest of the Iberian Peninsula – the longest continuous conflict of the Napoleonic Wars – was supposed to have been achieved peacefully. Napoleon saw the Spanish Royal Family as being weak and inept and the Spanish Government as unpopular and corrupt. With a little skilful diplomacy and a 'few cannon shots', the Emperor of the French believed that he could topple the Spanish monarchy and the country would fall into his hands.

In many respects Napoleon was correct, but he failed to take into account the pride of the ordinary Spanish people. Their government may have been irretrievably incompetent but it was still *their* government, and, when they realised that the Royal Family had been removed to France, the Spaniards took to the streets. The Peninsular War had begun.

Unlike the other countries of Europe that the French armies had overrun, the Spaniards were not prepared to accept Napoleonic rule. In Holland, Belgium and the many Italian and German states, the people had been largely unaffected by the defeat of their armies and the acquiescence of their governments. Life for them carried on more or less as normal.

Not so in Spain. Even though vast tracts of its territory, including its capital, Madrid, were in the hands of the French, the Spaniards never considered themselves beaten because their government remained free and beyond Napoleon's reach. Nor was this a government in exile. The Spanish Regency continued to function openly in its own land, in Andalusia, Spain's richest province.

The British were quick to realise this and, when the French overran Andalusia and the Supreme Junta was forced to run to the fortress-port of Cadiz, Britain offered its help. A squadron of warships and a contingent of troops were soon helping turn Cadiz into an impregnable sanctuary for the Spanish Government.

The Supreme Junta stood aside to allow a nationally elected Cortes to assume legislative powers. Safe behind the walls of Cadiz, the Cortes was able to issue decrees and pass laws as if there was not a single French soldier on Spanish soil.

Providing the Allied forces defending Cadiz took no chances the place would never fall, and Napoleon's 'Spanish ulcer' would continue to bleed dry the blood of his reluctant levies.

The Spanish, though, are a proud people. Not for them was the slow process of attrition. They baulked at being blockaded within the confines of Cadiz and, though their armies had known little other than defeat every time they had engaged the French, the Spaniards concocted ambitious schemes to drive the enemy from their lands.

Their allies, in the form of Lieutenant General Graham, who commanded the British forces at Cadiz, urged caution. As long as Cadiz remained powerfully garrisoned and a Royal Navy fleet rode at anchor in its harbour, it could not be assaulted. Eventually the French would be compelled to withdraw. The Emperor Napoleon had turned his attention to preparations for the invasion of Russia and the Peninsular War had become a sideshow, with many troops being withdrawn to join the forces assembling in France and Germany. All the Spaniards had to do, therefore, was wait.

However, rather than viewing the weakening of the French forces in Spain as a vindication of Britain's prudent policies, the Spaniards saw it as an opportunity to strike a crushing blow against the invader. They envisaged a grand assault upon the French forces besieging Cadiz, one that at a stroke would crush the enemy and raise the siege as a prelude to the liberation of Andalusia and all of Spain. This was all very well, but what if this magnificent operation failed?

Though the Spaniards were capable of great patriotic fervour, the grim reality was that the defence of Cadiz and the security of the Spanish Government depended upon the dour but dependable British. If they were drawn into a battle beyond Cadiz and were defeated, that place, and more importantly the Cortes, would be placed in grave danger. It was not a risk worth taking but this was ignored by the Spaniards who thought only of glorious victory.

Graham repeatedly refused to take part in any such reckless adventures but in the spirit of cooperation he finally succumbed to the appeals of the Spaniards. At the beginning of March 1811 a large Anglo–Spanish force left Cadiz to face the French. A successful sortie would considerably disrupt French operations in the south of Spain, but was unlikely to achieve any more than this. Defeat, on the other hand, would render Cadiz defenceless and might result in the capture of the Cortes and the effective end of organised Spanish resistance. Defeat might well mean victory in Iberia for Napoleon. Never in the course of the entire Peninsular War was there so much at stake.

INTRODUCTION

When, therefore, the opposing forces met on the gentle slopes of the Cerro de Barrosa they engaged in one of the most important battles of the Napoleonic Wars. Victory for the allies would be a fine achievement, anything else would spell disaster.

Raise high the battle-song
To the heroes of our land;
Strike the bold notes loud and long
To Great Britain's warlike band.
Yonder's Barrosa's height
Rising full upon my view,
Where was fought the bloodiest fight
That Iberia ever knew.

The Battle Song William Glen (1789–1826)

Map 1: The Siege of Cadiz 5 February 1810 to 24 August 1812

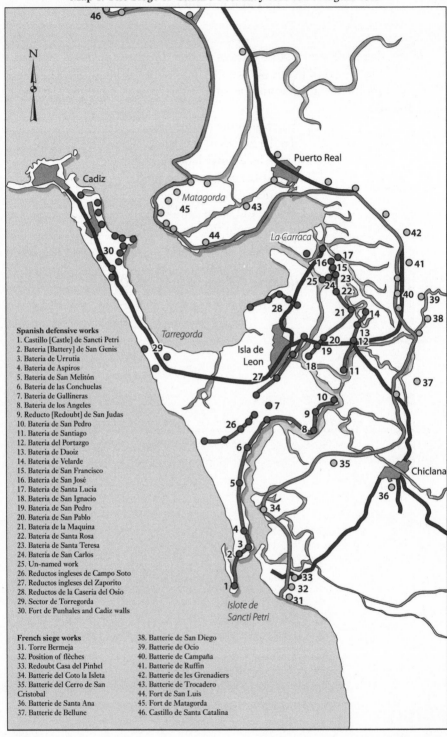

N

46

Cadiz

Puerto Real

Matagorda
45

43

44

La Carraca

42

30

16   17
15
25   23
24   22

41

40

39

38

28

21   14

13
12

Tarregorda

29

Isla de
Leon

20
19

18

11

37

27

10

7

9

26

8

35

Chiclana

6

36

5

34

4

3

2

1

33
32
31

Islote de
Sancti Petri

Spanish defensive works
1. Castillo [Castle] de Sancti Petri
2. Bateria [Battery] de San Genis
3. Bateria de Urrutia
4. Bateria de Aspiros
5. Bateria de San Melitón
6. Bateria de las Conchuelas
7. Bateria de Gallineras
8. Bateria de los Angeles
9. Reducto [Redoubt] de San Judas
10. Bateria de San Pedro
11. Bateria de Santiago
12. Bateria del Portazgo
13. Bateria de Daoiz
14. Bateria de Velarde
15. Bateria de San Francisco
16. Bateria de San José
17. Bateria de Santa Lucia
18. Bateria de San Ignacio
19. Bateria de San Pedro
20. Bateria de San Pablo
21. Bateria de la Maquina
22. Bateria de Santa Rosa
23. Bateria de Santa Teresa
24. Bateria de San Carlos
25. Un–named work
26. Reductos ingleses de Campo Soto
27. Reductos ingleses del Zaporito
28. Reductos de la Caseria del Osio
29. Sector de Torregorda
30. Fort de Punhales and Cadiz walls

French siege works
31. Torre Bermeja
32. Position of flèches
33. Redoubt Casa del Pinhel
34. Batterie del Coto la Isleta
35. Batterie del Cerro de San
Cristobal
36. Batterie de Santa Ana
37. Batterie de Bellune

38. Batterie de San Diego
39. Batterie de Ocio
40. Batterie de Campaña
41. Batterie de Ruffin
42. Batterie de les Grenadiers
43. Batterie de Trocadero
44. Fort de San Luis
45. Fort de Matagorda
46. Castillo de Santa Catalina

Map 2: The Barrosa Campaign

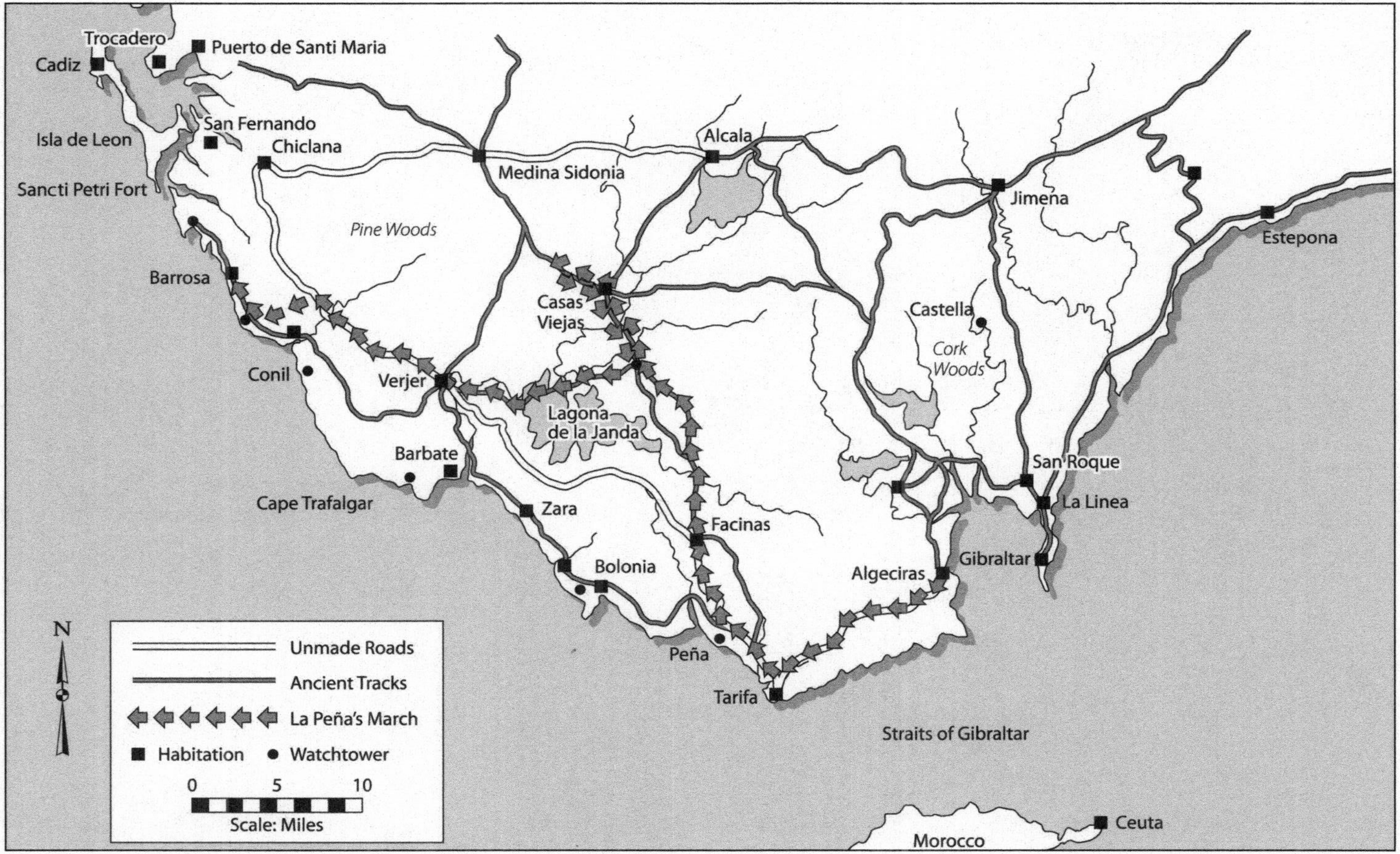

Legend:
- Unmade Roads
- Ancient Tracks
- La Peña's March
- Habitation
- Watchtower

Scale: Miles
0 5 10

Locations shown:
Cadiz, Trocadero, Puerto de Santi Maria, Isla de Leon, San Fernando, Chiclana, Sancti Petri Fort, Barrosa, Conil, Cape Trafalgar, Barbate, Verjer, Zara, Bolonia, Peña, Tarifa, Facinas, Casas Viejas, Lagona de la Janda, Medina Sidonia, Alcala, Algeciras, Gibraltar, San Roque, La Linea, Jimena, Castella, Cork Woods, Estepona, Pine Woods, Straits of Gibraltar, Ceuta, Morocco

Map 3 The Battle of Barrosa, 5 March 1811

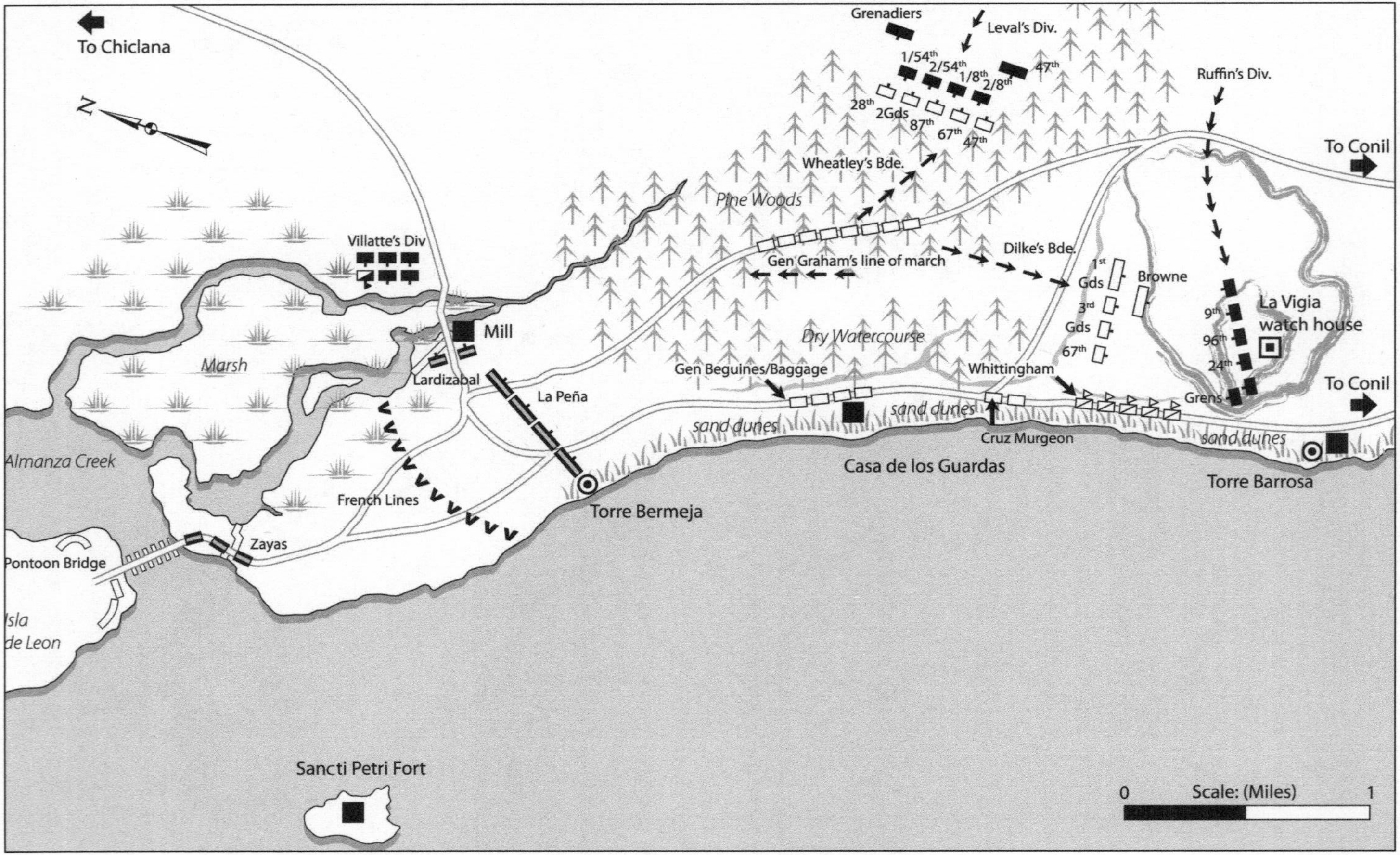

To Chiclana

N

To Conil

Ruffin's Div.

La Vigia watch house

To Conil

9th
90th
24th

Grens.

sand dunes

Torre Barrosa

Grenadiers

Leval's Div.

47th

Browne

1/54th
2/54th
1/8th
2/8th

1st Gds

3rd Gds

67th

Dilke's Bde.

Whittingham

Cruz Murgeon

28th
2Gds
87th
67th
47th

Wheatley's Bde.

Gen Graham's line of march

Pine Woods

Dry Watercourse

sand dunes

Casa de los Guardas

Gen Beguines/Baggage

sand dunes

La Peña

Torre Bermeja

Mill

Lardizabal

French Lines

Villatte's Div

Marsh

Zayas

Almanza Creek

Pontoon Bridge

Isla de Leon

Sancti Petri Fort

Scale: (Miles)

0   1

CHAPTER 1

Saving Spain

A coach drew away from the Royal Palace in Madrid. It was early morning and the departure of the daughter of King Charles IV aroused little interest. Later, another coach pulled up outside the Palace. This time the response would be different. When the *Madrileños* learnt that *Infante* Don Francisco, the last important member of the Spanish Royal Family, was leaving for France, their worst fears were confirmed. Their leaders were abandoning them.

It is said that it was a master locksmith called Molina Soriano who first raised the cry of 'treason'. His call was taken up by the crowd and a group of around fifty Spaniards forced its way into the Palace and confronted the *Infante*. Driven by the excited mob to present himself at a window, Don Francisco's appearance only served to increase the disorder in the streets.

To quell the disturbance, and to make sure that the *Infante* left Madrid as planned, a battalion of French grenadiers marched up to the Palace. It took three volleys from the French infantry to disperse the mob. Around a dozen *Madrileños* were left behind, dead or wounded. It was 2 May 1808 – *El dos de mayo* – the first day of the Peninsular War, of Spain's *Guerra de la Independencia*.

*

Just six weeks earlier, the increasingly unpopular Charles IV had been forced to abdicate the Spanish throne in favour of his son Ferdinand, Prince of the Asturias. But, by then, Charles had already agreed to the passage of French troops through Spain to attack Portugal. It proved to be a terrible mistake as large numbers of French troops were allowed to march into northern Spain. Before the Spaniards realised what was happening, the French had seized control of many of the major fortresses and an army of 20,000 men under Joachim Murat had reached Madrid.

Spain was nominally an ally of France but, in Napoleon's view, one that could not be trusted. Corrupt and inefficient, Spain's government had been entirely dependent for decades upon treasure from its South American colonies. By taking over Spain, Napoleon could secure his southern flank and, at the same time, gain access to the riches of the New World.

So, with northern Spain in French hands and the capital policed by French soldiers, everything seemed set for Napoleon to install a new puppet regime. Indeed, Murat himself, as Napoleon's brother-in-law, expected to be offered the throne of Spain. All that was required now was for the Spanish Royal Family to quietly acquiesce. Prince Ferdinand, however, had other ideas. The day after Murat had arrived in Madrid Ferdinand himself rode into the capital and declared himself King.

This sudden and unexpected turn of events presented Murat with an unforeseen problem – whom should he deal with, the father or the son? Whilst considering his options, the situation became even more confused when Ferdinand's sister sent a message to Murat claiming that her father and mother had been compelled to sign the act of abdication under duress, thus rendering the document invalid.

This was perfect. Nothing could have served the French better than such confusion amongst the Royal Family. At this most crucial moment in Spain's history, with French troops occupying the capital, there was no clear, legitimate head of state. Murat quickly despatched a letter to Napoleon explaining the situation.[1]

It would be weeks before advice could be received from Paris and Murat needed to act quickly before Ferdinand's position became unassailable. Ferdinand was young and popular and far more likely to oppose the French occupation of Spain than his weak, imbecilic father.

Murat therefore prepared two documents for Charles to sign. One was a letter to Napoleon in which Charles begged for the French Emperor's intervention in the royal feud, the second was a proclamation withdrawing his abdication: 'I protest and declare, that my decree of the 19th of March, in which I renounce my crown in favour of my son, is a deed to which is therefore to be considered as of no authority.'[2]

Murat withheld these documents for possible further use, but sent copies to Napoleon. Murat had manipulated the situation very cleverly and, he hoped, for his own ends. With both Charles and Ferdinand refuting each others' right to the crown, it could be argued that the Spanish throne was vacant. Who better placed to accept this vacancy than the man on the spot, the Grand-Duke of Berg, brother-in-law to Napoleon the Great – Joachim Murat?

Napoleon concurred with Murat's assessment of the situation, but it would be someone with Bonaparte blood in his veins that would be King of Spain, not just one of the in-laws. The throne would be offered to one of Napoleon's brothers. Though his younger brother Louis would wisely refuse the honour when approached by Napoleon on 27 March, his elder brother Joseph was later bullied into accepting – and Spain would have its third king in almost as many weeks. All the Emperor had to do now was encourage the Spanish Royal Family to quietly leave the country and place itself in French custody and, incredibly, that is exactly what happened!

Ferdinand and his parents, and most of the senior members of the Royal Family, were persuaded to travel to Bayonne in southern France to settle the dispute, with Napoleon as arbiter. The only royals left in Madrid were one of Charles' second cousins, the Archbishop of Toledo, Ferdinand's younger brother Don Francisco, and his sister, the former Queen of Etruria. Though none of these were figures of any real consequence, Napoleon wanted to remove any member of the Bourbon dynasty around whom any resistance movement could be formed.

But Napoleon did not quite get away with it. The departure of the last members of the Royal Family sparked the riot in Madrid on 2 May. Soon news of the riot spread around the country. Similar uprisings occurred in those northern regions already occupied by French troops. The discontent amongst many sections of Spanish society, which had been brewing for some years over the mismanagement of the country, suddenly found an outlet. An opportunity presented itself for all manner of malcontents to get together and overthrow the old order, each driven by their own agenda, all under the pretext of support for the new regime, for Ferdinand.

When, on 20 May, the official gazette formally announced that Ferdinand had abdicated and that Joseph Bonaparte was to be the new king, the whole of Spain was thrown into a state of utter turmoil. As any imposed government in Madrid would be considered illegitimate, local self-governing, and usually self-appointed, bodies were quickly formed. These juntas became the focal point of the revolt, hastily raising their own armies, combining both the regular forces in their areas and local levies.

These uprisings had to be quickly and mercilessly suppressed before they became too firmly established, and Napoleon ordered his generals in Spain to march against the main centres of resistance. This included a strong force sent into Spain's richest and most influential province, Andalusia. The French column, under the command of General Pierre Dupont, initially numbering 10,000 but later reinforced to a total of 18,000, marched from Madrid, crossing the Sierra Morena to reach Andujar on 5 June.

Dupont's original objectives were to secure Seville with its great cannon foundry, and the port of Cadiz where the remnants of the French fleet under Rear-Admiral Rosily, which had been defeated at Trafalgar in 1805, still remained blockaded in the harbour by the Royal Navy. He was now ordered to extend his operations to deal with the insurgent forces in Andalusia which had formed under the Junta of Seville.

At Andujar, Dupont heard that the whole countryside had taken up arms against the invaders and he sent a message for further reinforcements. Dupont continued his march southwards, eventually forcing his way to Cordoba. After a short, confused fight in the streets of the city, the insurgents fled down the road to Seville, pursued by French chasseurs.

The arrival of the fugitives at Seville caused widespread despair amongst the inhabitants and, if Dupont would have pressed on with his advance, the city would have fallen to the invaders, and Andalusia would have been lost. But the French Commander, magnifying his danger, remained at Cordoba and repeated his earlier appeals for reinforcements. These letters were intercepted by the partisans, giving them fresh hope, and as the days passed and Dupont continued to linger indecisively at Cordoba their fear evaporated and plans were made to surround the French.

For ten days Dupont waited at Cordoba for help to arrive until, on 17 June, he decided to retreat. He made his decision too late. The Spanish General Castanos, in command of some 7,000 regular troops and nearly 30,000 fresh levies, had already sent detachments to occupy the passes of the Sierra Morena and to cut off Dupont's line of communication with Madrid.

With a small Spanish force following cautiously in his wake, Dupont reached the walled town of Andujar without serious incident and he resolved to hold his ground there until he was reinforced. News at last reached Dupont that the first of the reinforcements was coming from La Mancha with a convoy of provisions.

The approach of the French reinforcements prompted Castanos into action before the two French forces could unite. It was arranged that Castanos with 12,000 men would attack Dupont at Andujar whilst another body of 18,000 men under General Reding crossed the Guadalquivir upstream and descended upon Dupont from the rear.

Though another column of troops arrived from Madrid bringing Dupont's force up to almost 20,000 men, it was Castanos who attacked first. Dupont, therefore, moved out of Andujar to Bailén where the second Spanish force under Reding was waiting. But instead of concentrating his forces he sent his battalions into the attack as they arrived on the battlefield.

Dupont's piecemeal assaults were beaten back with considerable loss and Dupont himself was wounded. Dupont called off his attack and proposed an armistice and Reding, who was scarcely able to hold his ground, happily agreed.

Dupont offered to withdraw peacefully to Madrid, but Castanos, thanks to another captured dispatch, was fully aware of Dupont's isolation. He demanded not only Dupont's surrender but also that of the other French forces in the region that had been sent to help him – which Dupont calmly accepted! Though Castanos agreed to permit the French troops to return to France, this did not happen and, with the exception of Dupont and some of his generals, all 18,000 men that surrendered became prisoners of war and never saw France again. It was the first time that one of Napoleon's Imperial armies had laid down its arms and the Emperor raged that 'there has never been anything so stupid, so foolish, or so cowardly since the world began.'[3] When Dupont finally returned to Paris he was imprisoned for the remainder of the war.

The consequences of Dupont's surrender at Bailén were profound. The immediate result was that the newly crowned King Joseph Bonaparte, who had only arrived in Madrid on 20 June, took fright and evacuated his new capital. Imagining that Madrid was about to be engulfed by vast hordes of angry Spaniards, Joseph fled north towards France and did not stop until he was beyond the River Ebro. This was followed by the capture of Rosily's squadron at Cadiz, all six of his warships being seized along with more than 3,500 men.

From that time, Andalusia acquired an ascendancy over the other regions of Spain which only diminished in the latter stages of the war. Seville became the home of the Supreme Junta, begrudgingly acknowledged by the rest of Spain as the nation's provisional government. Andalusia earned its position by force of arms; it retained it by fortune and geography.

The insurgents across Spain were inspired by the French defeat at Bailén, and at Saragossa and Gerona the French forces sent to seize these places were repulsed. 'The unhappy business of Bailén', wrote Count Dumas, 'had, in the space of a few days, changed the position of the French army, animated the nationalist and anti-French factions, and disconcerted all the Emperor's plans.' It was clear that Napoleon would have to go to Spain himself 'to get the machine working again' as he put it.[4]

After settling affairs in central Europe, Napoleon marched into Spain at the head of around 130,000 of his finest troops, including the Imperial Guard. He cut his way through the hastily assembled Spanish forces and re-occupied Madrid. Now was the time to avenge Bailén and conquer Andalusia. But there was a problem; a British army had landed in Portugal and cut across his lines of communication in northern Spain. The Spaniards had realised that they could not defeat the French army with their own limited resources, but, with most of Europe under Napoleon's control, finding an ally meant turning to one of Spain's traditional enemies – England.

In the last week of May, the Seville Junta approached the Governor of

Gibraltar, General Sir Hew Dalrymple, with a request for weapons and money. The request was passed onto London where delegates from Asturias in northern Spain had also arrived with a similar appeal for assistance in defeating Napoleon. Nothing could suit the British more.

Peace was declared between the two countries and money and arms were made immediately available to the insurgents. Together Canning, the British Foreign Secretary and the Secretary of State for War, Castlereagh, assembled a small expeditionary force from the troops that could be made available quickly and despatched them to Spain.

Command of the expeditionary force was entrusted to Major General Sir Arthur Wellesley. He set off ahead of his troops in a fast frigate to assess the situation on the ground in Spain. Wellesley first landed at Corunna but he found that no one had any idea what was happening elsewhere in the country. He therefore sailed on to Portugal, landing at Oporto. Here Wellesley learnt that the French occupying forces had concentrated in and around Lisbon and that the north of the country was relatively free of enemy troops. Wellesley had found the perfect place for his troops to land with limited risk of the French intervening.

The British Expeditionary Force disembarked in Montego Bay before the French were able to respond. The small force sent by General Junot, the Duke of Abrantes, to try and delay the British army was defeated at Rolica and the victorious Wellesley marched upon the Portuguese capital.

Junot had no choice but to gather together as many troops as he could and face Wellesley on the battlefield. The two forces met at Vimeiro and the French were comprehensively beaten. Junot almost immediately requested an armistice in order to negotiate the French evacuation of Portugal.

At this moment in time Wellesley, the most junior Major General in the British Army, was superseded by Hugh Dalrymple, the man to whom the Spanish insurgents had first made contact at Gibraltar. Dalrymple was only too happy with the prospect of liberating Portugal without further bloodshed and he agreed to allow the French troops to return to France, carrying with them much of the loot they had plundered from the Portuguese. Under the terms of what was known as the Convention of Cintra, the French were taken home in British ships and, upon their return, they were free to take up arms once again. Dalrymple and Wellesley were recalled to face a Board of Inquiry!

With Portugal successfully liberated, the British Government urged the new commander of the Expeditionary Force, Sir John Moore, to carry the war into Spain to help the insurgents. With reinforcements from Britain bringing his force up to 25,000 men, Moore marched into northern Spain hoping to seriously disrupt Napoleon's operations. He succeeded.

When Napoleon heard that Moore had dared to trespass into Spain, all thoughts of completing the subjugation of Spain by continuing south into Andalusia were abandoned. Instead he turned his troops around, and force-marched them northwards in the hope of catching the British.

As it transpired, Moore's army escaped through the mountains of Galicia, reaching the coast at Corunna. After fighting a successful delaying action, in which Moore was fatally wounded, the British troops were able to embark upon the waiting transports and return safely to England.

Napoleon returned to France believing that he had driven the British out of the Peninsula and that the Spanish uprising had been crushed. Joseph was reinstated upon his throne in December and French forces set about asserting their authority across Iberia.

This proved a far harder task than Napoleon had expected. Though the Spanish armies had been scattered by the Emperor they had not been destroyed and, with much of the population behind them, and all the advantages of the terrain in their favour, they proved an elusive and resilient foe. 'They were everywhere we were not,' wrote an officer in one of Napoleon's Polish regiments, 'they disappeared upon our approach, escaped our clutches and reappeared behind us.'[5]

The French forces found themselves tied down in a vicious guerrilla war that gradually sapped their resolve and their resources. With the *guerrilleros* stubbornly defending the passes and the hills of Galicia, Aragon, Navarre and the cities of Catalonia, King Joseph's rule extended no further than the reach of a French musket ball.

Andalusia, in particular, still remained free, and Canning sought to support the Supreme Junta by sending a considerable force to join the Spaniards. The terms under which he was willing to send British troops into Andalusia, however, proved too exacting for the Spanish people to accept. Canning wanted British troops to garrison the fortress-port of Cadiz in order to guarantee a safe point of departure should the French attack in overwhelming numbers, and the British be compelled to retreat back to their ships: 'Without the security to be offered by that fortress,' he told John Frere, the British ambassador to Spain, 'it is impossible to hazard the army in the interior.'[6]

Without waiting for an answer from the Supreme Junta, Canning despatched a brigade of infantry under General Mackenzie to Cadiz. When the ships carrying this force arrived in Cadiz harbour, Frere was placed in a highly invidious position – because the local authority in Cadiz refused to grant the British permission to land![7]

Right in the middle of this embarrassing hiatus, a battalion of the 40th Regiment, which had marched from the Portuguese border to strengthen Mackenzie's force, tramped across the isthmus that joins Cadiz with the mainland. This angered and frightened the locals. In their eyes the British saw Cadiz as another Gibraltar. If they let the British into their city they would never leave. So the mob rushed down the streets and barred the gate.

Whilst the Junta accepted that 'the loyalty of the British ministry and the generosity of its efforts to assist Spain were beyond suspicion', they recognised that they had to 'respect national prejudices'. After wallowing idly in the transports for four weeks, Mackenzie's force set sail for Lisbon just as a convoy of additional troops from England tried to enter Cadiz harbour! They too had to turn around and the whole force went to join the small British army at Lisbon.

In the wake of this embarrassing episode, the British Government concentrated its efforts on supporting the Portuguese. Castlereagh appointed Sir Arthur Wellesley, who had been exonerated at the inquiry over the Convention of Cintra, as commander-in-chief of the Anglo-Portuguese army, with the defence of Portugal as 'the first and most immediate object' of his attention.[8]

Wellesley's first and most immediate concern was in fact with the French II Corps under Marshal Soult which had invaded northern Portugal and had occupied Oporto. With a mixed force of barely 20,000 men, Wellesley attacked and drove Soult out of Oporto and chased the II Corps back over the Spanish border.

With Portugal at last free of French troops, Wellesley was granted permission to extend operations into Spain. In conjunction with the Spanish army of General Cuesta he arranged to advance into Spain to attack Marshal Claude Victor's I Corps, which was stationed at Talavera.

On 22 July, the combined Spanish and British armies reached Talavera, taking Victor completely by surprise. Outnumbered two-to-one, I Corps was in a perilous situation. But Cuesta refused to attack, and Victor made good his escape two days later. Seeing the French withdraw inspired Cuesta into action and he recklessly set off in pursuit.

Wellesley, without the food and transport that the Spaniards had promised to provide, would not be drawn any further into Spain. He took up defensive positions around Talavera to await Cuesta's inevitable return.

Wellesley did not have to wait long. Three days after chasing off down the highway to Madrid the Spaniards came running back with the combined forces of I Corps, Sebastiani's IV Corps and the bulk of Joseph's Madrid garrison at their heels. On the night of 27 July 1809, Victor led the French attack upon the Allied lines at Talavera. The fighting continued throughout the following day, with every French attack being beaten back.

With other Spanish forces threatening Madrid, the French disengaged and returned to the capital, leaving behind seventeen guns and 7,000 of their dead and wounded. Despite being able to claim a victory, Wellesley was forced to retreat back to Portugal as other French armies menaced his communications with his Lisbon base.

After this experience Wellesley vowed 'not to have anything to do with Spanish warfare, on any ground whatever, in the existing state of things.' His future plan, he announced, a week after escaping across the border, 'is to remain on the defensive . . . I must be satisfied with maintaining myself in Portugal.'[9]

Following Talavera, the British Government again asked the Spaniards to allow Cadiz to be garrisoned by British troops and the Supreme Junta was informed that the admission of British forces to Cadiz would be 'integral to any further British advance into Spain'.[10] British forces would not be risked on operations beyond the Portuguese border unless they could be certain of a secure line of retreat should their communications with Lisbon be severed. Cadiz was the ideal place to cover an embarkation of the British Army, both in the nature of its defences and its location far to the south, deep in Spanish-held territory. Wellesley even undertook a flying visit to Seville in support of this and then down to Cadiz where the British Ambassador had taken up his post. But the Supreme Junta remained unmoved. Cadiz would not be garrisoned by British troops.[11]

As it transpired, the French forces in Spain were in no position to follow Wellesley and there was no possibility of his Lisbon base being threatened. The problems that the French were experiencing in retaining control of central Spain reflected the difficulties that they were encountering elsewhere in the country. By the summer of 1809, French forces had evacuated Asturias and Galicia as well as Portugal. Bonaparte was losing the war in Spain.

The Emperor, though, had other worries on his mind. Austria had been preparing for war for many months and on 10 April 1809, with no formal declaration of hostilities, its forces crossed the River Inn and advanced into Bavaria.

Napoleon, well aware of Austria's intentions, moved far more rapidly than his enemy and was able to block the Austrian thrust. The subsequent series of engagements resulted in the hard-won Battle of Wagram.

Twenty thousand French soldiers died in the battle but their deaths brought a fragile peace to central Europe. This meant that Napoleon could reduce his forces in Germany and send them over the Pyrenees. The French armies in Spain were to be reinforced to an unprecedented level and the insurgency crushed by sheer weight of numbers.

*

The first of the reinforcements marched into Spain in December 1809, relieving Joseph's garrisons and releasing thousands of men for field operations. Joseph saw this as his opportunity to finally subjugate Andalusia. The 'Intrusive' King was all too well aware of the importance of Andalusia and he had been contemplating a move against Spain's southern province for months. The Supreme Junta in Seville pronounced itself the legitimate government of Spain and its very existence posed a direct threat to his authority. Andalusia was also Spain's richest and most populated province and Joseph was in a desperate financial position (the pay of his troops was thirteen months in arrears) and still dependent upon grants from his brother in Paris.

All the time that the Spaniards held the passes of the Sierra Morena in force Joseph dare not risk a second Bailén but the Spaniards themselves provided the 'Intrusive' King with the opportunity he sought. Instead of remaining safely on the defensive, the Supreme Junta threw caution, and common sense, to the wind by launching a new offensive.

The Supreme Junta devised a wildly-ambitious scheme to commit almost its entire disposable force to a direct assault upon Madrid. A body of 50,000 men, under the command of General Areizaga, descended from the heights of the Sierra Morena on 3 November. After a rapid advance to La Guardia near Aranjuez, Areizaga lost confidence and halted. He dithered at La Guardia for three days, which enabled Marshal Soult and Joseph to concentrate the bulk of the IV and V Corps, three cavalry divisions and the strategic reserve.

Areizaga began a precipitate retreat but was brought to battle near the town of Ocaña. The result was a catastrophic defeat for the Spaniards, who lost 18,000 men. The consequence was that Andalusia was now defenceless and the Supreme Junta was utterly discredited. Bowing to public pressure the members of the Junta promised to surrender their powers to a nationally-elected Cortes.[12]

The Spaniards had played right into Joseph's hands and he began to plan his attack upon Andalusia. On 14 December, his chief-of-staff, Marshal Soult, wrote to Napoleon requesting permission to invade Andalusia: 'At no time since the Spanish war began have circumstances been so favourable for invading Andalusia, and it is probable that such a movement would have the most advantageous results.' Five days later he wrote again to Paris: 'The government of Seville is at the last gasp; the hour is upon us; and I mean to profit by it.'[13]

Napoleon, however, was less concerned with Joseph and the Spaniards than he was with the British, and Soult waited in vain for a reply from Paris. In the Emperor's eyes the British were the 'only danger'. As one French staff officer explained, if the British could be driven out of the Peninsula 'they would lose all their influence in Spain. Portugal would submit and Spain, exhausted and discouraged, would follow its example as soon as it was abandoned.'[14]

Soult and Joseph waited a month for a response from Napoleon and then they took matters into their own hands. Their plan of campaign was typically Napoleonic, both in its scale and its design, consisting of a frontal attack combined with a wide encircling movement.

To defend the south of the country, the Spaniards had just two small armies. General Areizaga commanded the 23,000 strong Army of La Mancha which held the passes of the Sierra Morena and guarded the road to Sevillle.[15] He was supported to the west, in Estremadura, by the Duke of Albuquerque with the 12,000 men of the Army of Estremadura. By contrast Joseph had three full army corps available for the campaign in Andalusia, plus his own Royal Guard and other detached troops totalling more than 60,000 of all ranks. To deter the British army in Portugal from taking advantage of Joseph's absence and to prevent the junction of the Army of Estremadura with the Army of La Mancha, Marshal Mortier with the French II Corps, was detailed to capture the fortress of Badajoz on the Spanish-Portuguese border and crush Albuquerque. A single French division was left to hold Madrid.

Joseph's march upon Andalusia began on 7 January 1810. Four days later the French column halted at Almagro. Here Joseph's forces divided, with Marshal Victor and I Corps moving to the west through the central ranges of the Sierra Morena to Cordoba. Joseph allowed six days for Victor to descend upon Areigzaga's rear before marching directly upon the main Spanish positions.[16]

Areizaga's front stretched for 150 miles and he had split his small force into three divisions to cover the principle routes from the north. Joseph had also divided his army, intending to attack on all points. Against a powerful enemy such a policy was extremely hazardous (as Napoleon had shown in his early campaigns in Italy) but Areizaga was weak everywhere and the French drove the Spaniards from the mountain passes with relative ease.

By this time, Victor had also brushed aside the small Spanish body opposing him in the mountains and I Corps was now descending upon Cordoba. Defeated at every point, Areizaga's Spaniards, no longer an army, scattered in all directions. A large proportion of these troops stayed with Areizaga and retired to the province of Murcia. Others fell back into the Sierra de Ronda and then to Gibraltar from where they were shipped to Cadiz. Many of the remainder withdrew into the Condado de Niebla to conduct guerrilla operations against the invaders.[17] But now the road to Seville was open and Joseph and Soult marched upon the Andalusia capital convinced that the campaign was all but won.

The Supreme Junta now sent 'wild and impracticable' orders to the Duke of Albuquerque to fall upon the rear of the advancing French columns. Realising that he could not comply with his orders, Albuquerque marched instead directly upon Seville.

The Andalusian capital had been in a state of chaos for days. The Supreme Junta had scampered off to Cadiz shortly after receiving confirmation that the French were marching upon Cordoba. The Junta, which due to its repeated failures was viewed as being 'universally obnoxious', had acceded to the call for it to relinquish its authority to a national Cortes which was due to assemble at Cadiz on 1 February. This event needed to be prepared for, claimed the members of the Junta. It seemed the perfect excuse to get away from the enemy.

But the proud Andalusians were not so easily deceived. Many of the Junta's members were waylaid, some taken captive, some murdered. Only twenty-three fortunate individuals found their way to Cadiz. 'Andalusia generally, and Seville in particular, were but one remove from anarchy,' wrote William Napier, 'when the intrusive monarch reached the foot of the [Sierra] Morena with a great and well organised army.'[18]

The defence of Seville was taken up by another unrepresentative and non-elected body, the 'Revolutionary Government'. The leaders of this new assembly, when the imminence and scale of the French advance became apparent, followed the example of the Supreme Junta. After just five days in office, they slipped out of the city during the night of the 28th. The next day the leading French dragoons arrived before Seville. Despite an initial display of bravado, the leaderless citizens surrendered without a fight.

The Duke of Albuquerque, meanwhile, had reached the River Guadalquivir, about fifteen miles north of the city, where he received further instructions sent earlier by the Junta to move upon Cordoba. So the Duke crossed the river and turned south-eastwards, being joined at Carmona by about 2,000 troops that had retreated from the Sierra Morena. Advancing eastwards, Albuquerque came into contact with Victor's cavalry and he saw that he was facing a far greater force than his small army could possibly contend with. By this time the Duke was aware of the flight of the Supreme Junta and he knew that Cadiz had practically no garrison. He also knew that if adequately defended the fortress-port could be rendered virtually impregnable. So Albuquerque marched upon

Cadiz as quickly as he could travel. The Duke's 'wise resolution', as Sir Charles Oman was later to write, 'may be said without hesitation, saved the cause of Spain.'[19]

Joseph Bonaparte entered Seville in triumph on the afternoon of 1 February. After all the years of claiming to be the spirit of the insurgency, the Andalusia capital did not just succumb to the enemy, it welcomed him with open arms. The scenes of rejoicing which met Joseph at Seville were repeated throughout Andalusia as the King made a grand tour of his newly won province: 'It is impossible to convey an adequate ides of the joy with which the population of Ecija, Jérez, Santa Maria, Ronda, Málaga, Granada and Jáen received the new king', remarked General Bigarré, Joseph's aide-de-camp, 'In every town, the nobility, formed up as a guard of honour, came to congratulate him on his happy arrival . . . Following their example, the people kissed his horse and prostrated themselves on the ground, crying, "Long live King Joseph!"'[20] Never, declared one of his supporters, had Joseph I of Spain felt more certain of his throne.[21]

An excited Joseph wrote to Napoleon, 'All the towns are sending me deputations; Seville is following this example. The Junta has retired to the Isle de Leon. I am about to enter Cadiz without firing a shot.'[22] Though this last statement was entirely incorrect, Joseph believed it to be true. Yet the campaign to conquer Andalusia, which the King thought won, had already been lost. 'The tide of French conquest,' wrote Professor Oman, 'reached its high-water mark, when Soult appeared before the walls of Cadiz.'[23]

*

When the French reached Cadiz they found that Albuquerque's army had arrived before them and put the place into a hurried state of defence. Unlike the other Andalusian cities which had fallen so easily to the invaders, Cadiz, if adequately garrisoned, was practically unassailable. This single fact provokes two questions concerning the early stages of Joseph Bonaparte's Andalusia campaign.

The first question is, if such a stronghold lay in their rear, why did the Spaniards try to hold all the passes of the Sierra Morena? Surely a small holding force in the mountains was all that was required to give the bulk of the Army of La Mancha time to retreat upon Cadiz from where they could defy the French almost indefinitely?

The second question is, with the mountain passes breached, why did Joseph not send a strong column to capture Cadiz before any Spanish troops could retire

13

into that great fortress? Seville was certain to fall as the city was too large to defend but Cadiz could be secured with a comparatively small force.

In General Napier's opinion, Joseph believed that such was the 'moral influence' of Seville, 'the possession of that town would produce the greatest moral effect, in Andalusia, and all over Spain.' But the influence of Seville was simply transferred to Cadiz and Seville became just another occupied city.

'Marshal Soult did not avail himself of the terror, spread among all classes of inhabitants, by his passage of the Sierra,' complained one of Napoleon's own generals, Jean Sarrazin, 'but he seemed to hesitate, and advanced with the slowness of a tortoise.' Sarrazin argues that instead of sending Sebastiani to Granada and Mortier towards Badajoz to secure both flanks of his advance, Soult should have pushed on with his whole force upon Seville and then Cadiz. He had no need to worry about his communications with Madrid as affluent Andalusia possessed all he could need to support his army.[24]

Yet Seville was a city of 100,000 inhabitants and the people gave all the outward signs of being prepared to resist the invaders. If Joseph had marched directly upon Cadiz without subduing Seville, he ran the risk of the Spaniards falling upon his rear. It could have been a second Bailén. It was a risk he could not take.

As it transpired, Seville succumbed without a fight but the Andalusia capital's 'ephemeral' resistance saved Cadiz.[25] It was not until the day after Joseph's entry into Seville that Victor was directed to pursue Albuquerque and take possession of Cadiz. Victor reached Cadiz on 5 February. Albuquerque had arrived on the 3rd. Those two days gave the Spaniards just enough time to make the place secure from a *coup de main*. As Sarrazin commented, from 29th January until 3 February the French might have entered Cadiz 'without any obstacle'. All they had to do was march six leagues a day and the war in Andalusia would have been won and with it organised resistance in Spain would have ended. 'It is difficult to exaggerate the good service rendered by Albuquerque,' the historian of the British Army, John Fortescue observed, 'in thus marching upon his own responsibility to Cadiz.'[26]

Joseph had raised the question of advancing straight upon Cadiz, rather than Seville, with Soult whilst at Carmona on 30 January. They were both aware that Albuquerque was moving in that direction with a considerable body of men. Yet Soult, inexplicably, silenced Joseph with the words, 'If anyone will answer to me for Seville, I will answer for Cadiz.' It was probably the Marshal's gravest error in his entire military career.[27]

CHAPTER 2

Enter the Lion

Cadiz sits on an island – the Isla de Leon – separated from the mainland by the estuary of the Rio Sancti Petri. This river is between 300 and 400 yards wide and is further broadened by salt marshes that border it which, in 1810, could only be traversed by means of a narrow causeway which was carried across the Sancti Petrie on the Puente Zuazo. This was the only permanent bridge over the river. The front of the island facing the mainland runs for around seven miles from the isolated arsenal of Carraca at the northern end, to the Castle of Sancti Petri at the south. Somewhat confusingly, a small township on the Isla de Leon close to the Sancti Petri was also called Isla.

Heavy batteries had been erected on all the commanding points overlooking the channel between the island and the mainland. Beyond these defences, at its south-western tip, the island shrinks to form a sandy spit of land which, at its narrowest point, is only 200 yards wide. Here a line of entrenchments had been built that stretched across this isthmus from the Atlantic to the waters of Cadiz's Inner Harbour. This defence line, the Cortadura (or Battery of San Fernando) was also armed with heavy guns.[1]

A further two miles along this spit is the outer enceinte of Cadiz itself. All but surrounded by water, the fortress sits near the very end of this long peninsular which forms the western arm of the port's Outer Harbour in Cadiz Bay. The Inner Harbour offered a deep-water refuge for ships. It was protected from the surf by the Isla de Leon and it offered 1,600 yards of anchorages.

Another significant feature is a sandy peninsula, called the Trocadero, which stretches from the mainland into Cadiz Bay and defines the Outer Harbour from the Inner Harbour. The tip of this peninsula is only 1,200 yards from Cadiz, and three forts had been built to defend this narrow passage, Fort Matagorda and Fort San Luis on the landward side and Fort Puntales on the Cadiz side. However, the city's military governor, General Venegas, had demolished and abandoned the forts on the Trocadero, leaving the French to occupy the ruins if they so chose.[2]

The main, central span of the Puente Zuazo had been pulled down by Albuquerque and all boats in the vicinity removed from the mainland by Venegas. Unable therefore to attack Cadiz, Victor sent a summons into the city which was promptly rejected. With Spanish gunboats patrolling the channel and four British warships anchored in the harbour, there was simply nothing else he could do other than report back to Soult and Joseph.

When Soult reached Cadiz he likewise invited Albuquerque to surrender. In reply the Spanish general made clear Soult's mistake in not taking Cadiz when the city was undefended: 'The fortress of Cadiz', wrote Albuquerque, 'has nothing to fear from an army of one hundred thousand men. There is no comparison between its present state of defence, *and the situation in which it was a few days ago.*'[3] For his part, the King, still revelling in what he believed was the great success of his Andalusia campaign, insisted on seeing the situation for himself. What Joseph saw, when he arrived in the Bay of Cadiz, he did not like. It was apparent that the fortress could only be taken by an amphibious assault and Joseph had no ships. But Napoleon had a fleet.

On 18 February, Joseph wrote to his brother requesting the assistance of the Toulon fleet. Yet, such was Britain's supremacy at sea, Napoleon dare not risk his principal naval force, in what must have appeared at the time to be a minor cause. Joseph's request was denied. As it transpired, Cadiz would come to symbolise the determination and the ability of the Spanish people to resist the invaders. As long as the Spanish flag flew from the Iglesia de San Felipe Neri, Spain would remain unconquered.

Napoleon made a disastrous mistake in not helping his brother. All the defences along the Isla de Leon could easily be bypassed by a sea-borne force landing close to Cadiz itself, but without a large naval force this was never going to be achieved.[4] He certainly preserved his fleet by not sending them to sea but what good was a navy that could never sail? As one historian has already made clear, if the French would have been able to cross the Sancti Petri at this early stage of operations 'no-one could have felt much surprise had Cadiz surrendered to the French.' In view of all that was later to occur, it could be argued that this was one of Napoleon's worst decisions. For in failing to capture Cadiz he allowed Spain to consider itself still an independent sovereign state under the authority of its own government. The Spaniards could justifiably claim that they were still fighting a war against an alien invader, not a civil war against its monarch, which is how Joseph wanted to portray the actions of the Spaniards.

Though he had not been in favour of the invasion of Andalusia whilst a strong British army remained in the Peninsula, Napoleon knew that now Joseph had committed himself to that course of action he must not be allowed to fail: 'The slightest retrograde movement of any corps in the Andalusia expedition,' he wrote to Joseph at the end of January, 'will be contrary to all military ideas, will embolden the insurrection, and will discourage the French Army.'[5] This makes Napoleon's decision not to send Joseph all the means at his disposal all the more inexcusable.

If Cadiz had fallen, and the Spanish government deposed, the war in Spain would have been over. The only recognisable authority would have been that of Joseph Bonaparte, King of Spain. Sir Arthur Wellesley (recently elevated to the peerage as Viscount Wellington of Talavera) might have been able to defend Portugal and maintain its independence, but he would not have been able to drive the French out of Spain with his small Anglo–Portuguese force alone.

Napoleon, however, would not let his fleet go to sea and Victor was left with responsibility for blockading Cadiz, whilst Joseph returned to Madrid. Soon control of Andalusia was taken from Joseph by his brother with Soult being given independent command of the I, IV and V Corps as the Army of Andalusia.[6]

The blockading forces were placed at San Lucar de Barrameda, at the mouth of the Guadalquiver, Rota, Puerto de Santa Maria, Puerto Real and Chiclana, which became Victor's main base. A strong garrison was also established at Medina Sidonia. The Marshal commanded some 28,000 troops, considerably more than manned the defences of the fortress.[7] But if the French had been slow to recognise the importance of Cadiz, the Allies were not. In addition to Albuquerque's 12,000 men and the Cadiz civic militia, reinforcements from both Spain and Portugal were being hurried into Cadiz from across Iberia. A force of 3,000 regular Spanish troops, that had been in garrison in Seville, and had escaped westwards after the surrender of the city, were the first to arrive. Though pursued by Mortier's V Corps, they managed to reach the port of Ayamonte at the mouth of the Guadiana from where they were shipped to Cadiz. Next came the British and the Portuguese. Despite their earlier reluctance to allow British troops into Cadiz, the situation had changed completely and the Spaniards were now willing to accept British help in the port's defence. Lord Liverpool, the British Secretary of War, was keen to help the Spaniards and, on 13 February, he wrote to Wellington asking him if he could send a body of troops to Cadiz: 'Could you supply it from your present force, consistently with the security of Portugal; and if an option must be made between the two objects, which of them ought to be preferred?' Even though he asked Wellington's advice, Liverpool made it clear that he placed a 'higher value' on Cadiz than he did on Lisbon. 'But even if the value of the two objects were equal,' continued Liverpool, 'is not true that Cadiz and some part of the south of Spain might be defended if Portugal were for the time lost, but that Portugal could not long be defended if Andalusia were in possession of the French?'[8]

Wellington had already made his mind up about the Spaniards, after his earlier experiences, and he was not willing to sacrifice Lisbon for Cadiz. He was certain that Napoleon would soon send a mighty force to drive the British from the Peninsula, whether they were situated in Portugal or Andalusia. But he had already begun work on the vast, and highly secret, defences of the Lines of Torres Vedras and he had no intention of abandoning them at this stage of the war. He estimated that it would take an army of more than 100,000 men to break through the Lines of Torres Vedras and Wellington did not believe that the French would be able to hold down the insurgents in Spain and also find a field army large enough to penetrate the Lines. Equally, if the British were to withdraw from Portugal, the French would seize Lisbon without difficulty. 'Cadiz would then be attacked by the whole French army,' explained Wellington, 'and even if we should be admitted to take a share in its defence, it might be in such a [poor] state as to render all our efforts hopeless.'[9] Wellington also believed that Lisbon was strategically better placed: 'I am decidedly of opinion that the largest British army which Great Britain can afford to supply would do better to carry on its operations through Portugal, and make Lisbon the point of its communications with England, than carry on its operations through the south of Spain, communicating with Cadiz . . . we can advance with safety nearer the centre of the scene of operations, and retire with greater ease.'[10] Wellington was willing to send some of his troops to Cadiz but the bulk of his army would remain in Portugal.

He immediately despatched three British battalions and one Portuguese regiment, amounting to approximately 3,500 men, under the command of Major General William Stewart. A further 1,000 troops were detached from Gibraltar. Wellington made no conditions as to their service, except that on points of discipline they should be subject to their own officers and that they should not be detached from Cadiz.[11]

This meant that, along with the existing civic militia, Cadiz was now held by around 20,000 men. Victor had barely 8,000 more, but the Allies also had the men and the guns of the Spanish and British warships. Victor was out-gunned and stood no chance whatsoever of taking Cadiz. But this would not stop him trying.

*

The British ships arrived at Cadiz late in the evening of 11 February. Stewart had been told by Wellington that the defence of Cadiz was so important that he should not let anything delay the deployment of his troops, and the disembarkation of Stewart's force began as soon as dawn broke the following morning.[12] Even before the troops had stepped foot on Spanish soil they had formed a poor opinion of their new hosts. The British knew that, ultimately, the defence of Cadiz would depend upon them. 'We will have a regular fire day and night until they [the French] are either driven away or destroyed', wrote an officer of the 87th Foot whilst still on board his ship in Cadiz harbour, 'which is not at all unlikely, as the Spanish soldiers are behaving in the most cowardly manner.'[13]

Likewise, the arrival of the British troops did not provoke universal rejoicing amongst the citizens of Cadiz. It was only five years since the Battle of Trafalgar and the shattered remains of some of the Spanish vessels still lay in the bay. They stood as a stark reminder that their Allies were their enemies only two years before, and until that time Cadiz had been held in a tight blockade by the Royal Navy. As the troops were marched to the bomb-proof barracks under the ramparts, there was the occasional 'Viva Englese' shouted from the crowd, the majority of whom received their Allies 'with a gloomy suspicious silence'. Others made provocative jibes such as 'what fine-looking and well-disciplined soldiers the British are! What a pity they cannot fight!'[14]

Stewart's force consisted of the 79th, 87th and 94th Foot, as well as two companies of the Royal Artillery under Major Alexander Duncan. The 79th were between 900 and 1,000 strong and the 94th numbered 670. The second battalion of the 88th Regiment was sent to Cadiz from Gibraltar, arriving at approximately the same time. The Portuguese Regency also offered their help and the 20th Portuguese Regiment, totalling some 1,300 men, was shipped from Lisbon just a few days later.[15] So, within days of receiving the call for help from the Spaniards, her Allies had landed a substantial force of around 3,500 men. The men were to be supplied with food and drink by the Spaniards (which included an issue of wine) and all purchases by the Commissariat had to be recorded and the bills passed onto the Spanish authorities.

Stewart organized his force into two brigades. The 1st Brigade, under Lieutenant Colonel Cameron, consisting of the 79th and the 20th Portuguese and the light companies from all the battalions formed into a composite battalion, was moved down to the Isla de Leon and was quartered in the San Fernando Barracks. The light battalion was then sent to occupy the outposts by the Sancti Petri.[16]

The remaining battalions forming the 2nd Brigade were placed in barracks in Cadiz itself where, it cannot be said, they were treated as the saviours of Spain. 'For the first two days we got leave to lie on brick floors,' Lieutenant Wright Knox of the 87th complained, 'the Spanish Government then issued a mattress, a chair and a small table to each Officer but nothing to cover us, so we are obliged to sleep in our clothes.'[17] Duncan's artillery also took up key posts around the defences. This included the company under Lieutenant Brett which took over the guns in Fort Puntales.[18]

A network of ships was quickly established to enable regular communication between Wellington and his new command. Three times a week a packet ship sailed to and from Faro in the Algarve and from the Algarve boats sailed round to Cadiz. Gibraltar, though entirely independent from Wellington's force, also maintained frequent contact with Cadiz by ship.[19]

Britain's presence at Cadiz became even more prominent with the arrival of three ships-of-the-line and four frigates of the Royal Navy under Admiral Purvis. Along with the Spanish warships of Don Ignacio de Alva this made a formidable total of twenty-three men-of-war anchored in Cadiz Bay.

Though the arrival of the British troops and warships had helped make Cadiz more secure, things were not well in the city. Albuquerque's troops were in a 'deplorable' state. They had received no pay for a very long time, and the greater part of them lacked arms, accoutrements, ammunition, or in some cases even clothes!

There had been no attempt to recruit or arm any of the citizens of Cadiz, even though the enemy was, quite literally, at the gates, and not a single person had volunteered either to fight or even labour on the city's defences. 'The Spaniards are of a disposition too sanguine,' complained Wellington. 'Every man who knows anything of the state of Spain, must be certain that if Cadiz should hold out . . . the Bonapartes may have the military possession of the country, but sooner or later they must lose it.'[20] Nothing, though, could stir the Spaniards into improving the city's fortifications.

Beyond the walls of Cadiz, Victor set about establishing his landward blockade of the city. The works encompassed the whole of the perimeter of Cadiz Bay and included three principle entrenched camps.

The first of these was formed around Chiclana. It ran for a distance of eight miles along a range of thickly wooded hills from the sea near the Torre Bermeja, across the Chiclana and Almanza rivers to the Zuraque. This line bordered a marsh that met the Sancti Petri river and which varied from one to three miles in breadth. The marsh was broken by not only the Chiclana and Almanaz but also by many other small creeks, some of which were navigable to large boats.

The second, and central, camp ran for some seven miles from the Zuraque to the town of Puerto Real along a ridge that skirted the marsh. Puerto Real was itself entrenched but of much greater importance was the Trocadero which projected into the bay from the town. The Trocadero is four miles long and at its farthest point stood the fort of Matagorda. The fort, being only 1,200 yards from Cadiz, was therefore within cannon shot of some of the city's fortifications. As mentioned above, the fort had been abandoned by the Spaniards, its guns removed and its defences blown up, but it had not yet been occupied by the besiegers.

The final French camp followed the sweep of Cadiz Bay round to the castle of Santa Catalina at the extreme left point of the Outer Harbour. In the centre of this line is the town of Santa Catalina which sits at the mouth of the River Guadalete. Victor entrenched the town, which was further protected from assault by rugged ground around its landward side. In total, when completed, the siege works ran for a remarkable twenty-five miles.

A covered way, concealed by thick woods, was formed to connect the three camps and, when finished, no less than 300 guns were placed in battery. Strengthening this line were the towns of San Lucar de Barameda and Rota, which were occupied and fortified. Beyond the blockading line, Latour-Maubourg's division was stationed at the town of Medina Sidonia some fourteen miles to the north-east, to protect the rear of the besieging force and secure its communication with Seville. From Medina Sidonia pickets were pushed as far as the passes of the Sierra de Ronda.[21]

To supplement the ordnance the French had brought with them, which at first were just field guns, Victor's engineers 'fished up' the guns of the French and Spanish ships that had been wrecked upon the coast after the Battle of Trafalgar. Over time, large ordnance was brought to Cadiz from across Spain, particularly from the arsenal at Seville which housed the country's only gun foundry.[22]

Soult also set about extending his control across all of Andalusia. Sebastiani (IV Corps) was directed towards the east and occupied Malaga after limited resistance. To the west Marshal Mortier's V Corps marched into Estremadura. Mortier reached the fortress of Badajoz on the Portuguese/Estremadura border on 12 February, but found the place well garrisoned and its governor determined to resist. Nevertheless, Mortier's presence in Estremadura ensured the security of Victor's west flank.[23]

Though the Spanish politicians had escaped from Seville by the skin of their teeth only days earlier, and despite the fact that the defences of the Isla were far from adequate, they were already proposing sending troops from Cadiz to attack the French! This greatly alarmed Wellington and he wrote to General Stewart on 27 February to explain his concerns over the defence of Cadiz: 'Without adverting to the enormous armies which are daily pouring into Spain, in addition to those which were before in the country, and were already superior in number to the allies; or to the fact that there is now no army in the field excepting the

British army, they [the Spaniards] are thinking of offensive operations from Cadiz; and they appear to me to hold the Isla de Leon more as the intrentched camp (and hardly even deserving that name) of an army, than as a fortified post, upon the possession of which everything is to turn in future.'[24]

Whilst accepting that the defence of Cadiz was of paramount importance, Wellington urged his political masters not to abandon Lisbon for Cadiz: 'If we should withdraw from Portugal . . .,' he advised Lord Liverpool, 'Cadiz would then be attacked by the whole French army, probably before the Isla could be fortified as it ought to be.'

Even if the British Army continued to hold out in Portugal Wellington was convinced that 'sooner or later' Victor would make a 'most serious' attack upon the Isla de Leon which 'it would be in vain to resist, without having recourse to all measures for the defence of these points which art can suggest.' Wellington made it clear that 'if the Isla de Leon is lost, the town of Cadiz will not, and probably cannot, hold out a week'.

He consequently advised Stewart to order the senior engineer present, Captain Landmann, to devise a plan for the strengthening of the defences of the Isla and Cadiz as quickly as possible. Landmann was reminded to pay particular attention to ensuring that the works he recommended would not be more extensive than the troops available to man them. These plans, when drawn up, were to be submitted to the Spanish Government. Yet, as Wellington conceded, 'In the existing temper of the times, the loss of this place will be set down to our account, however little is in our power.'[25]

Wellington's main concern with the defence of Cadiz was with the Trocadero, as he knew that from there the French could cut off the communication between the Inner and Outer harbours. Wellington accepted that such an occurrence could not be avoided so he advised Stewart to move all the boats which would be needed to protect Cadiz into the Inner Harbour before the French batteries became established.

Wellington continued to be worried about the Spaniards' apparent wish to undertake offensive actions beyond Cadiz, and he advised Stewart that he must be 'in every respect the best judge' of any undertaking that involved the troops under his command, and that he should not allow himself to be coerced by the Spaniards into detaching any part of his force if he was unhappy with the proposed operation.

As it transpired, Stewart's first offensive act was taken on his own initiative. This action was the recovery of Fort Matagorda. This outwork which Colonel Napier considered to be 'infinitely the most important post' was close enough to the French lines on the Trocadero to pose a real threat to the besiegers' operations if an Allied force could be established there. Equally, if the besiegers decided to occupy and re-arm the fort they would be able to bombard the isthmus of the Isla de Leon whilst providing defensive cover for any boats that the French might collect in the Trocadero creek.[26]

On the night of 22 February, the first three men of each company of the 94th Regiment (making a total of sixty-seven men) were turned out to make the night assault upon Matagorda. They were marched down to the quay where they were joined by a detachment of twenty-five Royal Artillery gunners with three cannon. This force was transported across the bay in boats from the men-at-war of the Royal Navy squadron under the cover of a storm. A small contingent of sailors and marines led by Captain Maclean joined the raiding party, taking the total of the assault force up to approximately 150 men. The party included subalterns, a lieutenant of artillery, a midshipman and a surgeon.

The raiders crept quietly into the fort, careful not to wake the enemy. But the French had failed to defend this vital post and the raiding party took possession of Matagorda without opposition. The British went to work immediately. A picket was stationed outside the fort whilst the other troops hauled up the three guns. The men managed to make a solid lodgement before daybreak.

When dawn broke, the fort's new defenders were able to take stock of the situation. The building was about 150 yards square. Each wall of the fort had been damaged by gunfire from the Allied warships and the side facing the sea was almost completely demolished. The bomb-proof shelters were all but ruined leaving scant protection from the French guns, which opened fire upon the fort as soon as they saw that the building was in the hands of the British.

With fascines, gabions and sand-bags brought over from Cadiz, the defenders were able to form some cover to protect them from the French artillery. They were also able to mount more guns on the ramparts until there were six cannon and two mortars facing the French batteries. Supported by a Spanish man-of-war and between six and eight gun-boats, the guns of Matagorda bombarded Fort San Luis and repeatedly harassed the French working parties moving down the road from Porto Real. Because of its isolated position, and because part of its garrison included sailors and marines, the fort soon acquired the nickname 'HMS Matagorda'.

This was a considerable achievement by Stewart, but his time at Cadiz was to be short-lived when, on 19 February, Lieutenant General Sir Thomas Graham was notified that he was to supersede Stewart in command of the British forces at Cadiz, for the defence of 'that most important place'. The new commander was told to make his way there 'with the least possible delay', though it would be more than a month before he would reach Cadiz. To assist him on his staff Graham was given Major Cathcart as Assistant Quarter-Master General and Captain Hare of the 23rd Foot as Deputy Adjutant-Assistant General. He was also granted full authority to convene general courts-martial.[27]

To strengthen Graham's position Wellington ordered a brigade of six-pounder field guns complete with carriages and ammunition as well as a squadron of the 13th Light Dragoons to be shipped to Cadiz. Wellington also sent four skilled corporals from other squadrons of the 13th Light Dragoons to help Brigadier General Whittingham, who had been seconded to the Spanish Army, improve the swordsmanship and horsemanship of the Spanish cavalry.[28]

Though he was shortly to be superseded, Stewart maintained an aggressive approach to the defence of Cadiz. He had observed the French works developing on the Trocadero and it was clear that they would soon make an attempt to capture Matagorda. On 15 March he planned a raid against the Trocadero timed to coincide with a diversionary attack against the French outposts at Sancti Petri. Led by Major Sullivan, four companies of the 79th Regiment with some light troops assembled for the diversionary attack, but, as the men tried to embark in the boats on the western bay of Puntales for the assault, they found that the surf was too heavy. The attack was cancelled.[29]

Eleven days earlier, on 4 March, Henry Wellesley arrived at Cadiz to take over the role of British representative to Spain from his elder brother Richard, who had been promoted to Foreign Secretary and had returned to London. Wellesley (whose other brother was Sir Arthur Wellesley) was received 'with every possible mark of respect and attention', and was met at the quayside by Generals Albuquerque and Venegas and the new commander of the Spanish fleet, Admiral Villa Vicencio. The garrison was drawn up under arms to salute the new Ambassador.[30]

The next day there was a meeting of the Regency Council, which had been formed to oversee governmental affairs until a Cortes could be convened. Wellesley was the honoured guest and, of course, both sides said all the right things. But after the sitting of the Council, Wellesley asked for a private meeting with the Regents. Wellesley wanted them to realise that subsequent meetings might not always be conducted in such cordial terms: 'I trusted whenever I should in future have occasion to converse with them upon affairs relating to their own country, or more immediately connected with the interests of Great Britain, they would allow me to express my opinions in the most frank and unreserved manner, and that they would observe the same line of conduct in all their communications with me.'[31]

Naturally the Regents agreed and Wellesley felt that the meeting was a success. However, after little more than a week at Cadiz, he made the following notes about the Regents in his dairy: 'It is impossible not to perceive that they have many of the same defects which so strongly characterised the proceedings of the Supreme Junta and which have hitherto baffled every effort of the Spanish nation to deliver itself from the tyranny of foreign usurpation.'[32]

Wellesley was equally alarmed by the lack of enterprise shown by the Spaniards: 'Although nearly six weeks have elapsed since the Spanish Army arrived at the Isla de Leon', he wrote on 12 March, 'and that since that period they have been unmolested by the enemy and in a manner secure from attack, no attempt has been made to render them more efficient, excepting in the case of the cavalry which, being placed under the direction of General Whittingham, will no doubt become an efficient corps. No progress has been made in the improvement of the infantry. They continue to be ill-clothed, ill-paid, ill-fed and their discipline totally neglected.'[33] It was quite clear, as he told his other brother, Wellington, that 'Cadiz must depend for its defence upon the British and upon the British alone.'[34]

Relations between Albuquerque, initially hailed as a 'deliverer', and the newly formed Regency deteriorated rapidly. When Albuquerque, being denied food for his men, published evidence that showed there was food available, matters were brought to a head. The result was that Albuquerque was soon to be sent out of the way, by being appointed Ambassador to England.[35]

Cadiz was not only vitally important as the home of the Spanish Government, it's preservation was also seen as providing Britain with a second operational base against the French if Wellington was eventually driven from Lisbon. The war in the Peninsula could still be maintained, regardless of events in Portugal, providing Cadiz remained in Allied hands. 'In the event of the evacuation of Portugal', Liverpool told Wellington on 13 March, 'it will be a great object to make Cadiz as strong as possible. It is believed here that 15,000 or 20,000 British troops might make it secure for the remainder of the war, and such a garrison would either oblige the French to evacuate the south of Spain or would compel them to keep in that part of the country an army of at least three times the amount of the British force.'[36]

With Cadiz viewed as being so vital to British operations in the Peninsula, Henry Wellesley continued to be concerned with the state of affairs in what was now effectively Spain's capital. He expressed his anxiety in a letter to Wellington: 'I entirely agree with you in all your reasoning upon the importance of the defence of this place, but I fear that it will at last depend upon the exertions of the British troops, and upon their exertions alone. It is for this reason that I am anxious for further reinforcements from England.' Wellesley wanted another 5,000 men.[37]

Wellington, however, saw the situation somewhat differently. There was, he had been informed, 'a party at Cadiz very adverse to receiving the assistance of the British troops in its defence; and considering the troops already there sufficient for its defence against any attack which may now be reasonably expected, I do not deem it expedient to incur the risk of the refusal of the people of the town, instigated by this party, to admit any reinforcement of British troops which I might send.' So, apart from another battalion from Gibraltar and the cavalry and artillery already promised, there was to be no further aid for Cadiz. The fate of Spain and its Government rested, just as Wellesley feared, in the hands of just a few thousand British troops.

*

The next significant development was the long-awaited arrival of Thomas Graham. The military career of Thomas Graham, later to become Sir Thomas, Baron Lynedoch, began in 1793 when as a volunteer he helped in the defence of Toulon against the French Revolutionary forces. The following year he raised his own regiment, the Perthshire Volunteers, which later became the 90th Foot. His rank was that of lieutenant colonel.

After a brief period on secondment with the Austrian Army, and serving with Sir Charles Stuart in the Mediterranean, he became the aide-de-camp to Sir John Moore. Graham served as Moore's aide-de-camp throughout his operations in Spain in 1808. He was by Moore's side when he was mortally wounded at the Battle of Corunna and it is said that it was Moore's dying wish that Graham should be promoted to full colonel.

The wish was granted and it was back-dated to the time that he raised his regiment. With this Graham immediately became a major general by seniority, with effect from 25 September 1803.

The newly elevated general took command of a brigade and later a division at Walcheren, from where he was invalided home after contracting the infamous 'Walcheren Fever'. With his appointment at Cadiz he was given the local rank of lieutenant general (Spain and Portugal). This was later made substantive with seniority from 25 July 1810. He was sixty-one years old.[38]

Graham's instructions were to assume command of the British troops already in Cadiz and the reinforcements due to be sent there shortly. Though he had been asked to communicate directly and separately with both Lord Liverpool and the Commander-in-Chief of the Army, Sir David Dundas, he was still under

Wellington's command and he was 'liable to any orders received from Lord Wellington, whose military authority extends over all the troops in the Peninsula, the garrison of Gibraltar excepted.'[39]

Graham reached Cadiz on 24 March, meeting first with Admiral Purvis on his flagship, and then on into the city itself to see Wellesley and Stewart. He returned to his ship overnight, disembarking the following morning to have breakfast with Wellesley before meeting an old friend of his, General Castanos, who had been appointed President of the five-man Regency Council. Castanos, with typical Spanish pride, declared that the city's defences were quite adequate to meet the French threat. However, in a surprising act of humility, the President said that he was willing to accept any suggestions on improvements to the fortifications that Graham might offer.

Graham and Wellesley then went to meet the Duke of Albuquerque who still commanded the army. He learnt of Albuquerque's deteriorating relationship with the Junta of Defence and of the 'paper battle' that was being fought between them. On their way back Graham and Wellesley stopped to look at the new defences being erected across the peninsula and at the French works on the Trocadero and opposite Fort Matagorda.[40]

Graham then undertook a tour of the rest of the defences – and he was shocked with what he saw. With a French assault likely at any time, Graham realised that unless he could strengthen Cadiz very quickly the city was in real danger. 'Our tenure here at present', he wrote to Lord Liverpool, 'depends more on the inactivity of the enemy than on any resistance that could be made to a vigorous attack.' Indeed the Spaniards continued to appear indifferent to the progress of the enemy and, in Graham's own words they wished the English would drive away the French only so that 'they might go and eat strawberries at Chiclana'! [41]

The next day Graham was taken by a Royal Navy boat over to Matagorda, which at high tide was completely surrounded by water. Stewart had devised a plan to form a counter-guard to protect the fort from attack by sinking ships in the mud and to establish a flanking battery on boats to the left of the fort. But Graham considered Matagorda to be a 'miserable place and which must fall whenever seriously attacked' and he doubted the wisdom of maintaining a garrison there.[42]

Though Graham had not found time to inspect the troops under his new command, he had seen enough to be able to compile his first report to Lord Liverpool. He explained that the existing British force could not hold the weak defences of Isla de Leon by itself and that no reliance could be placed upon the Spanish troops. Though most of the British troops were deployed upon the defences of the Isla de Leon, two battalions were held in Cadiz itself and used as reinforcements for Fort Puntales. The barracks formed two squares, one on each side of the main gate into the city of the road which travelled down to Isla. It was, in Graham's words 'undoubtedly the most important point of any in the place.' There was also a sally port from one of the barracks into the ditch that surrounded the city walls.[43]

Despite his concerns, Graham's new command was an exciting one, as Wellington was quick to point out. He told Graham that he believed the operations in Portugal would not 'hold out a prospect of anything very brilliant. I must maintain myself on the Peninsula till it is necessary to withdraw from it; and when it is necessary to withdraw, I must carry off the army without disgrace, if possible . . . On the other hand, the state of affairs at Cadiz is highly interesting, not only to the Peninsula, but to Great Britain and to the world.'[44]

Graham was told by Lord Liverpool that his first concern was with the security of the Spanish warships and the captured French prizes in Cadiz harbour. This was likely to mean taking control of the Spanish ships by Admiral Purvis and would have to be handled very sensitively. Nothing was more important that preventing the ships falling into enemy hands and Graham was instructed to conduct this 'delicate' matter in such a manner 'as will afford the least possible ground of jealousy to the Spanish authorities and people of Cadiz.'[45]

With the large population of Cadiz swollen by refugees from the adjacent provinces, one of the most pressing concerns was with the supply of food and fresh water. If, upon his arrival, Graham found that the French had managed to cut or restrict the city's water supplies he was instructed to arrange with the local authorities for the removal of as much of the 'inefficient population' as possible, either to the Balearic Islands or the Canaries. After this had been put in hand, Graham was to make sure that the remaining garrison was adequately supplied with food from the Mediterranean. If necessary, a shuttle service of ships carrying water was to be organised between Cadiz and the nearest watering stations.

Graham was also asked to detail the nature of the existing defences of Cadiz and to assess what measures would have to be undertaken to defend the city of Cadiz alone and/or the entire peninsula including the Isla de Leon. This would be undertaken by the contingent of the Royal Engineers at Cadiz, which consisted of ten engineers under the command of Captain, later Major, Lefebvre, assisted by around fifty Royal Military Articifers. Graham soon learnt that he could expect little help from the Spaniards and that the British troops, having been so hastily despatched, were poorly equipped. Despite urgent appeals for picks, shovels and wheelbarrows, nothing could be obtained from the civil authorities.

Graham also learnt that the Brigade of Guards, which was to form the backbone of the expected reinforcement, was not going to be as strong as previously indicated. The news was a blow to Graham: 'The superiority of that corps makes a diminution of its numbers a subject of great regret,' he complained to Liverpool. 'No situation can require more steady or determined troops than the Island of Leon. Whenever the enemy can penetrate into it, the contest must be expected against a great superiority of force, and probably under circumstances of a very discouraging nature, for it will be deceiving ourselves to depend upon the Spaniards not showing a very bad example in the open field. The only hope of their behaving well must rest in the works being completed before an attack is made.'[46]

Graham considered the bend of the river, opposite to the Isla, to be a vulnerable spot. If the marshland proved firm enough for the French to pull artillery across it then batteries could be established there. The fire from these guns would then be able to cover the building of a bridge across the river. The security of this sector was therefore crucial. But the point which concerned Graham the most of all was Sancti Petri. 'Opposite to it', Graham explained to Lord Liverpool, 'the enemy has an extent of hard sandy ground with the advantage of a navigable creek which forms a natural approach quite covered from outside, and within a short distance of our batteries.' Sancti Petri was also at such a distance from the barracks where most of the troops were stationed that it might prove impossible to reinforce it in the event of an attack.[47]

Graham observed that if an entrenched camp with artillery batteries were built behind Sancti Petri on the heights on which the town of Isla stood, this point might be rendered more secure. He also thought that this fortified camp could be connected with the narrowest part of the isthmus (Torre Gorda) by a chain of redoubts. The line of redoubts would stretch along the beach and along the road between Torre Gorda and Isla and provide cover for the defenders should they be forced to retreat if the French broke through the outer defences. But for the present, Graham wrote, 'it must remain an object of great apprehension till some better plan of defence can be adopted and executed.'[48]

Yet Graham believed that the capture of Isla, and that part of the Cadiz peninsula, would not necessarily mean the loss of Cadiz itself. The seizure of the Inner Harbour with all its facilities would very likely result in the French being able to build a large number of small vessels which, if armed with cannon, could harass the city. But, Graham concluded, 'with determination on the part of the inhabitants, no real danger is to be apprehended [however] I would by no means answer for the perseverance of the inhabitants after the loss of the Isla.'[49]

The French could clearly be seen busily building boats and rafts but it was evident that it would take a very long time for them to make enough vessels for Victor to mount a serious attack upon Cadiz. Graham was far more concerned with the marshy plains of the Sancti Petri, which the Spaniards regarded as too insubstantial for the French to be able to pass a large force across, but which continued to cause him great anxiety: 'By means of the many navigable creeks which intersect the marsh, and which chiefly lead from the side next to the high ground occupied by the enemy towards the river, there may be opportunities for the establishment of posts and batteries near the banks of the river with more facility than the Spaniards are aware of.' Graham continued to press the Spaniards on the vulnerability of this area but, as he told Lord Liverpool on 12 April, 'The Spaniards, with that fatal confidence that has so often hurt them, will not be persuaded of the possibility of such an attack being made.'[50]

Wellington, who understood Cadiz's topography, was generally in agreement with Graham, and he confirmed this in a letter three days later. 'My notion of the defences required for the Isla is founded upon the species of attack which the enemy will probably make upon it. My opinion is that they will make roads across, and establish themselves upon the salt marsh, in order to force the passage of the river.'[51]

Over the course of the next few days Graham noticed that even though the French made no attempt to establish themselves on this ground, the batteries they were erecting on rising ground near Chiclana were taking on a more substantial shape and some were already armed with heavy ordnance. The French guns could reach the Allied batteries on the Isla de Leon and were able to command the most important stretches of the Sancti Petri.

Graham wanted to secure this sector by digging a canal, some three miles long, along the edge of the marsh, as a barrier which would be under the guns of the Isla. As little could be expected from the Spaniards, Graham asked Lord Liverpool to send out 'a good set of English canal diggers'.[52]

At the beginning of April, the first of the British reinforcements arrived. These troops comprised the weakened brigade of the Guards, three companies of artillery, two companies of the 95th Rifles and one company of the Staff Corps which landed on 1 April, and two days later the 2nd Battalion of the 44th Regiment arrived.[53]

Finding accommodation for this sudden influx of men into a place already over-crowded by refugees created real problems. Unlike the rest of Spain the inhabitants of Cadiz, the country's foremost naval base, were not accustomed to dealing with the billeting of troops and the locals showed little interest in opening up their houses, even to officers. Castanos provided some help by offering to put his own troops into tents, providing enough could be found, but lack of suitable quarters remained a subject of much dissatisfaction among the British soldiers.

For the troops at Isla, the only accommodation was in tents but Graham, after repeated appeals for wood and hides, was able to have huts built for the men, which was infinitely better than leaving them sweating under canvas throughout the long Andalusia summer.[54] The two companies of the 2nd Battalion of the 95th Rifles which had served at Walcheren were in such poor physical condition that they contracted 'intermittent fevers' and had to be sent into Cadiz where they were placed in barracks.

Graham's force was further reinforced at the end of May with the arrival of three troops of the 2nd Light Dragoons (Hussars) of the King's German Legion (KGL). If Graham was obliged to undertake any offensive action, he now had his own cavalry arm. Just three days later the 2nd Battalion 30th Regiment arrived from Gibraltar. On 4 June there was a *feu de joie* for King George's birthday and some 4,500 British troops stood for the salute. Graham now had a fair body of men – infantry, cavalry and artillery under his command. Soon it would be called into one of the most desperate encounters of the entire Peninsular War.[55]

CHAPTER 3

A Common Cause

The siege of Cadiz continued quietly. There was some skirmishing by the light companies at the outposts, but the French were primarily engaged in building their batteries and their boats, and the people of Cadiz were untroubled.[1]

There was, however, a severe on-shore gale which blew a large number of vessels across Cadiz Bay. The ships, which included three Spanish line-of-battle ships (amongst which was the 100-gun, three-decker *Concepcion*), grounded on the French side of the water where they became stranded. They were fired upon by the French with red-hot shot; all the ships were destroyed and some amongst the crews were killed. The survivors struggled ashore and were taken prisoner. More than thirty merchant ships were destroyed in the storm including a transport ship carrying the flank companies and the staff of the 4th Foot, some 130 men. They ran aground near Port St Mary and the entire contingent was taken prisoner.[2]

Many of the stranded vessels were laden with cargo which the French were able to recover. The men on the ramparts of Matagorda, watching the enemy stripping the ships, could not resist the temptation to join in the looting. The soldiers from the fort could only attempt such a venture at night, running the risk of stumbling into a French piquet in the dark. Yet many times the soldiers and sailors from Matagorda crossed the dangerous marshes and reached the wrecks. On many of these night-time expeditions the British troops encountered French soldiers, also using the cover of night to search the wrecks for valuables, but rarely was there any trouble between the two nationalities. Indeed, when wine or spirits were found, they often sat down and drank together![3]

Though things appeared to be quiet across the Sancti Petri, Victor was actually planning to regain Fort Matagorda. At first Victor's engineers believed that they could bombard Cadiz into surrender by erecting batteries as far forward as they could on the ground they occupied around the harbour. The French trundled their artillery along the causeway which carried the highroad from Seville across the salt marshes of the Sancti Petri. They tried to erect batteries along the banks of the river but found the boggy ground, cut with channels and inlets, utterly impracticable. They could dig no deeper than three feet without water seeping into the trench.

The British troops were camped close to the Sancti Petri by the broken Bridge of Zuarzo. Guards were posted to watch the river, which is very narrow at this point, though not fordable. The only approach to the bridge was along a causeway that traversed the salt marshes and pickets were pushed over the river to keep the French at bay. Regarded by the troops as the 'Post of Honour', these outposts were held by Barnard's five companies of the 95th Rifles and a six-gun artillery battery, along with a small contingent of Spanish cavalry. Directly opposite the bridge was a French battery which was well within range of the British guns, but the opposing artillerymen seldom exchanged fire. Because of the narrowness of the causeway the French could not mount a serious attack on the outposts and none was attempted.[4]

The two other key positions along the river were held by the Spaniards. These were the two extreme ends of the Isla side of the isthmus opposite the Arsenal of Carracas and the Punta de Sancti Petri. In the town of Isla itself was Graham with the British Brigade of Guards to act as a general reserve.

Faced with such opposition Victor pulled back to Chiclana which became the headquarters of the blockading force and where Ruffin's division was permanently based. Yet Victor was determined to find some way of threatening Cadiz and the next point of attack which the French considered was further north opposite the La Caracca where the river was very narrow, or against Fort Puntales. For the latter to be possible they would need to retake Matagorda.

Secretly batteries were built on high ground on the Trocadero, hidden from view by a complex of buildings. By 21 April the batteries were armed and ready to begin their bombardment upon Matagorda. That night the French blew up the buildings, exposing the batteries. At 02.00 hours, according to Sergeant Donaldson, the French batteries – forty-eight of the largest calibre guns and howitzers – opened fire, and 'the silent gloom of the night was broken by the rapid flash, and the reverberating thunder of the cannon.' The first French salvo was directed at the Spanish man-of-war which was stationed off Matagorda. The warship caught fire and she was forced to slip her cable and move down the bay out of range from the French guns. Further volleys of heated shot then dispersed the gun-boats, leaving them to face the French batteries alone. 'Death now began to stalk about in the most dreadful form,' remembered Donaldson. 'The French soon acquired a fatal precision with their shot, sending them through our embrasures, killing and wounding with every volley.' The fort's defenders attempted to retaliate, but, as increasing numbers of the trained artillerymen were killed or incapacitated, the British counter-fire became increasingly less effective. 'The carnage now became dreadful; the ramparts were strewed with the dead and the wounded; and blood, brains, and mangled limbs, lay scattered in every direction.'

The bombardment continued all through the day. 'Our guns had been well directed at first,' continued Donaldson; 'but, towards evening, most of the artillery who had commanded them were either killed or wounded; and the direction of them was then taken by men who knew little about it. The consequence was that much ammunition was used to little purpose.'[5]

The battle between the batteries continued until the early hours of the following morning. As the firing had died down Donaldson took stock of the situation: 'I saw the ramparts covered with the pale and disfigured corpses of those who, a few hours before, were rioting in the fullness of health and strength, and others writhing in agony, under the severe wounds they had received.'[6]

When Donaldson went below into the bomb-proof shelter, he was shocked to find that the wounded filled the whole place. The surgeon was assisted by a woman – Mrs Reston – who had volunteered to join the fort's small garrison. This lady became known as 'the heroine of Matagorda' and she later achieved some degree of celebrity status.

At dawn the French guns recommenced their bombardment of Matagorda. By this time the French gunners had their sights well adjusted and almost every shot hit its intended target. The Spanish flag, which flew above Matagorda, was repeatedly cut down by French shot. Each time the flagstaff was repaired and the flag raised again, only for it to be shot down within minutes. Eventually, one of the frustrated sailors replaced the flag with a Royal Navy ensign from one of the boats. There was a great cheer as the ensign was raised above the fort. But the officer commanding ordered it to be pulled down, before it too was hit by the French cannon. The Spanish flag was raised once more but when it was shot down again it was left lying in the dust.

By the middle of the morning, three of the fort's guns had been disabled and General Graham crossed over the bay to see for himself the situation at Matagorda. He saw that the fort was in such a ruinous state that the garrison would not be able to fight off an assault by the French, and he ordered an immediate reinforcement from Cadiz. But the more men there were in the fort, the greater the casualty list grew. Graham decided that occupation of Matagorda was no longer justified, and he ordered his men back to the safety of Cadiz. It had defied the French for fifty-five days.[7]

The French had evidently been watching developments in Matagorda and they decided to make a move as soon as the defenders were seen preparing to withdraw. A column of infantry advanced across the open ground towards the fort. The British engineers had prepared a number of mines to demolish what was left of Matagorda's defences, but the sight of the approaching French column proved irresistible. There were only three cannon still serviceable. These were 'stuffed' full of all the loose powder, grapeshot and ball cartridge that could be found. When the French column was just 200 yards from the fort, the guns erupted their masses of metal 'into the very middle of their column, and laid the half of them prostrate on the earth.' The rest of the column wheeled right about and marched rapidly back to the French lines.[8]

The battered defences were then blown up under the direction of Major Lefebre, but he too was struck down before he could escape back to Cadiz – the last man whose blood wetted the ruins of Matagorda. The unfortunate Lefebre was leaving the fort with Captain Maclean, these being the last two men to descend the ladder to the waiting boats. Sir Richard Henegan described what happened next: 'A point of etiquette here suddenly arose between these gallant officers as to which should be the last to quit the scene of danger. The commanding officer, drawing back, politely offered the precedence to the Major, who, equally polite, was anxious not to concede it to the Commandant of the Fort. As thus they stood, irresolute, a thirty-two pound shot, in violation of all good rules of breeding, struck off the Major's head, and so the question was decided.'[9]

The loss of Matagorda dismayed the Spaniards and there was another set-back when, on the night of 15/16 May, the French prisoners held in the rotting hulks in Cadiz Bay since the capitulation of Bailén managed to overpower the crew of the sloop *Castile* during a heavy storm. They cut the sloop's cables with axes they had stolen from workmen who had been patching up holes in the old ship and, with the help of a make-shift sail which they had put together from their hammocks, the ship was blown ashore to the French side of the bay to the northwest of Matagorda. A number of boats were hurriedly sent after the *Castile* but the escapers were prepared. The ballast of the sloop consisted of cannon balls (24-pounder and 36-pounder) and, as the boats approached, the French threw the cannonballs down on their pursuers, who quickly withdrew.[10]

The Spaniards were so 'incensed' at the escape of the poor wretches who had been incarcerated for two years, and who had been half-starved by their captors, that their gunners continued to fire upon the hulk even after it had run aground. Lieutenant Brett, commanding the guns in Fort Puntales, refused to fire at the unarmed prisoners. Altogether thirty-four staff officers, 337 officers and 348 soldiers escaped.[11]

The storm lashed the whole of the Spanish south-west coast for four days and resulted in more than forty merchant ships as well as warships being driven on shore. 'The coast exhibited the lamentable spectacle of several thousand unfortunate individuals, struggling against the waves, on the wrecks of ships,' wrote Jean Sarrazin, 'but the sea was so heavy, not more than six hundred could be saved.'[12] The French prisoners in the remaining hulks in Cadiz Bay were completely cut off from the land. 'The storm was so great that we could not receive our supply of provisions from the land,' wrote one of the captives. 'Our signals of distress were wholly disregarded by the Spanish authorities; and had it not been for the humanity of the British . . . who sent his boats to our relief, many more of our miserable men must have perished.'[13]

Remarkably the Spaniards did not take any measures to prevent a recurrence and ten days later the prisoners of the *Argonauta* attempted a similar break for freedom during another south-west gale. This time they were less fortunate, the ship being grounded on a mud-bank. Though French boats from the mainland were able to recover many of the prisoners, a number were still on the ship when it was set on fire by the Allied guns. Others died when the French boats plying between the ship and the shore were sank by Allied gunfire. 'To me this is a most disgusting event in war,' C. B. Vaughan wrote to Charles Stuart; 'there were also eleven officers' wives on board.' Following this second escape, the prisoners were shipped to the Balearic and Canary islands.[14]

After the French had occupied Matagorda they re-built its shattered walls and rearmed the fort. They also re-established the ruined forts of San José to the north of Matagorda and San Luis on the Trocadero, which had been inaccessible to them all the time Matagorda had been in Allied hands. These were the most advanced points from which the French could bombard Cadiz and these forts were armed with the heaviest calibre guns they possessed. It was found that from the Trocadero the French 12-inch mortars could reach the outermost parts of Cadiz, as could the 36-pounder cannon when elevated at an angle of from thirty to forty-three degrees.[15]

This caused considerable unrest in Cadiz as the townsfolk believed that the French guns would be able to drop their shells directly into the heart of the city. Graham knew differently and he was determined to show the locals that even if some shells could reach Cadiz they had little to worry about. With some difficulty, he moved a large mortar into the ditch of the left bastion of the land-front of the city. The mortars were loaded with a 20-lb charge and fired several times by British gunners towards Matagorda. None of the shells reached the fort. 'This trial', Graham reported, 'which the Spaniards seemed afraid to make, has satisfied people that the town cannot be bombarded from that point.'[16]

The reason why the French had devoted so much effort at establishing themselves in the forts was that they hoped to be able to demolish Fort Puntales and to drive the Allied ships from the Inner Harbour. As Graham had demonstrated, the distance was too great for the French guns to do much harm to Puntales, but the ships in the Inner Harbour were vulnerable and they had to move either into the Outer Harbour or eastwards close to Isla.

With the French guns unable to do any real damage, the only danger to Cadiz would come from an amphibious attack and Graham continued to press the Spaniards to put more resources into building the island's defences – but with little effect. His frustration with the lack of energy displayed by his allies fill his despatches: 'The works at Puntales not carried on with the spirit and exertion required,' he wrote on 25 April. 'The situation of things here does not improve', he lamented five days later, 'for the energy of the different authorities does not rise with the difficulties. It would be endless to enumerate the instances of want of foresight, of inattention, and of indifference that occur.'[17]

Manning the defences at Isla required just 500 British rank and file to be under arms each day, and this allowed a thousand British troops to be employed at any one time in building the entrenched camp on the Isla heights. The men worked for a week at a time before being relieved. They were given an allowance of six pence a day for eight hours' labour under the direction of the engineers. In principle, this payment was for the 'wear and tear of necessaries' whilst working, but it clearly gave the men some much-welcome extra cash because many of the men volunteered to work extra hours at the same equivalent rate of pay. The only restriction imposed upon the men was that they were not allowed to work overtime during the stipulated afternoon break when the sun was at its hottest. 'In this way', Graham was able to report in the first week of June', 'the work has gone on cheerfully, and a great deal has been done.' Strangely, very few of the local population were employed on the defences and those that did work were paid 'extravagant wages'.[18]

The work was not without danger and a man was appointed to watch the French batteries, and when a gun was discharged he would call out 'shot' or 'shell'. Sometimes these shells would fall in a battery and explode, an experience familiar to Thomas Bunbury, a captain in the 20th Portuguese Regiment: 'The best way of avoiding the splinters was to lie down flat; for if it fell near you a better chance of escape might be afforded than if you were more distant from it, as the splinters generally fell wide after a shell had burst . . . I was once a spectator in one of the batteries, where a Spaniard was lying asleep under one of the banquettes, when a shell from the enemy fell into the battery. We had all thrown ourselves flat on our faces as distant from the danger as we possibly could on so short a notice. Unfortunately, the noise awoke the sleeping Spaniard who was before safe. He now ran about rubbing his eyes, and placed himself nearly over the shell, which, in exploding, killed him on the spot.'[19]

On 13 May Graham learnt that the British force at Cadiz was to be considered part of Wellington's army and that the heads of the various military departments were to report directly to their respective heads in Lisbon.

Wellington himself was uncomfortable with this arrangement and he expressed his wish 'to leave to the decision of the general officer on the spot all those matters referred to in his instructions.' He also told Graham that he wanted him to continue to make all the arrangements for the British forces at Cadiz as he had before this ruling was in place, 'in the perfect confidence that I shall concur in them all.'[20]

At the same time Wellington expressed his worries about the health of the troops during the 'great heats of the summer at Cadiz'. With Cadiz so over-crowded he doubted that a suitably healthy place could be found to establish a military hospital anywhere on the island. He advised Graham to form a hospital at Ceuta (an autonomous Spanish town on the North African coast) and, if he did so, Wellington would send some hospital ships from Lisbon which could be used to transport the sick and the wounded to the hospital.[21]

This was a sensible idea, but politics intervened. The Spaniards were far from happy with the presence of British soldiers in Cadiz and if Graham tried to establish yet another British base on their territory it would seem to confirm the suspicions of many that their so-called allies were out to grab as much Spanish land as they could get their hands on. Until a more satisfactory solution could be found, the British had to make use of the local general hospital, the 'Hospicio', which was situated in a 'very airy situation' near the ramparts at St Sebastian. Though only a small place, part of it was given over to the British troops.[22]

On 27 July Sir Richard Keats arrived at Cadiz to take command of the British squadron. The first objective that Lord Liverpool had set him was the removal of the ships of the Spanish fleet to a place of safety. The Spanish warships were anchored in the middle of Cadiz Outer Harbour where, Liverpool observed 'they will probably be driven by the first gale of wind to the opposite shore, and in that case, unless they can be burnt by us, the enemy will gain possession of them.' This would answer all Victor's prayers, enabling him to attack Cadiz from the sea.[23]

Surprisingly, Liverpool was also worried about the safety of the British troops amidst a city full of Spaniards. Though he regarded the majority of the population as being 'well disposed and attached to the British interest', he admitted to Graham that it was impossible 'to divest one's mind of the suspicion of a possibility of treachery on the part of some of the persons in power.' He advised Graham to make sure that his troops occupied the city's main strongpoints, particularly to secure a safe retreat to the harbour. Keats had also been briefed by Liverpool before he sailed for Cadiz on the possibility of a sudden evacuation.[24]

Graham was able to set Liverpool's mind at ease as the only post held jointly with the Spaniards was the bridge of Zuarzo and the adjacent battery. Every other strongpoint was already exclusively in British hands. With regard to Cadiz itself, Graham replied, 'I am so much convinced of the impossibility of any successful attempt being made by traitors while the great body of the inhabitants are hostile to the French and well inclined to us.'[25]

*

It was now the middle of summer and far to the north the most decisive campaign of the Peninsular War was beginning. Napoleon knew that if he was to conquer Iberia he had to drive the British out of Portugal. For this task he sent his most experienced commander, Andre Masséna.

With a nominal force of some 130,000 men, allowing a field army of little more than half that number, Masséna laid siege to the Spanish border fortress of Ciudad Rodrigo. Wellington was well aware that 'the first and great objective', of the French, 'will be to get the English out' and he had prepared well for the attack which he knew was inevitable. He had constructed a series of fortifications stretching across the neck of the Lisbon peninsula. Behind these defences, the famous Lines of Torres Vedras, Wellington would make his stand.[26]

After a siege lasting seventy-six days, Masséna had forced the garrison of Ciudad Rodrigo to surrender. Wellington had made no attempt to raise the siege. His Anglo-Portuguese army was inferior to that of France's most successful marshal and Wellington was not going to cross swords with the enemy in the open terrain around the frontier.

This was not appreciated by the Spaniards who felt betrayed. The newly invoked Cortes in Cadiz even discontinued communications with Wellington for a while but soon relented, acknowledging that an attempt to save the fortress might have been 'attended by the most disastrous consequences.'

Masséna crossed the Portuguese frontier on 24 July but, as Napoleon had instructed him not to invade Portugal until the autumn, he was in no hurry. The next obstacle facing the optimistically named French Army of Portugal was the Portuguese fortress of Almeida, and it was almost three weeks before the French troops broke ground to start the siege trenches. This time, though, there would be no protracted siege.

On 23 August, the French siege guns opened fire. That night, as the artillery duel continued from the siege batteries and the ramparts of the fortress, there occurred a disaster that Professor Oman considered to be 'unparalleled in magnitude during the whole Peninsular War'. A French shell ignited the fortress' main powder magazine which contained some 150,000 pounds of gunpowder, and in excess of 1,000.000 prepared charges. [27]

In an instant a great part of Almeida had disappeared and the rest was a pile of rubble. Portugal's northern gateway had been blown open. Nothing now, it seemed, stood in Masséna's way. Wellington, and the British troops, would be driven into the sea.

With the French moving ever closer to Lisbon, Wellington needed every man he could and Lord Liverpool, believing that Cadiz was now safe, advised Wellington that he could take a number of men from Cadiz to help in the defence of Lisbon: 'Under the present circumstances of the contest in the Peninsula I can see no reason why you should not draw about 2,000 men from Cadiz. The British and Portuguese garrison consists at present of 9,000 men. It will consist of 7,000 when these corps are drawn from the place; and, considering the improved state of the defences, that all Victor's efforts appear to be directed rather to his own defence than to an attack, and that the force in Andalusia with all its detachments is hardly equal at the present moment to any serious and decisive operations in that quarter. I should certainly think that the 7,000 men to which I have referred will, for the present, be amply sufficient, together with the Spanish forces already there, for the defence of the place.' Liverpool closed the letter by stating that 'they might always be replaced at Cadiz if circumstances should afterwards render it expedient.'[28]

The troops that Liverpool wished to send to Lisbon were the 13th Light Dragoons, 109 men; 95th Rifles, 100 men; the 79th Foot of 1,020 men, and the 700 men of the 94th Foot. This was a total of 1,980 effectives. Wellington also arranged for reinforcements sent from operations in the Mediterranean which were expected to land in Cadiz, to be sent on to Lisbon.[29]

As well as bolstering the forces under his direct command, Wellington was advised to make sure that if he failed to hold back the French in Portugal he would still be able to evacuate to Cadiz to continue the war against Napoleon. One of the greatest problems in such an eventuality would be the safe removal of all the army's horses. Because of a severe lack of suitable transport, if an evacuation appeared probable, the horses would start being shipped before the bulk of the troops. Wellington, therefore, ordered Graham to prepare a magazine of 30,000 rations of straw and 30,000 rations of forage corn just in case.

Wellington, though, remained opposed to a withdrawal to Cadiz, and he repeatedly expressed this view to Lord Liverpool, using every argument he could to emphasize his point. His main objection was that the introduction of more British troops into Cadiz would not be appreciated by the Spaniards. ('It may be expected that the people of Cadiz, and possibly even the Spanish Government, would refuse us admission, which would be an awkward occurrence, and might render uncomfortable the situation of those already in the place.')[30] As this reasoning failed to move Liverpool, Wellington tried a different tack, and one which revealed his real fears if he was forced to abandon Portugal: 'I will do whatever the King's Government think proper to order me to do; but I wish you to consider whether it may not be deemed a hardship upon General Graham that I should go there, and supersede him in the command of the operations for the defence of Cadiz, at the moment when the measures for the defence will be completed, and the serious attack is about to commence.'[31]

Wellington was clearly worried that if he was forced to evacuate from Portugal there would be no role for him in Cadiz ('I think that I shall myself stand in a very awkward situation at Cadiz,' he eventually conceded), and he urged Liverpool to consider either Gibraltar or Ceuta as an alternative base of operations for the British Army. However, Wellington soon found himself fully occupied with the defence of Portugal as the war in the Peninsula reached its most critical stage.[32]

As Masséna's army advanced deeper into Portugal, so Wellington retreated. Ahead of the retreating Allied force, the Portuguese were abandoning their homes and destroying their crops. The French found themselves marching through a virtual desert with food becoming ever harder to obtain.

On the formidable heights of Busaco, Wellington paused in his retreat and stood to face his pursuers. The result was a resounding victory for the Anglo-Portuguese Army. Yet Wellington continued his withdrawal and the French pushed on after the Allies, believing that they would soon be at Lisbon. Then they stumbled into the vast ranges of forts and strongpoints known as the Lines of Torres Vedras.

After his defeat at Busaco, Masséna was not prepared to assault the Lines of Torres Vedras with the force at his disposal. Equally he had no intention of admitting defeat and withdrawing. He believed that he could still drive Wellington into the sea and win the campaign. But to do this he needed a considerable reinforcement, and so he appealed to Napoleon for more men. Meanwhile Masséna settled down in the bleak Portuguese countryside hoping that soon the Emperor would send him the men he so desperately needed.

*

Napoleon's armies had now reached the limit of their expansion in the Peninsula. Operations had stagnated in Portugal as they had at Cadiz, where there were no significant moves by the besiegers, and the lack of aggression demonstrated by the French encouraged the Spaniards to consider offensive action against the invaders. In typical Spanish fashion, General Blake, who had now been placed in command of the Spanish troops at Cadiz, proposed a large-scale sortie against the French lines. Graham considered the idea dangerous as he had no confidence in the Spanish troops when operating openly in the field. The history of the war in Spain had been one of recklessly ambitious schemes by the Spaniards which invariably led to disaster.

Graham, therefore, preferred rather to adopt small-scale hit-and-run attacks along the adjacent coast against the French posts. General Campbell at Gibraltar had already signalled his willingness to cooperate in such operations with the detachment of troops under his command based at the port of Tarifa some seventy miles along the coast. Graham saw that, by conducting a continual program of harassment, the Spaniards' need for action would be satisfied without jeopardising the security of Cadiz. Yet, above all other considerations, Graham wanted to preserve the goodwill that existed between himself and General Blake. If, or when, the French finally attacked Cadiz, Graham needed to know that the Spaniards would stand shoulder-to-shoulder with their British allies. So when Blake asked Graham to march with him in an assault upon the French positions, Graham felt that he simply could not refuse.

Naturally, Graham informed both Wellington and Liverpool of the proposed enterprise which he believed 'does not promise success according to any calculation I can make.'[33] Initially, Wellington also rejected the idea and he urged Graham to oppose the scheme. His reasoning was that it was known that Victor's force when it crossed the Sierra Morena was between 20,000 and 25,000 strong and was likely to still be more or less the same. This meant that the Anglo-Spanish field force that could be sent from Cadiz, after deducting the numbers needed to be left guarding the Isla, would be inferior to the French. 'The success, in this view of the case,' Wellington concluded, 'is not promising.'[34]

Likewise Lord Liverpool replied on 12 July to council caution. 'The object of His Majesty in sending a force to Cadiz was the security of that city and the Isle of Leon. If the situation . . . should render an attack upon the enemy advisable, the advantages might be of such a nature that it would not be right that you should decline affording the assistance of the force under your command for such an expedition. But you will consider yourself possessed of a discretion to abstain from co-operation in any offensive operation which may appear to you to be unnecessary or inexpedient, and you are fully at liberty to make use of the authority of His Majesty's Government in this respect.'[35]

Wellington had already made his views clear. Though he saw that the French forces in Andalusia might be ordered to lift the siege of Cadiz to help support Masséna's offensive in Portugal, he did not want the Allied force at Cadiz to conduct an operation from that place: 'The failure of the operation might, according to the circumstances attending it,' he told Graham on 20 June, 'endanger the safety of the place itself, from the loss sustained, and the want of confidence which it would create.'[36]

Blake, however, continued to press for his offensive plan to be adopted. Graham, as diplomatically as he could, stated that he 'could not be desirous of the operation taking place', but if Blake insisted on undertaking the scheme 'he would find me ready to obey his orders in co-operating in any way he wished.'

This worried Wellington who continued to argue against the plan, telling Graham that 'the French officers, who are by no means satisfied with their situation in Andalusia, would probably call out for reinforcements, when they should find that the allies had begun to make sorties from Cadiz.' In other words an attack upon Victor's corps might well bring matters to a head and compel Napoleon to bring an overwhelming force against Cadiz, which would prove ruinous to the Spanish cause. Nevertheless he understood the difficulty under which Graham laboured in opposing this and other similar schemes, and he therefore advised Graham to refer Blake to the article in the conditions on which the British Government agreed to send troops to help the Spaniards, i.e. that no detachments should be made from the British force defending Cadiz. By doing this Graham would be able to decline any involvement in a sortie from the Isla without offending Blake: 'This will relieve you from all difficulties, which you might otherwise feel, in discussing with General Blake the merits of the plan which he might propose.'[37]

After much discussion a plan of operations was decided upon. Graham would lead a combined Anglo-Spanish force against the French line at Chiclana. The force would be split into two columns. One would cross the Sancti Petri by boat bridge to deliver a frontal assault upon Chiclana, whilst the second column would be landed upon an open beach to the south to attack Victor's positions in the rear. At the same time a diversionary attack would be made by the small British force at Tarifa and the Spaniards at Algeciras which would be shipped round to land and assault Medina Sidonia, a few miles east of Chiclana.

As it transpired, the plan was repeatedly delayed because of frequent gales which made disembarkation on an open beach extremely hazardous and therefore too unpredictable. This could mean that the frontal assault might attack only to find that the supporting column was unable to land in time to join the battle. Then, on 18 July, a captured dispatch sent from Victor to Berthier gave details of the strength of the French forces opposite Cadiz. It showed that I Corps had been reinforced since February. This settled matters for Graham as he was now 'more than ever convinced that the projected offensive operation would have been attended with disaster.'[38] When he learnt that the offensive had been cancelled, Wellington expressed his relief in a letter to Graham: 'I am glad to find that the great plan of attack at Cadiz upon the enemy's lines is relinquished; it would have undoubtedly failed.'[39]

Surprisingly, the subject continued to be discussed and it was even proposed that additional troops could be sent from Sir John Stuart's Mediterranean force to provide Graham with a larger army. Wellington was quick to dispel any thoughts that even with this reinforcement Graham should consider offensive action: ' . . . even if all the troops expected from the Mediterranean should be added to your corps, I should still be of opinion that the attempt to raise the siege of Cadiz is one of considerable risk.'[40]

Even Blake's enthusiasm for an offensive was evaporating, and when Liverpool next wrote to Graham he spelled out exactly how he should respond to any future requests from the Spaniards: 'You will state that the force under your command was in a great measure withdrawn from the army under Lord Wellington for the protection of Cadiz and the Isle of Leon, and your instructions do not permit you to take a part in any operations beyond these limits.' If Liverpool would have left the instructions at that, Graham's situation would have been completely unambiguous, but the Minister ended his note with this caveat, 'except in a case where the enterprise itself shall appear to you to be prudent, and when considerable advantages may be expected to arise out of it to the common cause.' This placed all the onus of responsibility squarely on Graham's shoulders. When the Spaniards next suggested an offensive operation to raise the siege – an objective clearly of advantage to the 'common cause' – Graham had no grounds upon which he could refuse to co-operate.[41]

Further concerns were raised by Wellington who drew Graham's attention to the information published in the British press concerning details of defences at Cadiz. 'I was astonished some time ago', Wellington wrote, 'to see in the English newspapers an accurate account of the batteries and works erecting at Cadiz and on the Isla, with the number of guns, and of what calibre, each was to contain, and their distance from each other, and from the enemy's works.' This information could only have come from a British officer in his letters home and it provided Napoleon with far more information than he could otherwise expect.[42]

Nevertheless, Cadiz's defences were growing stronger and Graham's perseverance and determination began to be acknowledged by the men under his command: 'We might defy the power of France to expel us from hence if all were done that might be done,' wrote Graham's Chief Engineer in a letter home, 'but we have only British troops at work on this important position, and our numbers will not permit the progress which the exigency of affairs requires . . . We have in our respected General a confidence which is daily on the increase . . . We may possibly retain our ground. If we do, although our success may have none of the brilliance of victory, yet his merits, who, by patience, prudence, and self-possession, shall have kept all quiet within our lines, preserved tolerable harmony, and kept an enterprising enemy off with very inadequate means.'[43]

The reality was, however, that Victor could never take Cadiz even if it was only lightly garrisoned and this fact was apparent even to the British Minister of War in London. As a result the troops ordered to be shipped to Lisbon were despatched on 17 August. Graham declared that he was happy to send Wellington more troops if required, but he advised Liverpool not to reduce the force at Cadiz below four British battalions of infantry, plus some companies of the 95th Rifles and all the artillery.[44]

Graham was also keen to leave Cadiz and join the British forces in Portugal where the next great battles were certain to take place. But the failures of the local authorities meant that both he and the British garrison were still needed to ensure the safety of the Spanish Government. As he explained to Wellington at the end of August, if the Spaniards had applied their energies towards the defence of Cadiz rather than on 'their restless system of warfare without any object' then 'a numerous army might have been created here, and its discipline been considerably advanced, the works of defence might have been nearly completed, and thus much of the greatest part of the British force, no longer necessary for security, become quite disposable.'[45]

At this time the Spanish forces defending Cadiz amounted to 13,892 infantry, 1,442 cavalry, 840 artillery, and 108 Engineers, a total of 15,291 of all ranks. In September, the authorities ordered the conscription of every male between the ages of sixteen and fifty-five. Depending upon their status they could either join the privileged *Voluntarios Distinguidos* or the ordinary *milicias urbanes*. Anyone who was unfit to serve had to pay a substitution fee proportionate to their income.[46] As a result of Graham's recommendations, and the expected increase in the numbers of the Spanish brought about by the conscription, two more battalions, the 30th and 44th, were shipped to Lisbon on 25 September.[47]

Because of the importance of Cadiz to the Allied cause, Wellington remained convinced that the French would mount a serious attack upon the place as soon as they were able. With this in mind, he asked Admiral Keats to consider how he would deal with the naval contest which there would be, sooner or later, in the Inner Harbour of Cadiz. It was known that the Spaniards had left what Wellington described as 'large naval means' in the merchants' yards on the Trocadero and that the French were actively employed in building boats. He suggested to Keats that he might 'strike a blowO' against the Trocadero before it was too late, though this idea was not immediately adopted by the admiral.[48] Wellington also told Lord Liverpool that if it appeared that at any time a French attack was imminent he would send troops from Lisbon to strengthen Graham's force.[49]

Graham, on the other hand, was becoming increasingly frustrated with his dealings with the Spaniards and he wanted to be with Wellington in the main theatre of the war. But these were difficult times for British arms in the Peninsula. Though Wellington commanded a force of more than 50,000 British and Portuguese troops and the British garrison at Cadiz numbered less than 10,000, Graham's prospects appeared better than those of Wellington who might well be driven out of Portugal by Masséna. As Wellington had explained to Graham in May, he did not expect 'anything very brilliant' in northern Spain. 'I must maintain myself in the Peninsula till it is necessary to withdraw from it; and when it is necessary to withdraw I must carry off the army without disgrace, and without loss if possible . . . On the other hand, the state of affairs at Cadiz is highly interesting, not only to the Peninsula, but to Great Britain and to the world. You may render the most important services there, and to withdraw you from that place might shake the confidence and damp the spirits of the Spanish Government and of the people of the town . . . However desirable, therefore, it might be to me that you should be in Portugal, I cannot but think that it would be most advantageous to the public interest that you should remain at Cadiz, at least as long as that place is seriously threatened by the enemy.'[50]

Liverpool agreed with Wellington and found a solution to the problem of Graham's position, by nominating him as Wellington's second-in-command, should Wellington ever be forced to relinquish his command at Lisbon, but keeping him at Cadiz until further notice. This was outlined to Wellington: 'As to the question of Second-in-Command in the Peninsula, it has been most seriously considered in the Cabinet. Graham was intended for that service; but we were all of opinion that the service at Cadiz is of such a critical nature that it could not be entrusted to any person so well as to him, considering his habits of acting with foreigners and his personal intimacy with General Castanos. He is certainly to be considered as Second-in-Command in the Peninsula. If anything should unfortunately happen to you, he should succeed to the command of the army. Under very special circumstances you might send to him to join you; but it is very much wished that, except in a case of emergency, he should remain where he is for the present.'[51]

Lord Liverpool was very worried about the security of Cadiz and he did not want Graham to leave. As the seat of Spain's government and principle port, Cadiz was vitally important as a source of money for the British forces in the

Peninsula. Though the American colonies no longer provided the great quantities of gold and silver of earlier times, Spain, and therefore Cadiz, still received considerable sums from its territories in the New World. It was this gold that fuelled the war in the Peninsula. Wellington knew this only too well: 'I must inform you that it is impossible to maintain an army in the Peninsula, and to perform the engagements into which the king has entered with the Portuguese Government, without the assistance of the money to be procured at Cadiz and Gibraltar for bills upon England.' If Cadiz fell into the hands of the French it would mean the end of Allied operations in Iberia. Spain would belong to Napoleon.[52]

CHAPTER 4

A Considerable Risk

S eemingly untroubled by events beyond the Sancti Petri, the great and the mighty in Cadiz were embroiled in their own conflict in the Real Teatro where, at last, the new Cortes sat in session, and from the outset, it was the scene of bitter wrangling. Originating in the twelfth century, the local Cortes of the various regions of Spain met separately, though infrequently, to vote on taxes and to discuss legislation. After the consolidation of royal authority in the fifteenth century, the powers of the Cortes were curtailed and they were seldom convoked. What was formed at Cadiz was the first *national* Cortes of Spain, composed of elected representatives from each province in the country. The Cortes ruled Spain, in principle if not always in practice, throughout the rest of the Peninsular War as its first democratic government.

So it was that, throughout the spring and summer of 1810, the deputies from all across Spain travelled to Cadiz. Such were the difficulties of communication and transportation across occupied Spain, however, it was not until 24 September that the Cortes sat for the first time, and even then less than half its members had reached Spain's new seat of Government.[1]

In theory there was to be a deputy for every 50,000 people throughout Spain. The method of selection, however, was somewhat convoluted. Each village chose an elector who would meet with other electors in the chief town of the district. They would select a body of secondary electors whose role was to choose a final committee for the whole province. It was this body, the *Junta provincial electoral* which, along with the Governor, the Archbishop and the Intendant of the province, would choose the deputies for the Cortes. This complex system could only be followed in those regions free of the enemy and every part of Spain was occupied by French forces, in whole or in part, except Valencia, Murcia, Estremadura, Galacia and the Balearic Isles.

The election of representatives for many occupied regions was by secret meetings between insurgent leaders or, if even this arrangement was not possible, representatives would simply be chosen by the five-man Regency Council from anyone who happened to be in Cadiz who came from that particular region![2]

To the Liberal reformers, the Constitution was 'the most formidable army that the French have had to face, for it has transformed . . . a horde of savages into a nation of free men.' Yet the endless debating of the Cortes meant that few positive decisions were ever achieved and the armies of Spain were in fact little more than ill-coordinated hordes. 'We say that the entire nation should not breathe anything but war', wrote one anonymous critic in Cadiz, 'but we wish to wage this war without subjecting ourselves to the severe discipline of a military government and idle under the rule of a democracy that comes very close to anarchy and is incapable of preserving tranquility and good order.'

If the actions of the Cortes were generally ponderous and slow, some of the new assembly's decisions were supported by all parties and quickly promulgated. One of its first acts was to decree a new levy of 80,000 conscripts and the Cortes declared that military service should be universal – a concept that would have been unimaginable two or three years before.

The principle of national unity was further fostered by removing the old provincial army titles. Thus the Army of Catalonia became the First Army; the forces in Valencia were re-named the Second Army; the Murcian forces became the Third Army; the troops in Cadiz, the Fourth Army: the Army of Extremadura, the Fifth; and the Galacian army was the Sixth. The old titles, however, remained in popular use.

Within just a few weeks of its inauguration the Cortes began to flex its muscles. One of its first acts was to allow freedom of the press. This, wrote Graham optimistically, was 'a death-blow to the inquisition and despotism in Spain'. The Cortes also disbanded the Regency in its then current form – though it still maintained its executive powers – and appointed a new Regency Council of just three members, including General Blake.[3]

This was good news for Graham, who expected that Blake would energise the locals into committing more resources to improving Cadiz's defences: 'I am most anxious to have an opportunity, before you are involved in the business of your high office, to lay before you some observations on what appears to me indispensable to be done without a moment's delay for the security of the position.'[4]

Blake did indeed meet Graham the following day to discuss these observations. But as the days passed into weeks and there was still little practical assistance coming from the Spaniards, it became apparent that Graham's faith in the new Regency was misplaced. It was only when Graham threatened to evacuate the entire British force from Cadiz that a measure of grudging help was finally given.

Such weighty matters seemed to trouble the ordinary citizens of Cadiz little as for much of the time during the siege there was a party mood in Cadiz. Richard Henegan recalled the atmosphere of some of the city's 'gay' parties, where 'the castanets and silver-toned guitar accompanied the light and graceful forms of the Andalusian women in their voluptuous and unrivalled dance. Sometimes the hissing rush of a death-winged messenger from the enemy would, for a moment, stop the dance [then] the lovely dancer would again resume the soft waltz as if forgetful of the past and present danger'.[5]

The Spanish were not alone in enjoying themselves. The hunting-crazy British officers, with no foxes or hares to chase, took to pursuing stray dogs. 'The worthless cur was to be seen winding through the redoubts that crowned the heights of the Isla de Leon', Henegan observed, 'and followed at full speed by the lovers of the chase, within the very outposts of the enemy, who wondered not a little at the "view hollao" that rung from the lungs of General Graham himself'.[6]

This happy mood changed abruptly when a new terror raised its spectral head – fever! Throughout October and November of 1810 an unspecified disease (possibly yellow fever which had affected the French prisoners on the prison hulks earlier in the year) ran rampant around Cadiz.[7] Many began to die and soon this became known to the newspapers, including those published in England. Deaths rose to twenty (some accounts say thirty) a day including members of some of those British regiments in barracks in Cadiz. 'Like a fearful scourge, it spread its devastating influence around,' wrote one member of the garrison, 'sweeping from the land of the living almost every object that it attacked.' By 5 November two lieutenants, one sergeant major and thirty other ranks of the 47th Regiment had died of the disease. The engineers were also affected with the two senior officers, Birch and Landmann, both seriously ill. Fortunately the fever, which became known as 'the black vomit' remained confined to Cadiz itself and none of the battalions on the Sancti Petri defences suffered any loss.[8]

After the fierce fighting over Matagorda the French forces outside Cadiz remained utterly passive until the arrival of three battalions of marines and shipwrights at Victor's headquarters in September. It was evident that the Marshal intended to launch an attack across the mouth of the harbour from the Trocadero.[9]

The long delay by Victor had done little to improve his chances of success whilst every day of every week was used by Graham to push forward the work on the defences of the great port. As the British General observed, 'the enemy, never having considered himself capable of making an impression on the position of Isla, when almost in a state of nature, can scarcely be supposed to calculate on success by an attack with the same force on the improved position – for improved it undoubtedly is.'

Yet by the beginning of October the French batteries mounted more than 300 guns, and the Trocadero, Puerto Real and Chiclana were powerfully fortified. According to Sarrazin, Soult still hoped to overawe the garrison with a continual heavy bombardment. Soult himself 'presided' over the building of these works because 'he wished to make amends by great zeal, for the fault he had committed of not marching rapidly enough to Cadiz.'[10] One of the British officers of the 87th Regiment in barracks in Cadiz explained how persistent the French attack was in letters home: 'Cadiz, September 5, 1810. Everything is going on as usual here, constant fire kept up, we have now been here for 8 months, every day of which I have seen the enemy's fire and many days exposed to it as we are kept at Cadiz for the purpose of giving fatigue parties to Fort Puntales against which all their fire is directed.'[11]

Unceasing though the bombardment was, its effect was minimal. The same applied to the return fire which was delivered from Fort Puntales against the French siege works. 'Constant firing took place every day,' remarked Graham's aide-de-camp, Lieutenant Colonel Stanhope, 'by which immense quantities of ammunition were wasted and no harm done to either party.' Despite the ineffectiveness of the Allied cannon fire, the Spaniards, Stanhope observed, happily believed that it was having a considerable impact, and they called it, '*Una demonstracion en que nuestras bateriasun fuego terrible con el mayor efecto* – a demonstration in which our batteries delivered a terrible fire with the greatest effect'.[12]

In August Wellington had advised Keats to attack the French boat-building facilities on the Trocadero, but this had not been carried out. In the intervening months it had been noticed that large quantity of fascines and other building materials gathered at Catalina indicated that the French were intending to develop their works there still further, with the aim of establishing batteries that would completely dominate the harbour. So, at last, Keats responded. On the night of 2nd October, he attacked the French store of fascines with guns, mortars and rocket boats. 'They accordingly advanced in good style,' wrote a British soldier, 'keeping as far, however, as possible out of the range of the French batteries at the point, which [they] could not easily bring their artillery to bear upon our boats.' Much hope was placed on the Congreve rockets being able to set fire to the fascines, but the rockets fizzled out prematurely and fell short. Very little was achieved and the failure of the attack led Keats to advise Graham that the only way he could ensure the safety of his ships was for them to leave Cadiz and cruise along the nearby coast.[13]

When news of Wellington's great victory at Busaco on 27 September reached Cadiz, Graham, and most of the British troops, felt even more frustrated at being stranded so far from the main theatre of operations. So when Major General

Disney sailed into Cadiz on 21 October, Graham hoped that the arrival of another senior officer would be his opportunity to leave Andalusia. But when Graham pressed Wellington on this subject, all that Wellington could offer was that, if the siege should be lifted, Graham and the majority of the British garrison would then be free to join the army in Portugal, or to take the field with the Spanish Army.[14]

There was, in fact, every prospect that the siege would soon be lifted if Soult was ordered to help Masséna, which was considered by many to be a distinct possibility. 'They may abandon the siege of Cadiz,' Graham noted in his diary on 7 November, 'and draw every man towards the Tagus, to try to attain the object of driving the British army out of the Peninsula; if possible, should that happen, they should be followed up as closely as possible.'

It seems remarkable that the British were so well-informed about not only the enemy's situation across the Peninsula but also the attitude of the French. Graham's letter to Wellington on 10 November exemplifies this well: 'There is a persuasion of Masséna and Soult not being on good terms. Soult, unless interrupted by a positive order from Paris, would much rather employ Mortier here than send him towards the Tagus.'[15] Nevertheless, such a move by Soult to join Masséna, or for him to at least send Mortier's V Corps into Portugal, could not be discounted and Graham needed to plan for this. As soon as it was obvious that the siege was being lifted and the French were abandoning Andalusia, the forces in Cadiz should be ready to pursue. Graham began to make his preparations and he asked the Regency how many men they could arm and equip for such an operation. On 24 November, Graham received a reinforcement of the regiment of Chasseurs Britanniques. The first detachment of this corps landed at Cadiz on 10 December, though elements of the regiment were held in quarantine for a further eight days before being disembarked. If Graham was to undertake offensive action he would still leave a small garrison in Cadiz and the Chasseurs Britanniques would form part of that force, thus releasing more British troops for field operations.[16]

All this was, of course, speculation. The reality was that there was no indication of any withdrawal of Soult's forces from Andalusia, and Victor appeared to be trying as hard as ever to find a means of taking Cadiz. On 18 November, word reached Cadiz that Soult aimed to undertake an amphibious assault upon Fort Puntales and the Cortadura as soon as Victor had built enough gunboats to be able to transport 4,000 soldiers across the bay in a single wave. The French had, so the report declared, already amassed a flotilla of thirty-nine boats. These were guarded by French soldiers only, no other nationals being allowed near them.[17]

If the French were able to land on the Cortadura and capture Puntales they would be able to sever Cadiz from the Isla. This could prove catastrophic and Graham repeatedly urged the Regency to entrench the rear of the Cortadura and erect two or three strong enclosed, mutually-supporting, redoubts placed so that their guns could cover the length of the beach. Graham also wanted to separate Fort Puntales from the Cortadura with a ditch.[18]

That Victor was assembling a considerable flotilla was confirmed at the beginning of November when twenty boats were moved out of the Sancti Petri. Twelve of the French boats were anchored at Rota and the other eight were berthed in Puerto de Santa Maria (though one of the latter struck the bar at the entrance to the port and was destroyed by British gunboats and gunfire from the shore batteries).[19]

Information from a 'confidential agent' also purported to claim that it was 'Buonaparte's positive orders' that an attempt must be made against Cadiz and that this attack would be delivered by Sebastiani's IV Corps. The attack would be made against the Sancti Petri whilst a diversionary move would be undertaken against the harbour.[20]

This seemed unlikely. Firstly an attack across the Sancti Petri against the heavy guns on the island's defences would be extremely hazardous and, secondly, if the IV Corps was to deliver an attack, this would mean Sebastiani abandoning the territory he had subdued in the east of Andalusia. Nevertheless, there were also reports that, rather than Mortier being sent into Portugal to help Masséna, he was making himself ready to join Victor immediately the 'naval arrangements' were completed. Graham did not believe that Victor could take Cadiz without being reinforced but these rumours seemed to indicate that is exactly what was being planned.

All this finally provoked the Spaniards into action but, instead of building the redoubts recommended by Graham's engineers, all they decided to construct was a continuous covered way from the rear of the Cortadura to the land front of Puntales. This trench line included two small five-gun batteries, which opened at the rear.[21]

Renewed fears of a French attack also prompted a large meeting of Spanish and British officers, of both the army and the navy, to agree on a course of action to considerably strengthen the island's fortifications. A plan was duly decided upon, but most of the inhabitants of Cadiz still refused to participate in any of the work.

Graham also soon learnt that the agreed plan was altered unilaterally by the Spaniards. The British general was furious and he threatened yet again to withdraw all the British troops from Cadiz. 'Nothing can be more unpleasant than the necessity of making this threat,' he wrote on 30 November, 'except being compelled by the obstinacy, ignorance, or treachery of the Spanish engineers.'[22]

Though Wellington was himself blockaded within the confines of the Lines of Torres Vedras, he remained conscious of the supreme importance of Cadiz and he wrote to Graham at the beginning of December to remind him that, if it appeared an attack by Victor was imminent, he would immediately send troops round from Lisbon to strengthen the garrison at Cadiz.[23] The force under Graham's command was increased, meanwhile, by the 2nd Battalion of the 67th Regiment which was sent by General Campbell round the coast from Gibraltar. Campbell followed this up with a detachment of 312 'drivers', this being the polite terminology for deserters from French foreign regiments. These were mostly Germans and they were formed into a provisional battalion that was attached to the Chasseurs Britanniques, which itself was a regiment composed of émigré Frenchmen. General Blake reported that there were many hundreds more such deserters at Alicante and other places along the coast. These were gradually brought into Cadiz, raising the total of this unit to than 700 men.[24]

Around the middle of December a deserter from the French 63rd Regiment made his way into Cadiz. He was able to give Graham details of the troops earmarked for the attack upon the Cortadura. The same day, as if to confirm the deserter's statement, all the French guns which had been established in batteries on the Trocadero – some thirty-five cannon plus mortars – fired a volley, seemingly to demonstrate their growing strength. Work was also seen to be progressing at Fort Matagorda and guns in Fort St Luis opened a desultory fire. There could be no doubt that Victor was going to try an assault as soon as he had built what he considered to be the number of boats he required, providing he also had enough troops at his disposal.[25]

Information of 'an authentic nature' was received in Cadiz on 31 December that Victor had managed to collect around ninety craft of all descriptions in the mooring of the Trocadero. Within view of the Isla there were another seventy or more. On the other hand, entirely contradictory information was received at almost the same time. Victor, it seems, had been ordered to release some of his troops by Soult. On 1 January it was reported that Victor had only eleven battalions available for front-line duties, though this figure proved to be wildly inaccurate.[26]

It seemed evident that something was afoot. If Victor's force had been substantially reduced it could only mean that Soult had drawn these troops away from the siege to conduct operations elsewhere. On 31 December, Wellington wrote to Graham telling him that he had learned from a number of sources that

Soult had marched northwards 'probably to operate with Masséna against the allies in Lisbon.'[27] Fearing, therefore, a renewed offensive against him, Wellington asked Graham to send the Chasseurs Britanniques to Portugal on the very next ship sailing to Lisbon.[28] On 14 January, confirmation that Soult was no longer in Andalusia reached Graham via General Lacy. Other reports indicated that Soult and Mortier had both marched for Estremadura to support Masséna in Portugal. Lacy consequently spoke to Graham about an operation against Victor as it was understood by the Spanish General that Soult had taken with him all his cavalry and a great proportion of his infantry.[29]

This information proved quite accurate. Soult had indeed marched out of Andalusia to help Masséna, who was in desperate trouble. He lacked the strength to break through the Lines of Torres Vedras and he lacked the resources to sustain himself in the empty Portuguese countryside. On 18 February Masséna called together his senior officers for a frank discussion. He asked his corps commanders if they thought they could hold on to their positions any longer. All agreed that they could not. This left them with just two options. One was to retreat back to the Spanish border where the army knew it could be supplied, and there wait for reinforcements from France before reinvading Portugal. The second was to force a crossing of the Tagus into the Alemtejo region, which had been untouched by the war, where the Army of Portugal would be likely to find food. This move also offered the prospect of joining forces with Soult if the Marshal could force his way into Portugal.

Napoleon, not wanting Masséna to withdraw from Portugal, ordered Soult to create a 'diversion in favour of the imperial army in Portugal'. This was vague enough for Soult to be able to interpret it any way he chose, and he had no intention of jeopardising his hold upon Andalusia to help his fellow Marshal. 'Was it likely that he would sacrifice half his own territory,' asked Oman, 'when no order to do so lay before him, in order that a colleague, sent on a separate task with forces no less than his own, might have every possible advantage?'[30]

Napoleon had first hinted at Soult providing some assistance to the Army of Portugal as early as the end of September the previous year. This ill-defined assistance amounted to no more than the request that Mortier should keep the Spanish Army of Estremadura (strictly speaking now called the Fifth Army) in check. Mortier was to keep pursuing this army and so prevent its commander, the Marquis de La Romana, from sending any troops to help Wellington's forces defending Lisbon.

No more was heard on the subject until Napoleon learnt in October that La Romana, with a large part of his force, had indeed joined Wellington within the Lines of Torres Vedras. The Emperor angrily assumed that Soult had disobeyed orders and he told Soult that Mortier should have followed La Romana march for march, even if this meant being led right up to Lisbon!

This, as one historian has explained, showed that Napoleon suffered from a 'complete misconception' of the situation in Estremadura and Andalusia. Mortier commanded only 13,000 men; La Romana could count on a field army of some 20,000 infantry and 2,500 cavalry with a further 6,000 men in garrison in the fortresses of Badajoz and Olivenza. When La Romana marched to Lisbon, he took with him some 8,000 men, leaving two strong divisions under Mendizabal and Ballesteros to keep Mortier in check. Even if Mortier could have forced his way through Mendizabal and Ballesteros and past the Spanish fortresses he would then have had to contend with the Portuguese border fortress of Elvas. Even then, once inside Portugal, there was a Portuguese cavalry brigade (led by Brigadier-General Madden) operating between the frontier and the Tagus. 'On this frontier,' Soult informed Paris, 'there are six fortified places – Badajoz, Olivenza, Jerumenha, Elvas, Campo Mayor, Albuquerque, in which there are at least 20,000 infantry and 2,500 cavalry. It is clear to me that if I thrust a body of 10,000 men forward to the Tagus, as his majesty has directed, that body would never reach its destination and would be cut off and surrounded before I could get to its aid.'[31]

Nevertheless, Soult knew he had to do something. Because of the long delay in receiving dispatches from Paris he was not likely to get an answer for many weeks, so he took it upon himself to undertake an expedition far greater than anything Napoleon had so far hinted upon, but one which was practicable and far safer.

Soult's plan was not to invade the Alemtejo but to capture Badajoz. This fortress sat astride the main Madrid to Lisbon highway and effectively barred the route between Spain and Portugal. If he was able to capture Badajoz it would send a signal to Wellington that Soult was preparing to invade Portugal from this direction. The British General would be forced to take some preventative action which must include withdrawing some troops from the immediate defence of Lisbon and the Lines of Torres Vedras. This, therefore, would be the 'diversion' in favour of Masséna's forces that Napoleon had asked for.

It may seem from this that Soult was acting quite altruistically, for he was embarking on a dangerous expedition to help his colleague. He could well be defeated and find himself surrounded by enemy forces many miles from Seville. But Soult had thought this operation through very carefully. He had always been worried about his western flank. Not only was this the area where the largest Spanish army operated – the Marquis de La Romana's Army of Estremadura which was based around Badajoz – but it was the avenue through which the

Anglo-Portuguese army could pass to attack Andalusia. If he could capture Badajoz he would both block this avenue and deny the Army of Estremadura its operating base. The security of his western flank would be immeasurably increased. If he was forced to help Méssena then he would help himself at the same time.

Soult had stripped his Andalusia garrisons to the bone and taken around 5,000 infantry plus the cavalry with him to join the 12,000 of the V Corps.[32] This gave him a field force of some 20,000 men with which he was marching towards Badajoz and the Portuguese border to help Masséna.

When he marched off on his enforced expedition, Soult failed to appoint Victor – a fellow marshal of the Empire – as overall commander in Andalusia in his absence. This meant that General Sebastiani with the IV Corps remained independently in the east of the province around Granada with responsibility for keeping the Murcians in check, and Victor continued to be concerned solely with the siege of Cadiz. Clearly, both commanders would look after their own interests before committing their forces to help the other. This would have serious consequences in the weeks to follow.

Victor was left with approximately 19,000 men. Of this number around 3,500 troops were engaged directly in the siege operation. These were 1,000 artillery, 800 engineers and sappers of the siege train, and 1,600 marine troops from the French flotilla. They were supported by three battalions of infantry – 2,000 men – to man and defend the trenches.

This meant that Victor had just twenty battalions of infantry, three regiments of cavalry and four or five field batteries, numbering approximately 15,000 men to fend off any attacks by the Allies. Around 3,100 of these soldiers (five battalions, a battery of artillery and a regiment of cavalry under Cassagne) were stationed some distance from Chiclana, principally at San Lucar and Medina Sidonia. This left Victor with little more than 10,000 troops available for field operations. There had not been such a weak force in front of Cadiz since Victor first galloped up to the Sancti Petri almost a year earlier. Now, at last, was the time for Graham and Blake to attack Victor and raise the siege. [33]

Over the course of the next seven days Graham held meetings with Keats and all the Spanish generals – Zayas, Anglona, Lacy, Lardizabal and La Peña – likely to be involved in any offensive operation. The discussions centered upon the direction of the attack upon the French lines. There were two possibilities. The first was an attack across the Sancti Petri by boat, the second was an amphibious operation by ship to land the troops in the rear of Victor's positions on an open beach some miles to the south.[34]

The most direct approach was across the Sancti Petri but this meant crossing a river under enemy fire and allowed for a possible counter-attack by the enemy when only part of the Allied force had been landed on the far bank. The advantages it offered over the second option, however, were that cavalry could be used and, in the case of a reverse, it afforded an easy avenue of retreat back to the Isla de Leon. Furthermore, the advice from those with local knowledge was that the weather conditions at that time of year were highly unpredictable, which could present considerable difficulties for an amphibious operation involving lengthy distances along the coast and a perilous disembarkation on an open beach. Transporting the cavalry and artillery by ship would also prove difficult. The first plan, therefore, was the one that was adopted.[35]

In this plan, the Anglo–Spanish forces in Cadiz under Graham's command would cross the Sancti Petri, timed to coincide with an assault upon Victor's rear outposts from a British battalion from Tarifa and the 'roving' forces of Ballesteros and Beguines. Richard Keats also planned a general attack by gunboats against the whole forward French line from Ronda to Santa Maria.

In support of the operation, Don Ballesteros's mobile command was to menace the weakened force at Seville, keeping the French garrison fully occupied. Towards the east, the *Partidas* would step up their activity and harass Sebastiani in the mountains around Ronda.[36] As it later transpired, this activity was so intense that Sebastiani thought that the main Allied attack was being delivered in his area! Also part of the plan was the involvement of the Spanish General Beguines's roving brigade based in the mountains to the east. Beguines was to attack the strategically important town of Medina Sidonia which he was to seize and hold until relieved by troops from Cadiz. Beguines was warned, however, that he might be expected to join La Peña's main body in the great attack which it was hoped the Allied force would deliver against Victor at Chiclana.

Graham had high hopes for the operation, particularly for his own future prospects, as he explained to Wellington: 'If it succeeds to the full extent I should hope that the effect would be favourable as a diversion in recalling the corps and detachments that have marched from Andalusia, or of enabling the Spaniards to operate on their rear, and at the same time might allow of much of the greatest part of the British troops here being removed to Portugal, in which case I should hope to be allowed to accompany them.'[37]

According to the account of an officer in the Tarifa garrison, Robert Blakeney, the raid by the Tarifa troops and Beguines' force was to begin on 26 January, with the main expedition from Cadiz starting three days later. Tarifa was actually part of Sir Colin Campbell's independent Gibraltar command and Graham had to request permission from Campbell to include the Tarifa garrison in the Cadiz-initiated operation.[38]

The objective of the British battalion based at Tarifa, Colonel Browne's battalion of the 28th (North Gloucestershire) Regiment, was to attack the French-held village of Casa Viejas and to support Beguines in his assault upon Medina Sidonia some fifteen miles further west. Browne received these instructions late on the 25th

At 1500 hours on 26 January the first moves in the great operation to attack Victor's I Corps began when Colonel Browne marched for Casa Viejas with the entire Tarifa garrison which included thirty Royal Artillery gunners and forty of the locally raised Tarifa Volunteers. Altogether Browne commanded 430 men. His line of march took them to Facinas, a distance of twelve miles, which the column reached at 2000 hours, despite encountering very poor weather.[39]

Browne's force rested at Facinas, posting a strong piquet to watch for any movements by the French. The next day, Browne's troops marched upon Casa Viejas which is approximately twenty-five miles from Tarifa. On the way they attracted the support of some mounted guerrillas who helped swell their numbers but were considered by Blakeney as being only 'of more or less use'.

Casa Viejas consisted of only the large *casa* (house) or convent and a few outbuildings. The convent, though, was sturdily built with high imposing walls. It was garrisoned by 100 men and had two 25-pounder cannon mounted on its flat roof.

The Allied force encircled the convent and opened up a brisk fire which was so intense, Blakeney noted, 'that even a sparrow could not live on its walls.' Impressive though the fusillade may have been, it had little effect upon the garrison. When Browne called for the garrison to surrender, the French, perfectly secure within the convent walls, refused and taking advantage in the lull in the firing sent off a galloper to Medina Sidonia to raise support.[40]

There was really nothing now that Browne could do. To storm the convent without scaling ladders was completely impracticable. Even if he were to find a means of forcing his way into the convent, he was not expected to retain possession of the place and it would not be worth the heavy casualties that would inevitably result.

Not really sure of what he should do next, Browne left a small detachment, including the Tarifa Volunteers, to contain the French garrison and then set off with the rest of his men to Medina Sidonia. The troops he left behind were well hidden behind a rise in the ground and, presumably, reasonably safe.

As Browne's men made their way towards Medina Sidonia, a troop of forty Spanish dragoons appeared and joined Browne's force. They proved to be of great assistance, as a troop of French cavalry, sent out from Medina Sidonia to find out what was happening, was driven off by the Spanish horse. There were several such encounters and sharp skirmishes, in which the Spanish cavalry acquitted itself well.

However, doubts about the determination of the Spaniards to carry out the operation against Medina Sidonia began to arise when a despatch from Beguines reached Browne stating that he was still held up at Alcala and he had not yet attacked Medina Sidonia.[41]

Around this time Browne received a despatch (actually two seemingly identical despatches, one from Graham and one from Keats) informing him that due to particularly poor weather the Cadiz force had been prevented from sailing. Though the despatches had been sent from Cadiz as promptly as was possible, when they arrived at Tarifa they were held up because there was no officer available to take the despatches forward to Browne. As a result, it was the Assistant-Surgeon, Johnson, who volunteered to deliver the despatches.

The surgeon galloped up to Casa Viejas but was fired upon by the defenders in the convent. Naturally he galloped away, but he was spotted by the Tarifa Volunteers riding from the convent. Unfortunately Johnson was wearing a blue cloak to protect him from the rain and, with his cocked hat covered by an oilskin, the Tarifa men took him to be a French officer![42]

The Spaniards rode after Johnson and the poor man was struck by a lance under the elbow which broke one of his arms and thrust him 'an incredible distance' from his horse. Now wounded and laying helpless on the ground, the Assistant-surgeon was attacked again and the Spaniards started to rob him of his clothes before they realised that he was British!

When the despatches finally reached Browne, the Colonel knew that he had no choice but to turn his column round and march all the way back to Tarifa in the pouring rain, picking up his detachment from Casa Viejas on the way. In all fairness to Browne he did send a message to Beguines asking the Spanish General if he had received the despatch from Cadiz and if so, was he still continuing with his operation against Medina Sidonia? Browne stated that he was returning to Tarifa but that he would turn back and help Beguines if the General asked the British to join him.

The British troops bivouacked in a 'comfortless and slobbery gorge' during the night to await a reply from Beguines, but no answer was received. The march to Tarifa was resumed the next morning.

By the time Browne's men tramped back into Tarifa they had been marching and fighting for five days constantly soaked through by rain, wading rivers and crossing lakes of water on the flooded plains. The plain of Tarifa was a sheet of water extending some three to four miles beyond the town.

As it transpired, Beguines did carry out his mission. He attacked and seized the partially fortified town of Medina Sidonia driving the French garrison of three companies out of the place. The Spaniards held Medina Sidonia until a strong French force was sent up from Chiclana and attacked the town. As there was no sign of the relieving force from Cadiz, Beguines, like Browne, had to withdraw; in fact the entire offensive had to be postponed amid utter confusion in Cadiz.[43]

The start of the main operation had been fixed for the morning of 29 January, but severe storms prevented the Cadiz contingent from sailing that day. As early as the 27th, Lacy had called on Graham to say that the weather was so bad that he believed the expedition should be postponed, but that he wanted to consult Graham before calling off the preparations. Graham agreed that 'so much depended on these naval co-operations that it became indispensable to delay.' He told Lacy that the officers commanding at Algeciras and Tarifa should be notified at once. This was done but, of course, it was too late to help Browne, who had already set off from Tarifa. The Spanish Admiral Villavicencio at Algeciras was also unsure what was happening and actually wrote to Graham on the 28th asking if the operation was going ahead as planned the next day. Graham rode off to speak to Keats and stopped on the way to see Blake. 'My astonishment was very great,' Graham later wrote, 'when on calling on General Blake, I found him uncertain whether the operation was or was not to take place'![44]

Amid the confusion, Keats and the Spanish naval forces at Cadiz had collected together all their boats and a number of floating rafts ready to transport the troops across the Sancti Petri for the proposed attack. All this was in full view of the French across the water. 'All this display of our naval means is most imprudent,' complained Graham.[45]

If this and Browne's and Beguines manoeuvres was not enough to warn Victor that the Allies were preparing some form of attack, the knowledge that the operation had been temporarily suspended was soon openly discussed around Cadiz. According to Graham's aide-de-camp, Lieutenant Colonel James Stanhope, the *secret* sortie was known by every child in the street.[46] 'Such publicity can only be accounted for by some traitorous breach of confidence,' Graham obviously was furious. 'How is it possible to expect success in an undertaking where there is not a chance of secrecy, on which so much depends at all times in war, but where here it is most essential to prevent the enemy's force from being collected to oppose the *débouché* by Sancti Petri?'[47]

There was nothing for it but to abort the enterprise and devise an alternative plan. Naturally Graham was 'much less sanguine of success'[48] than before but he was still willing to participate in an operation against Victor. 'I feel myself most unpleasantly situated,' he wrote in his dairy on the 29th, 'on one hand engaged so as to be exposed to much censure of the most disagreeable kind were I to retract; on the other, foreseeing how much the difficulties are increased by the strange conduct of our allies.'[48]

The ease with which Medina Sidonia had been taken, induced Graham to consider an attack against Victor's flank and rear from this direction as offering the greatest prospects of raising the siege. His main concern with this idea, though, was with the distances involved. A less ambitious, but more practical, alternative would be for a landing on the coast close to Cadiz from where an attack could be mounted against Chiclana. At worst, if the heights of Bermeja just beyond the Sancti Petri could be seized by the Allies in such an operation and formed into an entrenched camp, then a communication could be maintained between Cadiz and the rest of the countryside. It would mean that the French land blockade had been broken, effectively ending the siege.

The whole subject worried Wellington. He could see no advantage whatsoever in the operation. Victory might drive the French from Andalusia but it would only mean that Soult's entire force of 50,000 or more men would be available to be sent against the British in Portugal. Defeat at Victor's hands and the loss of Cadiz would be even more calamitous. 'And this is the part of the subject which gives me the greatest concern,' he told his brother Henry, 'and really grieves me.'[49]

CHAPTER 5

Manouevres in the Dark

However worried Wellington might be, and despite the previous debacle, the commanders at Cadiz were determined to strike a blow at the besieging forces. Time, though, was the critical factor. The Allies had to move quickly otherwise the opportunity provided by Soult's absence would be lost. On 11 February Graham went with Lacy and Zayas to examine the coast around Sancti Petri. They took a ship along the coast to where a landing could possibly be made between Barrosa and Bermeja where an entrenched camp would be formed. This would ensure a secure place on the mainland for the concentration of the Allied forces before their attack upon the besiegers.

But Graham was worried about a direct attack upon what he described as 'the enemy's very strong position' of Chiclana, 'where there might readily be assembled at least an equal number of the enemy's best troops, protected by several strong inclosed works.' He was also concerned that the route back to the camp after the attack would involve passing through a pinewood where the troops might be 'much impeded.' Nevertheless the Spaniards were determined to mount some form of operation and La Peña declared that he was going to undertake the expedition with or without the help of the British.[1]

As Graham could not prevent the Spaniards from embarking on an offensive move, he felt that the wisest course of action was for him to offer his support. 'It was left to my choice to go or stay,' he later explained to Lord Liverpool, 'and it being of the utmost importance that something in favour of the army of Portugal, and of rousing the spirits of the country, should be attempted, I considered my hearty co-operation in any enterprise for the attainment of these objects as essentially necessary towards a successful result.'[2] In reality Graham could not let the Spaniards go alone. If they were heavily defeated, which was a distinct possibility without the British, relationships between the two nationalities in Cadiz would be seriously damaged, possibly irretrievably so.

Though Graham really had little choice but to join La Peña, he was at least able to influence the plan of operations. In this new plan a large force – some 9,000 Spanish and almost the entire British Cadiz detachment – would sail to Tarifa, some fifty miles to the south-east of Cadiz. When that force had been disembarked it would advance upon Victor's rear via Medina Sidonia. With a

63

large Allied force cutting his communications Victor would have no choice but to leave his base and face the Anglo-Spanish army. This would place his Lines in a highly vulnerable state and, when it was certain that Victor had begun to move his field force to meet Graham and La Peña, a bridge would be thrown across the Sancti Petri and a body of 7,000 men from Cadiz would fall upon the forts and batteries of the siege works.[3]

Before all this could happen, shipping for this large body of men would have to be found and this would take time. Consequently, it was not until the middle of February that the expeditionary force was ready to sail.

As the Spanish forces involved would outnumber Graham's contingent by around two to one, the Regency insisted that a Spanish general should be in overall command – and that general had to be General Manuel La Peña, the senior Spanish officer on the Isla de Leon. They argued that, as the commander of the Spanish forces on the Isla, if he was not granted the command it would be seen 'as a reflection upon his character' and, perhaps more importantly, as Captain-General of Andalusia, La Peña would have the right to command the civil authorities through which the army would pass to provide it with the supplies it would require. This was a valid reason and, in fairness to the members of the Regency, they told Graham that they would understand if he chose not to place himself and his men under La Peña's authority.[4] They hoped that Graham would support the operation, however, because the Spanish soldiers would benefit from the steady influence of the British troops in battle. Graham could not refuse: 'I did not hesitate to determine to go', Graham explained to Liverpool, 'as otherwise it might have been considered as a peevish objection arising from the command having been withdrawn from me.' In a private letter to Lady Asgill he confided that 'I go because I was determined there should be no handle for it being said: "Since he is not in command, he will not assist."'[5]

Graham's magnanimity was welcomed by La Peña and he showed his appreciation by adding 3,000 Spanish infantry plus all the cavalry to Graham's division. It does seem, however, that Graham stipulated three conditions to his agreement to serve under La Peña. These were that the army should only make short marches, that the troops should be kept fresh for battle, and that they should never approach the enemy except in concentrated masses.[6]

As Colonel Napier made clear, there were some reservations concerning the new plan of operations. The main complaint was that Sebastiani's division at Granada could, 'by moving on the rear of the allies, have crushed them, and they had no right to calculate upon his inactivity.' Yet the distance between Tarifa and Chiclana is around fifty miles whereas Sebastiani's position was some 100 miles away from Victor's camp. For the French general to be able to influence the course of the operation he would have had to march as soon as the Allied force landed at Tarifa. But as Sebastiani was fully engaged with the insurgents in his area of responsibility, it would not have been possible for him to gather his troops together in time to reach Chiclana until long after any battle had been won or lost.[7] (Victor did in fact ask Sebastiani to march to his assistance as soon as he was aware of the Allied expedition but there was no response from Sebastiani who, as we have seen, was under no obligation to help his brother officer.)[8]

Another worry was that the Allied field army would be no greater than Victor's and the bulk was composed of Spanish troops. The hope was that Victor would leave a considerable proportion of his force to protect his siege works, giving the Allies a numerical advantage in the field. Nevertheless, how the Spaniards would perform in battle remained to be seen.

There were also justifiable concerns over La Peña's ability to lead such an operation. Considered to be more of a diplomat than a soldier, his most notable military engagement was at the Battle of Tudela in 1808 where he failed to support Castaños, who was under attack from a superior French force. Though Castaños was only four miles away, La Peña made no attempt to help his fellow general and found a safe retreat for himself and his troops. Possibly more worrying was that even the Spaniards considered him to be 'an old woman', giving him the nickname *Doña Manuela*![9]

Graham's division was the first to embark on the great operation on 19 February, but the KGL Hussars did not embark at Cadiz until two days later because of the limited accommodation provided for the transport of horses and strong winds which made loading difficult. Few horses were embarked uninjured.[10] Many of the troops were placed into small feluccas where they were so tightly together that the men barely had room to move. They were left in these conditions for thirty-six hours as the continuing bad weather prevented the first transports from sailing until the 21st.

Graham left behind at Cadiz only the battalion companies of the 47th Foot and the 20th Portuguese, along with the battalion of foreign deserters, under the command of Major General Disney. In addition there were some 4,000 or 5,000 local volunteers in the city and General Zayas commanded 8,000 Spanish troops on the Isla where the 20th Portuguese were actually stationed.[11] Graham also managed to increase the numbers under his own command by appealing to General Campbell at Gibraltar for assistance. Campbell unselfishly provided 1,000 infantry, which took the form of a composite 'flank' battalion made up from the Grenadier and Light Companies of the 1/9th, 1/28th and 2/82nd regiments, in addition to the remaining battalion companies of the 28th North Gloucestershire Regiment, which was still at Tarifa after its return from the earlier aborted mission.[12]

The British artillery, under the command of Major Alexander Duncan, comprised three brigades. These were the brigades of Captain Hughes and Captain Roberts, each of three six-pounders and one 5.5-inch howitzer, and Captain Gardiner with three nine-pounders and one howitzer.[13]

The convoy arrived at Tarifa around midday on the 22nd in rough seas and heavy rain. The persistent wind, coupled with a strong current, caused the transports to drag their anchors, carrying them into the straits. There was no immediate prospect of any improvement in the weather and, equally, no imminent possibility of landing the troops in such adverse conditions. So the convoy set sail for the sheltered port of Algeciras where Campbell's troops from Gibraltar were waiting.[14]

On the 23rd, the ships reached Algeciras and the disembarkation began. All the troops were landed except the artillery, and with no break in the weather it was decided to unload the artillery into small boats and then transfer them along the coast to Tarifa. After landing, the troops bivouacked on rising ground a little to the south of the town but were unable to march on to Tarifa early on the 24th, because the rations (bread and wine) which Graham had been assured would be made available for his division were not ready. The boats to transport the artillery were obtained from Gibraltar and added to those available at Algeciras and, at last, the laborious tasks of rowing the guns and horses along the coast to Tarifa began.

Graham bought what rations he could (at very inflated prices) from the locals and the British division set off for Tarifa at 1030 hours.

The road to Tarifa, which climbed for more than fifteen miles over two precipitous ridges, each about 1,300 feet high, was found to be in very bad condition and far too narrow for wheeled vehicles.[15] The division reached Tarifa at 1730 hours, but lacking its guns, supplies and transport, the British force, alone behind enemy lines, was not in a comfortable position. With no wine or barley and just enough flour for another two days, Graham knew that he might soon be forced to go back to Algeciras, especially as a boat arrived from Cadiz that evening which reported the Spanish convoy had sailed that morning but had probably been forced to put back to port because of the severity of the weather.

A despondent Graham wrote to Keats the following morning stating that 'what might have succeeded under favourable circumstance, now became hazardous' and he asked the Admiral to do all that he and Henry Wellesley could to persuade the Spaniards to abandon the operation.[16]

La Peña's troops had embarked in small Spanish boats but the convoy was driven back into Cadiz as predicted and the men were not allowed to disembark and return to their quarters. Instead they were left on the open boats with no protection from the elements. 'Their troops during this time were suffering the most extraordinary hardships,' wrote James Stanhope, 'exposed without cover to this terrible weather with no means of cooking their rations and were eating cold rice and oil with their bread.' When Stanhope raised this matter with one of the Spanish officers he was told that it didn't matter as the men were used to suffering![17]

However, the situation started to improve a little for Graham's force at Tarifa on the following day. A band of partisans joined the British force, which gave Graham some additional cavalry support, and the Royal Navy made a great effort and all the artillery was moved to Tarifa and unloaded. Graham was so impressed with the efforts of the sailors that he wrote to Keats expressing his 'astonishment at the great exertions made by the navy in rowing such a distance against such a wind.' In the evening thirty-three draught mules arrived with bread from Gibraltar and a few boats loaded with other supplies came in from Cadiz. Graham now had cavalry, artillery, food and drink, and he noted in his daily report that 'we may now remain without risk of starving.'[18]

The garrison of Tarifa was still the main body of the 28th Regiment, which was now under the command of Colonel Belson, who had rejoined the battalion a few days earlier, plus a detachment of artillery under Lieutenant Mitchell. These were added to Graham's field force to make a total of 5,217 men present under arms on the 25th. Graham divided this force into two brigades. The first brigade was placed under General Dilkes and consisted of the two composite battalions of the 1st Guards, Coldstream Guards and 3rd Guards, the flank battalion from Gibraltar which was placed under the command of Colonel Brown, and two companies of the 95th Rifles – making a total of 1,900 men. The second brigade was under Colonel Wheatley and it included the 2nd Battalion 67th, 2nd Battalion 87th and the battalion companies of the 28th Foot along with another flank battalion drawn from the 1/47th, 20th Portuguese and a further four companies of the 95th – altogether Wheatley's Brigade was over 2,500 strong. Graham also had two squadrons of the 2nd Hussars of the King's German Legion, and just ten of Duncan's guns.[19]

Duncan had decided to add Mitchell's detachment to his own force. Mitchell had accompanied Browne in his abortive expedition to Medina Sidonia and he possessed useful local knowledge. Duncan took all of Mitchell's mules but he did not take any of Tarifa's guns. This was because Duncan was so short of horses for his ammunition wagons and for the transportation of the reserve infantry ammunition that he reluctantly decided that he would have to leave behind two of his own guns at Tarifa. Graham insisted that all the larger-calibre 9-pounders had to be taken, so Duncan had to leave behind two of his 6-pounders. Graham's artillery was therefore composed of three 9-pounders, four 6-pounders and three 5.5-inch howitzers, with a complement of sixteen officers and 278 other ranks.[20]

With no indication of how long he might have to wait for La Peña to sail from Cadiz, Graham had to make his position at Tarifa secure from a possible French counter-attack. On the 26th he rode all around the hills that encompass the town and decided upon the most suitable points for the construction of field works. Following this he was able to write to Henry Wellesley declaring his confidence in being able to remain at Tarifa until the Spanish army arrived.[21]

But Graham did not have to wait long. With the weather moderating La Peña's convoy had sailed from Cadiz that morning and the first ships reached Tarifa during the night. At daybreak on the 27th the rest of the convoy could be seen approaching and by evening the whole force, amounting to around 500 cavalry and 6,000 infantry, had been landed.

Whilst the troops bivouacked outside Tarifa, the Allied officers poured into the old Moorish town. There was only one small *posada* or inn in the town and so the officers made full use of the garrison mess instead, with up to 150 men dining in the officers' mess. An examination of the mess accounts revealed that, including port, brandy and claret, 2,000 bottles were emptied in the officers' mess during the course of the week the army stayed at Tarifa. The sergeants' mess was just as busy.[22] 'All day we were busy in preparations for our morrow's march,' wrote Charles O'Neil of the 28th Regiment, 'expecting at its close to come within a short distance of the enemy's outposts.' That night the officers drank the cellars dry, leaving only porter and brandy. The revelry continued throughout the night with many 'inspiring songs of love and war'.[23]

By the following morning, the 28th, the entire Anglo-Portuguese-Spanish force was assembled and reviewed by La Peña. The Spanish General divided his troops into two divisions – one under General Lardizabal, the other under the Prince of Anglona. As promised, two unbrigaded infantry regiments, the 4th Wallon Guards and the Ciudad Real, commanded by General Cruz Murgeon, were graciously handed over to Graham to increase the strength of his command. Indeed, relations between Graham and La Peña were quite cordial at this stage. The Spanish and German Hussars were brigaded together under Brigadier-General Samuel Whittingham, an English officer who had raised his own regiment of Spanish cavalry. La Peña's two divisions were supported by fourteen cannon.[24]

Throughout the evening of 28 February, the combined force departed Tarifa. Before leaving the town La Peña delivered a speech to the assembled Spanish troops: 'Soldiers of the fourth army, the moment for which you have a whole year been longing is at length arrived . . . You have to combat in sight of the whole nation assembled in its Cortes; the Government will see your deeds; the inhabitants of Cadiz, who have made so many sacrifices for you, will be eye-witnesses of your heroism; they will lift up their voices in blessings and in acclamations of praise, which you will hear amid the roar of musketry and cannon. Let us then to conquer!'[25]

The Allied column was led by the Spaniards with the cavalry and five battalions under Lardizabal (considered by one officer as being far more worthy of commanding the Spanish force than La Peña)[26] in the van, followed by the Prince of Angola with six battalions, whilst Graham's infantry and his two Spanish regiments formed the reserve at the rear of the column. They marched out of Tarifa with sore heads but glowing hearts, 'while many a Spanish lady with waving hands and glistening eyes was seen on the balcony.'[27]

There were two routes available to La Peña. These were nothing more than tracks which led northwards on either side of a plain which was about two miles across and extended for about four miles. One of these ran to the east of the plain and travelled inland over the mountains and past the town of Casa Viejas to Medina Sidonia. It was a poor road and scarcely practicable for artillery but an Allied force stationed at Medina Sidonia, with its rear protected by the Sierra de Jerez, could cut Victor's communications at will. Victor would have no choice but to come out and fight at a considerable distance from his siege lines, which would then be exposed to an attack from Cadiz. The only disadvantage which this route presented was that Victor's force would be placed between La Peña and Cadiz, which meant that there would be the possibility of the Allied field force being unable to communicate with the garrison. The alternative route was nearer the coast, travelling through Vejer de la Frontera, Conil and then Chiclana. This road, which was considered the main route westwards from Tarifa, would bring La Peña close to Cadiz, allowing the garrison to co-ordinate its movements with the field force. But, by placing the army at Chiclana, Victor would be able to remain where he was and concentrate his troops in defence of his siege works. There was also a narrow defile along this road to the bridge across the River Barbate that ran below the steep cliffs at Vejer. There were no such obstacles on the inland road.[28]

The Allies marched from Tarifa until they reached the point at which the road split into two. This was at the small village of Puerto de Facinas, a pass through the mountains a little more than ten miles from Tarifa. From Facinas the ground falls to the great plain of La Janda. This plain was some twelve miles in length and three to five miles broad, and was intersected with a labyrinth of streams. In winter these streams overflow, flooding the entire plain, which was often submerged with water more than six feet deep for months at a time, forming an extensive lake known as the Laguna de la Janda. The winter of 1810–11 had been particularly wet and the Laguna was deep and wide.[29]

At the Puerto de Facinas the Allied force halted. Here the two routes went their separate directions around the Laguna. La Peña, quite rightly, decided upon the inland route and the Allied column turned northwards. As one soldier who lived at Algeciras for many years in the nineteenth century and knew the area well agreed, both strategically and tactically La Peña's choice of routes was a sound one. It was his methods that would later be open to question.[30]

La Peña also sent a detachment to seize Vejer and in doing so secure the main army's southern flank. The River Barbate was navigable up to this point and the town itself was held by a French force of three companies of infantry with 180 cavalry. The Spanish detachment, led by Colonel D. José Aymerich, included two 4-pounder cannon, and a squadron of cavalry under Major General Wall. As the detachment advanced directly upon Vejer, Wall rode his squadron on a wide march which took him across the Barbate and onto the road from Vejer to Medina Sidonia. The following morning Aymerich approached Vejer where the French showed every sign of defending the heavily fortified bridge over the river – until Wall's cavalry appeared riding up against their rear. The French immediately abandoned Vejer and fled up the road towards Conil. Though all the French escaped, Aymerich took possession of three artillery pieces and three French gun boats. More importantly, the Allied army's left flank had been secured.[31]

The main Allied army, meanwhile, had marched throughout the evening of 28 February and well into the night. La Peña believed that by continuing to march through the night he could surprise Victor by the speed of his movements. But the troops, stumbling along difficult roads in the dark, with a strong, cold wind (the 'Levanter') pushing at them from the east, were soon exhausted. 'Misled by the guides in quitting the Cortigo de la Jevas', complained Graham, 'and counter-marching made a most fatiguing march.'[32] According to Stanhope, La Peña's staff had sole responsibility for the procurement and management of guides.[33]

Towards morning Lardizabal's advanced guard reached Casa Viejas where the convent, which Browne had tried to capture in January, was still occupied by two companies of infantry.[34] Unaware that the Spanish cavalry was nothing more than a band of *guerrilleros*, the French manned their barricades, and as the

Spaniards approached the convent they were met by cannon fire. La Peña, who arrived at the village at around 1100 hours, did not want to bother assaulting the convent, the garrison of which gave the appearance of a determination to hold their ground, and the Allied column simply marched on past.

Graham, a more astute tactician than La Peña, was not happy with leaving a strong force of the enemy at Casa Viejas and he obtained permission from La Peña to eliminate this potential threat to the Allied army's rear. So Graham sent the Light Company of the 28th to deal with the problem.

As the 28th approached, the French, having now seen the size of the passing Allied army, evacuated the convent, leaving behind two pieces of artillery and some provisions. A party of the KGL Hussars under Lieutenant Cleve was sent in pursuit and they soon caught up with the fleeing Frenchmen. Normally, the infantry would have formed square when threatened by cavalry, but in the distance they could see the 28th Regiment's Light Infantry hurrying after the Hussars. The French chose to form line. Robert Blakeney saw what happened next: 'The French, seeing no possibility of escape, remained steady until the Germans were close upon them, when they deliberately fired a volley at them and then threw down their arms. Two of the cavalry were killed and others wounded. The Germans, enraged at their loss and justly considering it an act of wanton and useless bloodshed, charged the unfortunate defenceless wretches, sparing not a man; all were cut down.'[35]

When the wounded Frenchmen that had not been killed outright by the Hussars were carried back into the convent, the doctor of the 82nd Regiment attached to the flank battalion refused to dress their wounds as he considered it 'totally impossible' that any of them could survive. 'I have never in my life', confessed a shocked Blackeney, 'witnessed in so small an affair such mutilation of human beings.'[36]

A Spanish battalion was left in garrison at Casa Viejas, along with a number of mounted guerrillas. The column then moved on with the Allied cavalry being pushed ahead towards Medina Sidonia.[37] But news reached La Peña that Medina Sidonia had been strongly entrenched and was well-defended by General Cassagne with some 3,100 troops, including a battery of artillery and a regiment of cavalry. As Sir John Fortescue has explained, 'more welcome news could hardly have been brought to a general in such a position as La Peña.' The object of the entire operation was to bring Victor to battle at a distance from Cadiz that would allow the garrison to sally forth and destroy the French siege works. If the Allies were to attack Medina Sidonia, Victor would have no choice but to rush to Cassagne's aid – and La Peña would have his battle. Even if the battle did not go well for the Allies, Victor would still be drawn away from the Cadiz lines, exposing the siege works to destruction at the hands of Zayas's troops from the Isla de Leon. It was, according to one historian, 'the golden opportunity that the Spaniard ought to have been praying for.'[38]

La Peña, it would seem, saw things entirely differently. Instead of drawing Victor from his camp, the Spanish general chose to avoid Medina Sidonia altogether. Some have said that the prospect of a battle 'paralysed' him with fear. Others, rather generously, have found a more reasonable excuse. To assault such a place would not necessarily have brought Victor to battle and to attack a strong place without any heavy artillery would have taken time that La Peña felt he could ill afford. It has also been suggested that he wanted to join up with Zayas's Cadiz force and therefore bring together the greatest possible concentration of troops before engaging the French.[39] If this was the case, his plan therefore was to attack the entrenchments which formed the left of the French lines that rested on the Sancti Petri. This, in conjunction with Zayas's force, would secure the passage of the river and allow not only further reinforcements to join the Allied army but also provisions which La Peña's force was already in need of. Robert Southey supported La Peña's new plans as he argued that the combined force would have a far greater chance of securing a victory over Victor, whilst at the same time allowing a safe line of retreat back to the Isla in the event of a reverse.[40] Nevertheless, it was to 'everyone's astonishment' that La Peña instructed the column to turn away from Medina Sidonia and strike out across country towards the coast.

La Peña did at least allow his men some rest after their gruelling night march, but not until midday. The troops had been under arms and marching for some nineteen hours. The situation was even worse for the 2nd KGL Hussars – having been sent all the way to Medina Sidonia before being ordered back – as they had been on duty for an astonishing thirty-four hours.[41] La Peña ordered them to be ready to march again at dusk!

Graham was not impressed. He had seen just how exhausting the previous night's march had been for the troops. Victor was now little more than a march away. A repeat of the previous night would certainly present the Allied force before Victor – which was what was desired – but equally that body would be severely extended over many miles and utterly incapable of fighting. The weather was also terrible with a violent cold wind, and the men were instructed to bivouac in a poor location on some wooded hills.

Graham protested officially to La Peña. Even before leaving Tarifa Graham had repeated his plea to the Spanish general to make short marches to ensure that the troops were fresh and fit for action every day. He had also asked that a British officer be entrusted with the intended route one day before the day of march. His comments were noted. In actual fact they were ignored and if La Peña had any plan of operations he never divulged it to his Allies.[42] However, La Peña received reports that the road he intended to use, which skirted the northern bank of the River Barbate, was flooded and the Spanish general conceded that attempting to pass the inundated road in the dark would be dangerous.[43] So he waited until the next morning and at 0800 hours on 3 March, the Allied force was back on the road but, in another change of plan, La Peña decided to take the road that went round the Barbate's southern bank.[44]

The reason for this change was probably not just that the northern route was in parts flooded but also because of tactical considerations. By marching along the northern path, La Peña was presenting his exposed right flank to Victor. On his left was an impassable river, the Barbate being over twenty feet deep when in flood. If Victor would have attacked the Allies along this march they would have found themselves trapped on a narrow path with the Barbate at their backs. So although La Peña may have appeared indecisive he was in fact adjusting his operations to suit the prevailing conditions.

Further reinforcements in the form of Béguine's detachment of some 1,600 men reached La Peña during the night, taking the total force to 800 cavalry, 11,200 infantry and twenty-four guns.[45] As before Lardizabal's division led the way towards Vejer with Graham's mixed force in the rear. Unfortunately, the Spanish aide leading the column led the troops down the wrong road. The column was six miles off route before the mistake was realised. If Stanhope is to be believed, Graham had seen that they had taken the wrong route soon after the column had started. He rode up to the head of the column and tried to explain this to La Peña, who brushed aside his concerns. 'Having continued for some time,' Stanhope wrote in his journal, 'they found some peasants and it turned out that the circuitous route was impracticable but that the short and straight road which General Graham had pointed out was a very good one. It became necessary to counter-march the whole column.'[46]

More time was lost when the column came across a low-lying area where the Laguna overflowed unto the Barbate. This depression had a deep, muddy channel running down its centre and the only way across was along the top of a narrow causeway which had poles fixed at intervals to mark its edge.

The causeway, which was about six feet wide and 500 yards long, was in poor condition and when the head of the Allied column arrived the causeway was found to be completely submerged. With an east wind blowing straight across the Laguna (at this point over five miles wide) whipping up considerable waves, the Spaniards were reluctant to risk the crossing.

Rather than pass across in formed bodies, the soldiers took their shoes and socks off and picked their way individually across the stream and, worse still, the Spanish officers made their men carry them across on their backs![47] In this fashion it would have taken more than twenty-four hours for the whole column to pass across the river. The British troops at the rear were soon forced to halt and a frustrated Graham galloped up to the front to see what was going on.[48]

Without pausing for a moment, the sixty-one-year-old Graham sprang from his horse, dashed into the water, and scrambled over the causeway which was some three feet below the surface. The leading British regiment was the 95th Rifles and Graham ordered them to the front of the column and told them to 'go forward in regular sections, one man supporting another.' Without stopping, wrote Surtees, 'they went in and marched right through it, as if it had been plain ground, the water taking them generally about mid-deep.'[49]

Graham then encouraged a Royal Artillery gun team to take one of their cannon across the causeway. The rest of the British force followed and was across in less than thirty minutes. At one point the wheels of a small cart became stuck between some of the large stones in the river. Seeing this Graham dismounted and plunged into the river, put his shoulder to the wheel and 'fairly lifted' the cart clear of obstruction.[50]

This satisfied La Peña's men and, with much less caution than before, the entire Allied force crossed the stream with, in all fairness, the Duke of Anglona being the first Spaniard to cross.[51] The men had to take great care in crossing, however, as the causeway was so narrow that if anyone stepped a foot either way they would have plunged into the lake. Graham, accompanied by his staff, remained standing in the water pointing out the direction of the causeway until the whole column had passed safely across.[52]

Despite the fact that the men were now soaked, La Peña drove them on without a break. The soldiers were not even given time to check or dry their weapons or ammunition. The men marched on but the Allied force could not in the least be considered battle-ready. As Blakeney explained, all that La Peña allowed was frequent 'momentary' halts, which always tended to harass rather than refresh the troops.[53]

It was midnight before the combined force had navigated the causeway and marched into Vejer. It had taken twelve hours to march ten miles. Unbelievably, La Peña then proposed to continue the march throughout the rest of the night. Graham once again had to speak to La Peña, pointing out that they were now close to the enemy and pressing upon him the need for the troops to be fresh if they were going to meet the French. This time La Peña gave way.[54] The troops bivouacked in and around an olive grove. It was bitterly cold and the men could find little wood for fires to dry their wet clothing.

The Allies were now close to Victor's camp and a note was sent by ship the following morning to Cadiz advising Zayas that the field army was at last approaching the city.

The movements of the Allies had been observed throughout the day by a squadron of French dragoons on the Vejer heights. Almost all morning they must have had a clear view of La Peña's column. The dragoons vacated Vejer just ahead of the Allied cavalry.[55] Victor knew that the enemy was coming.

Graham agreed to send a number of his staff officers with a strong escort to reconnoitre the roads ahead whilst Graham himself rode to some high ground near Conil to see the area for himself. When he returned to La Peña's headquarters he found that the reconnaissance patrol had not been sent out. Worse still was that the guides which had failed so miserably the previous day had recommended that the Allied force should be split into two, with Graham's reserve body to take an alternative road which was further inland. Graham absolutely refused to allow the column to be divided now that they were so close to the enemy, but he sent two of his officers to examine the proposed new route. The two officers, Ferrar and Cathcart, soon reported back to say that the road was quite impracticable for artillery.[56]

At 1700 hours the KGL Hussars were back in the saddle, leading the column along the coast. It was an hour later before the reserve marched off. Just beyond the town of Conil the KGL came upon a French cavalry piquet. Both sides fired a few shots from their carbines and a few Germans and Frenchmen fell before the piquet withdrew to report back to Victor's headquarters.[57]

La Peña's movements had confused Victor, not least because of all 'the absurdities of our march', remarked Stanhope, 'and the error of our guides.'[58] The Marshal, who was fully aware of the Allied expedition having observed the ships depart from Cadiz the previous week, had already learnt on 2 March that the Allied force had cut up the garrison of Casa Viejas and was marching towards Medina Sidonia. He therefore told Cassagne to hold the town and he would march to support him with the whole of his disposable force. In anticipation of this Victor had moved ten battalions up to the Cortijo de Guerra, which was halfway between Medina Sidonia and Chiclana. But when, on the morning of the 4th, he learnt that his dragoons had been driven from Vejer he was puzzled. Had La Peña changed route or had the Allies split into two columns? Cassagne had informed Victor that Allied troops were still present at Medina Sidonia – La Peña had left a battalion of infantry and some guerrilla cavalry outside Medina Sidonia to watch Cassagne in case he should move out of the town and act against the Allied rear – and part of the Cadiz garrison had also crossed the Sancti Petri. Victor must have felt himself assailed from all sides.[59]

As per La Peña's original campaign plan, General Zayas had thrown a boat bridge across the Sancti Petri on the night of 2–3 March onto a hard beach on a narrow peninsula between the mouth of the river and the Almanza Creek. It was at this point that the coast road from Conil, after skirting the Bermeja ridge upon which the left flank of the French line of investment rested, reached the shore immediately opposite the southernmost part of the Isla de Leon.[60] A battalion of infantry (*Ordenes Militaires*) had crossed the bridge and had dug itself in on the mudflats directly opposite the French siege lines. Under the cover of the guns of the castle of Sancti Petri, and the batteries along the Isla de Leon, the Spaniards threw up a strong bridgehead which clearly indicated that the Cadiz forces intended to sally forth against the French in conjunction with La Peña's field army.

Victor knew that he would have to act quickly against the entrenchment before the small Spanish force was reinforced. At dusk on the 3rd, Victor sent a body of six companies of chosen *voltigeurs* from General Villatte's division to storm the bridgehead at bayonet point.

'The Spanish were on four arranged lines with 200 yards between them – their reserve was at the head of the bridge, their batteries and some cannons flanking the terrain they occupied,' wrote Colonel Eugene Lequetel, Victor's I Corps Engineer. 'The Spanish were overthrown in a tangle at their trenches; there the troops who guarded the bridgehead made a terrible fusillade holding for ten minutes, but our *voltigeurs* broke through. We took two flags, thirty-four officers of which five were colonels, and 495 enlisted prisoners.' In the fading light the Spanish artillery in the castle was ineffective and the French light infantry after overwhelming the defenders smashed down the earthworks and there was a real chance that the French would storm the bridge and open the way into the Isla. At what was described as 'the critical moment,'[61] Captain Hunt galloped up with his massive 10-inch howitzers and helped the Spaniards clear the bridge. The boat bridge was cut loose before the *voltigeurs* could make another attempt and it was floated back to the Isle de Leon.[62]

Zayas had followed his instructions. By the 3rd, La Peña was supposed to be preparing to engage Victor's forces, thus enabling the Cadiz troops to bridge the Sancti Petri with a strong chance of holding their ground. But Zayas had acted 'on mail-coach time', making no allowance for any delays that the field army might encounter, nor making any attempt to discover where La Peña was. As Blakeney put it: 'The proceedings of Zayas and La Peña offer a correct specimen of the manner in which the combined movements were executed by Spanish generals; all acted independently and generally in direct opposition to one another.'[63]

But there was no sign of the field army and it was not until the following day, the 4th, that a messenger from La Peña arrived at Cadiz by fishing boat from Tarifa to inform Zayas that the Allied force had been delayed. The boat had left Tarifa on the 1st but had been intercepted by a Royal Navy brig and the messenger, who was in disguise and without a British pass, was detained for some time.

Despite the lack of coordination between the Cadiz garrison and the field army, it was evident to Victor that the Allies planned to join forces and attack his positions from both sides. The French Marshal had to consider his options carefully, especially as Victor, by some 'curious point in military history', believed that the force opposing him was far larger than it really was. He thought that the British amounted to 8,000 men and the Spanish numbered 18,000.[64]

He could not prevent Zayas from crossing the Sancti Petri because of the weight of the Spanish guns on the fortifications that commanded the river. Such action by the Cadiz garrison, however, would take time to develop into a serious problem. The immediate threat came from the field army and it was this that Victor chose to deal with first.

Victor had at his disposal three divisions. He decided to place one of these – Villatte's Division of five infantry battalions and a regiment of dragoons – to block the road from Conil to Cadiz. This appeared to be the route along which the main body of La Peña's force was moving. As Villatte might be attacked by both La Peña in the front and Zayas in the rear, he was told not to dig in as it was likely that he would be expected to shift his position as the battle developed. The other two divisions would be held out of sight at Chiclana. As soon as La Peña's leading units became engaged with Villatte, the other two divisions would march into view and fall upon the flank the Allied column which would be stretched out along the narrow coast road. General Cassagne was also asked to find out exactly how large the Allied force was that was watching Medina Sidonia. If it was just a thin screen covering the movements of the main Allied force, which it was, Cassagne was to break out of the town and join Victor.[65]

La Peña left Vejer at 1700 hours on the evening of the 4th and marched on Conil, a small village on the Atlantic coast some eight miles away. In spite of promises from the Spaniards about how the march would be conducted, they marched for just five minutes at a time before halting and then by the time the men had got up and marched off again only a few yards had been covered before they halted once more. As with the previous night march, the Allied column staggered around in the dark and, predictably, took the wrong road.[66]

Graham was alarmed that the men were marching directly upon Victor's camp at Chiclana instead of keeping closer to the coast, and he galloped up to La Peña to find out what was happening. 'Coming up to the head [of the column] I saw the whole staff in the greatest confusion, from the contradictions of the guides . . . After some further rather ludicrous scenes of distress . . . it was agreed that the march should be continued as I had originally recommended, by a flank movement left in front, forming column of lines, the cavalry and rear guard on the right in first line, and so on.'[67] The guides had almost led the column straight into the French camp and when the Spanish generals, 'all in great dismay', realised just how close they were to the enemy they decided to turn round and counter-march the way they had come! Graham managed to persuade them to move down into the Chiclana plain where they would be only a short march from the Sancti Petri.[68] They moved off across the open heath in line of columns, as Graham had suggested, making, as Graham said, a remarkably pretty field-day.[69]

The straggling columns arrived weary, wet and hungry on the plain of Chiclana shortly after dawn but not before the advance guard of Spanish cavalry had encountered a troop of French dragoons. The French cavalry were drawn up on a wooded ridge about a mile and a half to the east of the Sancti Petri. There was a skirmish with the Spaniards being driven off to derisory shouts from the dragoons. The first victory of the day had gone to the French.

La Peña decided to push on along the ancient track that followed a line of sand dunes and passed a low ridge called *Cerro de Puerco*, or 'Boar's Neck', so named not only from its shape but also from the abundance of wild boar found there. Its highest point is about 800 yards from the coast and around six miles from Chiclana, and forms a prominent feature that rises about 160 feet above sea level but just eighty feet above the surrounding terrain. This sandy promontory is called Barrosa from the Spanish *barro* or mud, referring to the reddish or muddy colour of the rock. The mouth of the Sancti Petri lies some four miles to the west. On its summit is a small watch house or *vigia* which some accounts mistakenly refer to as a chapel. Below the heights, by the beach, is a lookout tower known as *Torres de la Barrosa* and towards Cadiz, just three miles distant, is a similar tower *Torre de la Bermeja*. These towers are both part of a coastal network of lookout posts built in the fifteenth century to warn of a reappearance of the Moors. The Bermeja heights, which are lower than the Barrosa heights, extend as far as the San Pedro river and beyond it Chiclana.[70]

The ground in front of the Barrosa promontory forms a wide plain which is fairly level apart from a few undulations, and was overgrown with low scrub. Generally this scrub was knee-high and in places even higher. There were several dry watercourses that became torrents during the winter rainy season and caused areas of low-lying ground to flood and form small lakes. To the right of the

Barrosa ridge, and covering the slopes of the *Cerro de Puerco*, were extensive and thick cork or pine woods. The woods stretched across the plain for four and a half miles until they reached the forest of Chiclana. The north end of the plain is bounded by the Almanza creek with, at the time, its mill and mill house. This joins the Sancti Petri to form a natural barrier with the marsh beyond making the area impassable.[71]

La Peña was anxious to make contact with the force from Cadiz and he sent Lardizabal with the vanguard directly to the mouth of the Sancti Petri. La Peña had promised Graham that he would only engage Victor when he had all his force concentrated. This was the only way that the Allies could make their superiority in numbers count in their favour. But the Spanish General sent Lardizabal ahead whilst the rest of the straggling column was still on the march.[72]

The Spanish cavalry, leading the way, mounted the coastal ridge unopposed shortly after daybreak on a fine, clear morning. Soon, however, they discovered Villatte's division blocking the road to Cadiz. The French force appeared to Lardizabal to be no more than a strong brigade of infantry with a squadron or two of cavalry. No other French troops could be seen.

La Peña, showing due respect to his subordinate, explained the situation to Graham. He told the old Scot that he intended to attack this French force without delay – even though the Allies had now been marching for fourteen hours.

With the rest of the Allied army drawn up to cover any possible movement by Victor from Chiclana, the five battalions of Lardizabal's vanguard division attacked what still appeared to be an isolated French brigade. The time was about 0900 hours.

Villatte in fact had 3,000 men, but because of the wood where his division was posted only four battalions were visible to the Spaniards. The first Spanish attack was driven off by Villatte but the apparent weakness of the French force encouraged La Peña, who reinforced Lardizabal with the leading brigade of Anglona's division, and the Spaniards renewed their assault. It was at this moment when Zayas threw the boat bridge back over the Sancti Petri. Soon Villatte found himself attacked from both front and rear, as Victor had feared. Villatte's orders allowed him to retreat if he was hard pressed so the French general quickly abandoned his position and fell back towards the Almanza creek, taking up a defensive position on the opposite bank from where he could defend the bridge. Villatte had extricated himself well from an extremely difficult situation. The affair had cost him 337 men yet he had achieved his objective as the unsuspecting Allied field force had been delayed and Victor was already on the march with the rest of his force. Likewise, La Peña had also achieved his objective as he had succeeded in his bid to unite his army with Zayas's force from Cadiz. It had also cost him no more than 300 men.[73]

At this stage of the battle both sides could feel that the opening moves had gone well, the only difference was that La Peña considered the battle to be over and Victor knew that it had only just begun!

CHAPTER 6

Barrosa's Blood-Drenched Hill

Victor had concealed his other two divisions, with their divisional artillery, in the Chiclana forest close to the north-eastern slopes of the Barrosa heights. These two divisions were to remain hidden in the forest until the Allied force was strung out across the plain. The French would move forward to occupy the high ground of the Barrosa ridge and then swoop down on the exposed flank of the Allies who would be trapped between the Bermeja ridge and the sea.[1]

At this stage of the encounter, however, the Allies were in two compact bodies. La Peña's Spanish divisions along with Zayas's contingent from Cadiz were close to the Sancti Petri, whilst Graham with the rearguard was firmly ensconced upon the Barrosa hill. Though separated by some three and a half miles of ground both Allied bodies were in reasonably secure positions. Then, at around midday, everything changed.

Graham, originally, had been asked by La Peña to move his division to the eastern slopes of Barrosa to act as the reserve to the main Spanish force as it crossed the open ground approaching the Bermeja heights. After just a short while in that position, at around 1200 hours, Graham was ordered to move part of his division from Barrosa to the Bermeja ridge to protect the recently re-established line of communication with Cadiz. La Peña was worried that his command was dangerously divided and, quite understandably, he wanted to concentrate his whole force.[2]

Graham was told to leave behind on Barrosa hill his two Spanish battalions under General Cruz Murgeon and Browne's Light Battalion which were to be joined by Beguines' three battalions. As soon as Graham's division had reached La Peña's main body, this rearguard force would move up and join the rest of the Allied army. Whittingham's cavalry, which was also on the hill, was to travel along the coast road to cover the flank of this rearguard force when it made its move.

Graham was very unhappy with this plan as it would mean that La Peña's Spaniards, the British division and the rearguard would be strung out across some three miles of ground before the whole force would be united. If Victor suddenly appeared in force and seized the Barrosa heights which dominated this narrow ground, he would be in a position from which he could strike down from the heights and cut the Allied army in two – which, of course, was exactly what Victor hoped to achieve. On the other hand, if Graham remained at Barrosa, Victor would not dare to assail any part of the Allied force.[3]

But it was the Allies that were on the offensive, not the enemy. As one British officer explained, 'the idea of the French leaving their stronghold to attack so formidable a force as the Allied army then presented, had never been contemplated.'[4] Yet, just in case there was a move by Victor, cavalry patrols had been sent towards Chiclana but no sign of enemy activity had been observed. Victor, however, was an experienced general and his troops were well hidden in the Chiclana forest. The French were much closer than anyone on the Allied side realised.

Earlier in the morning Graham had explained to La Peña the importance of Barrosa and he had advised the Spanish commander to occupy and hold the hill. Graham saw the heights as 'the key both to offensive and defensive movements'. Graham argued that, if Barrosa was held in strength, Victor would not be able to attack Bermeja because by doing so he would expose his flank to the force on Barrosa. Furthermore, abandoning Barrosa and moving all his troops towards Cadiz effectively ended the campaign as it meant that the Allies were back where they had started. It would seem that this was precisely what La Peña desired.[5]

Nevertheless, Graham had agreed to place himself under La Peña's command and he obeyed the Spaniard's instructions, even though they had been given somewhat discourteously after Graham had explained his objections. Now, in the face of the enemy, was not the time to show dissent. It was also true that with the Allied force united, and strengthened with the addition of Zayas's contingent, offensive action was still possible.

So, at around midday, Graham set off to join the Spanish main body, leaving the rearguard of Browne, Beguines and Cruz Murgeon, accompanied by Whittingham's cavalry, to occupy and hold Barrosa hill. There were two routes between Barrosa and Bermeja. One was through the woods, the other was along a narrow road which ran directly under the coast cliffs. The march through the woods was the better of the two as it was somewhat shorter and was just about practicable for artillery. By taking this route Graham would also avoid any congestion on the coastal track which was to be used by the baggage train of the army.[6]

As there was still no sign of Victor and the distance being little more than three miles the journey seemed safe enough and the road, though narrow, was quite good. The rearguard had orders to hold Barrosa until Graham's force had taken up a defensible position by the *Torre de la Bermeja*.[7] This latter position was described by Graham as being 'a narrow woody ridge, the right on the sea cliff, the left falling down to the Almanza creek, on the edge of the marsh. A hard sandy beach gives an easy communication between the western points of these two positions [Barrosa and Bermeja].'[8]

Graham's march towards Bermeja through the pinewood on the northern side of the Barrosa plain was recorded by Brigadier-General Dilkes: 'The column began its march, left in front, over the height, and descending the other side, encountered a fir wood, so thick as to be nearly impracticable for the guns and mounted officers.'[9]

It was whilst the British division was passing through the trees (according to Dilkes they were about a mile inside the wood) that Lieutenant von Gruben, who had been reconnoitring in the direction of the Chiclana forest with a small party of the KGL Hussars, sent a report to his commanding officer, Major Bussche, that the French were advancing through the wood towards Barrosa in two large columns. Graham had told La Peña that the Barrosa heights were the key to the entire Allied position – Victor did not need to be told.[10]

Forty-six-year-old Claude Victor-Perrin was a hugely experienced commander. He first joined the French Army in 1781 (as a drummer-boy), serving for ten years as a private. He rose to prominence, however, during the siege of Toulon in 1793, following which he was granted the rank of general of brigade. During Napoleon's successful Italian campaigns Victor's abilities led to his promotion to general of division. It was in that capacity that he fought in Napoleon's greatest battle at Marengo. In 1806, in the war against Prussia, he was Marshal Lannes' Chief of Staff. He distinguished himself at the crushing Prussian defeat of Jena and, at Friedland, he commanded I Corps with such determination that Napoleon made him a Marshal of the Empire. He became the 1st Duke of Belluno in 1808 and was sent to Spain. His I Corps had met the British at Talavera and he was well aware of their fighting spirit, but this time all the advantages lay in his favour.[11]

Victor believed that the perfect opportunity had presented itself. Though Cassagne's force had not set off from Medina Sidonia until mid morning and would not reach Victor for another two or three hours, he decided to attack immediately. His cavalry scouts had informed him that the Barrosa heights appeared to have been abandoned. There was nothing, it seemed, to stop the French from seizing Barrosa and falling upon Graham's column which was helplessly stretched out in line of march along a narrow path. Victor's moment had come and he was going to seize it.

The Duke of Belluno had taken the Grenadiers from the infantry regiments of his three divisions and formed them into three Grenadier battalions to act as reserves. He attached two of these elite battalions plus three squadrons of cavalry to General Ruffin's division and the other battalion was given to General Leval. Villatte's division, of about 3,000 men, was still posted close to the bridge on the Almanza river to cover the siege works and to watch La Peña's troops which had gathered on the Bermeja heights. With the remaining 7,000 men of Ruffin's and Leval's divisions Victor struck at Graham's column.

He ordered Ruffin to occupy Barrosa hill whilst the 1st Dragoons swung round the heights to the south-east to seize the coastal track. Leval's division charged straight towards Graham's division which was marching unsuspectingly through the pinewood.[12]

On the hilltop, Browne's men, who had been under arms for some twenty hours, were given permission to rest. They flung themselves down on the grass and almost immediately most of them fell asleep. Whittingham's cavalry, men and horses alike, also took advantage of this unexpected opportunity to relax, 'and a profound repose pervaded alike both animate and inanimate nature.' The reserve ammunition and baggage train was also on a plateau just below the summit of the heights.[13]

It was then that a lone horseman galloped up the hill to warn Browne and the Spaniards that the French were attacking! Beguines, Browne and Cruz Murgeon surveyed the scene below – and watched with horror as the main body of the British disappeared into the wood just as the French appeared in front of them. As the small Allied rearguard – just five Spanish battalions and one British – was stationed under the seaward-facing summit they were unseen by Victor who thought the hill was unoccupied.[14]

This rearguard had been ordered to evacuate Barrosa and join La Peña as soon as Graham was safely ensconced upon the Bermeja position. But now the Barrosa heights were about to be assaulted by the enemy. Surely they should hold this vital ground until the sound of gunfire brought La Peña and Graham back to help them? That, of course, would be contrary to orders. So Whittingham, with Cruz Murgeon and Beguines present, asked Browne what he intended to do. 'What do I intend to do, sir?' replied Browne. 'I intend to fight the French.' Whittingham responded to this by saying, 'You may do as you please, Colonel Browne, but we are decided on a retreat.' Undismayed, Browne told Whittingham that he was staying where he was, '. . . for it shall never be said that John Frederick Browne ran away from the post which his general ordered him to defend.'[15]

With that Whittingham, with his five squadrons and the five Spanish battalions, abandoned the heights and retired with 'firm tread' down the southern slope to join the army's baggage train which had already fled down to the coast road and was making off towards Cadiz. 'Thus a formidable corps,' remarked Blakeney, 'composed of two regiments of Royal Spanish Guards, three regiments of the line, a park of artillery and a strong force of cavalry, all well armed, clad and appointed, undaunted by the scowling frowns of their Allies and the reproachful taunts of their own countrymen, were not afraid to run away.' Alone on top of the bristling neck of the boar stood a single British battalion. [16]

Down in the plain below Barrosa, Graham, with the bulk of his division, was marching towards Cadiz through the pine wood blissfully unaware of the developing French attack. At the rear of the British column was the 2nd Battalion 95th Rifles.

When the Rifles were only about half a mile into the wood a sergeant of the KGL Hussars rode up to Lieutenant Colonel Norcott and asked for General Graham, and told him that 'the enemy had made his appearance in great force on our right and rear, and was pushing for the heights of Barrosa.' Norcott told the German Hussar to carry on and inform General Graham, who was at the head of the column. Without waiting for instructions from Graham, Norcott put his battalion right about and extended his front to a width of about 600 yards and retraced his steps to confront the enemy. [17]

Graham, leading his column, was more than a mile ahead of Norcott. One of his aides-de-camp, Ensign Frederick Colville, 3rd Foot Guards, relayed the information to Graham, saying that heavy columns of the enemy were moving towards the Barrosa heights. When he received this news Graham immediately gave the order, 'Right about face! Form as you can.' [18] A Spanish officer was with Graham's staff and he was urged to ride and let La Peña know what was happening (though La Peña should have needed no telling as the French flank would have been visible up the valley of the Almanza). 'He went,' wrote Captain James Stanhope, 'but no-body returned.' [19] In the mistaken belief that La Peña would soon be rushing to his aid, Graham turned his men around and marched them back towards Barrosa hill to support Browne and the Spaniards. 'A retreat in the face of the enemy', he later wrote, 'who was already in reach of the easy communication by the sea-beach, must have involved the whole Allied army in danger of being attacked during the unavoidable confusion, while the different corps would be arriving on the narrow ridge of Bermeja at the same time.' [20] What Graham saw was if his division attempted to hold its ground and face the French there was no possibility of forming any kind of cohesive fighting line in the dense pine forest. Worse still was the prospect that Victor would drive the retreating rearguard and the British division into the main Spanish body. If, in the ensuing confusion, the French were able to occupy La Bermeja the field army would be cut off once again from Cadiz. This, without question, was the decisive moment of the campaign.

It took Graham just three minutes to assess the situation and make up his mind. 'The enemy's numbers and position were no longer objects of calculation,' Graham later wrote, 'for there was no retreat left.' He saw that his only chance was to attack the French before they themselves had properly formed up. The French were attacking, they would not expect that they themselves would be attacked. Victor had taken Graham by surprise but now it was his turn to surprise Victor. 'To retreat was ruin,' agreed Lieutenant Colonel Ponsonby, 'but to attack a superior force in possession of strong ground with exhausted troops was almost as bad.' Nevertheless Graham had made up his mind. He decided to return to occupy Barrosa and join with the rearguard in the expectation that La Peña would also turn back to attack the French right flank and rear. Yet little did Graham realise that the battalions and cavalry he was moving to support were no longer on the summit![21]

Graham ordered his leading brigade, that of Colonel Wheatley, to march directly through the wood. At the edge of the wood he was to form line of battle and attack the French before him. Duncan's ten guns, which were in the centre of the column, were to drive up a side track and form up on Wheatley's right. The rear brigade, that commanded by Dilkes, was to march back along the forest track until it reached the foot of Barrosa hill. There it would form up and attack the French on the heights. As these movements would take time, Graham threw a force of light infantry ahead of each brigade to engage the enemy, regardless of formation or of casualties.

Browne, meanwhile, prepared to defend Barrosa. He ordered Lieutenant Sparks of the 30th Regiment, who was acting as an engineer, to loophole the small watch house on the summit. A few men were placed inside the watch house whilst the rest of the battalion formed three sides of an oblong, the watch house making the fourth face.[22]

By this time French cavalry had reached the coast road at the rear of the Barrosa heights. From here they turned and moved directly up the hill towards Browne's battalion. As the French horsemen trotted to within musket range of the Light Battalion they opened out to the left and right and rode around the flanks of the British formation. This revealed the enemy's artillery advancing behind the cavalry and, for the first time, Browne could see the dark masses of the French infantry. In full dress, and moving in single column of divisions, Ruffin's two brigades presented an imposing spectacle.[23]

Browne immediately realised that his proud boast that he would not abandon his post was unrealistic and he decided he should re-join Graham. He withdrew his men from the watch house, reformed them into close column and ordered them to march quickly down the hill towards the pine wood.[24]

The French Dragoons pressed closely round the retreating flank battalion. Browne dare not stop and form square because of the French artillery which was 'whipping over the plain' towards the hill. Browne sent out a few skirmishers from each angle of the column which kept the French horse at a safer distance, and a squadron of the KGL Hussars, led by Major Bussche, came to Browne's rescue and helped to hold back the French dragoons.

An orderly retreat was the most that Bussche could hope to accomplish and this he undertook, retiring by alternate half-squadrons – charging the French cavalry with one troop while the other retreated. Each time the Germans charged, the enemy horse withdrew behind their infantry who opened fire upon the Hussars. Despite mounting casualties, Bussche continued alternately charging and retreating for more than a quarter of an hour until Brown's battalion reached the foot of the hill. Browne formed his men in line with their flank resting on the wood and the cavalry drew away.[25] The Germans then fell back to join the rest of the cavalry and the Spanish battalions and the baggage train. The narrow coastal track became hopelessly congested and in the confusion some of the baggage mules broke loose and bolted away.

Though Whittingham had left Barrosa he had gauged the importance of the coastal road, and with the cavalry and Beguines's and Cruz Murgeon's Spaniards he blocked this route to prevent Graham's force being outflanked. Slowly Whittingham withdrew with the Spanish infantry maintaining formation in tight columns. 'The cavalry covered the retreat in the most perfect order,' Whittingham later reported, 'notwithstanding the continued skirmishing and repeated attack of the advancing enemy, whose force was at least a third superior to ours, and had the advantage of acting united.'[26] Beguines's three battalions with the remnants of the baggage train made their way along the coastal path to join La Peña, but Cruz Murgeon and Whittingham took up a position at the *Casa de las Guardias*, about a mile from the *Torre Barrosa*, where they were kept engaged by the French dragoons.[27]

Whilst Whittingham's force moved off westwards, Browne's battalion had just taken up its position at the foot of the *Cerro de Barrosa* when Graham rode out of the wood. Graham demanded to know if Browne had not been given orders to remain on the heights: 'Yes, sir,' said Browne, 'but you would not have me fight the whole French army with four hundred and seventy men?' Graham reminded Browne that he had with him five other Spanish battalions as well as artillery and cavalry. 'Oh!' answered Browne, somewhat uncharitably, 'they all ran away before the enemy came within cannon-shot.'

'Well,' said Graham, 'it's a bad business, Browne; you must instantly turn round again and attack.' Browne's flank battalion began to deploy in skirmish order for the attack, but Graham considered this would not do. 'I must show something more serious than skirmishing,' he told Browne. 'Close the men into compact battalion!' With the battalion formed ready, Graham ordered Browne to attack immediately.[28]

So Colonel Browne rode to the front of his battalion, took off his hat and called out to his men: 'Gentlemen, I am happy to be the bearer of good news: General Graham has done you the honour of being the first to attack those fellows. Now follow me, you rascals!' With that, Browne pointed towards the enemy, drove his horse forward and at the top of his voice started singing 'Hearts of Oak'.

'Thus we moved forward', wrote Blakeney, 'with four hundred and sixty-eight men and twenty-one officers to attack the position, upon which but three-quarters of an hour previously we had stood in proud defiance of the advancing foe, but which was now defended by two thousand five hundred infantry and eight pieces of artillery, together with some cavalry. To this force were added two battalions of chosen grenadiers.'[29]

Seeing such a small force moving towards him, Ruffin – described by one British trooper as 'an immense and fine-looking man, about six feet two or six feet three inches high' – told his men to hold their fire until the British were well within range. Colonel Browne, who knew that the French could bring to bear many more muskets than his own men, dared not stop and engage in a firefight. So he ordered his composite battalion to attack with the bayonet. 'As soon as we crossed the ravine close to the base of the hill and formed on the opposite side', wrote Blakeney, 'a most tremendous roar of cannon and musketry was all at once opened, Ruffin's whole division pointing at us with muskets, and eight pieces of ordnance sending forth their grape, firing as one salvo.'

Under the dense hail of that first French volley nearly 200 men and more than half of the officers of the composite battalion were mown down.[30] The battalion tried to close ranks to present once again a solid line, but a second volley smashed into the light infantry and another fifty men fell. 'The men were fast falling,' continued Blakeney, 'and it required the utmost exertion to keep the survivors together, exposed as they then were, to a murderous fire of round-shot, grape and musketry.'[31]

The men would not stand and face another fusillade from the French, and the remainder of the battalion scattered. They took cover behind trees or the few shallow watercourses and broken banks on the hillside, and began a sporadic return fire. Browne, who was still unhurt, could not persuade his men to reform and, leaving the wounded Blakeney with the remnants of his battalion, the Colonel rode off to join the Guards Brigade which had just marched into view at the bottom of the hill ready to join the fight.

It would be expected that the French would have charged down the hill to finish off Browne's wrecked battalion, but Dilkes' main body, with Norcott's Rifles in front, had just emerged from the wood 'looking more like a chain of *tirailleurs* than a line' and had reached the foot of the hill.[32]

The Guards exited the wood in 'little order indeed, but in a fierce mood', as Dilkes described, and he quickly reformed his men ready to attack up the hill. 'The deployment was soon effected, under all disadvantages, the detachment battalion [the Coldstream Guards and the 3rd Guards] forming in second line to the 2nd Battalion 1st Guards.'[33] Instead of following Browne's path up the hill, Dilkes chose a route more towards the south where there were more trees and bushes to provide a degree of cover and where the gradient of the hill was slightly steeper.

The Guards and the 67th Regiment, with Dilkes at their head, began their climb up the *Cerro de Barrosa*. Norcott split his two companies of riflemen and placed each one on either flank of the column. Ruffin had, by this time, got his artillery into action on a knoll 300 yards north-east of the summit but, because of the severity of the slope, the first rounds from the French guns passed over the heads of the advancing infantry as they crossed the dead ground.[34]

'The line was advanced obliquing [*sic*] to the right towards a body of the enemy already occupying the height we had so lately passed over,' continued Dilkes, 'a heavy fire of artillery and musketry being kept up on both sides.'[35] Blakeney watched their progress from above: 'Surmounting all difficulties presented by the roughness and inequalities of the ground, heedless of the enemy's menacing attitude, reckless of the murderous fire which swept their still unformed ranks, they bore steadily onward and having crossed a deep broad and rugged ravine, wherein many a gallant soldier fell to rise no more, they climbed the opposite bank.'[36]

As they rose from the ravine, the Guards met Rousseau's two Grenadier battalions and two battalions of the 24me *Ligne*, with the 96me *Ligne* in support, which had marched down from the summit of the hill to throw back the redcoats. The Guards were strung out in line formation which had struggled to maintain order as it had climbed the hill. Dilkes' brigade numbered less than 1,400 men. They were opposed by more than 2,000 Frenchmen charging downhill in column. 'By all the rules of military art,' Oman declared, 'four battalion columns, fresh and well ordered, charging downhill, should have been able to break through a disordered line of decidedly inferior strength pushing upwards against them.' Yet, as the professor put it, the impossible happened! [37]

With drums beating and bayonets levelled, the French infantry rushed down the slope confident of success. Then the 1st Guards opened fire. Stanhope had watched the Guards improve the order of their formation as they advanced and with practised control and accuracy the British infantry unleashed a hail of lead that cut down the front ranks of both battalion columns of the 24me *Ligne*. The ranks following behind stumbled into bodies of their fallen comrades and were brought to a standstill. Shocked and disorganised, the French infantry attempted to return fire but with little effect. It seems that at this time the 67th caught up with the Guards and Norcott's Rifles, adding their weight to the intense fire that was concentrated upon the Frenchmen. [38]

Victor, watching from the crest, rode down the hill and placed himself at the head of the two Grenadier battalions, waving his large white-plumed hat above his head to urge them on, as they marched down the slope and moved towards the right of Dilkes's line. As they moved downhill they came within range of the 3rd Guards and the wing of the 67th. Volley after volley was delivered against the Grenadiers but still the Frenchmen strode forwards until they were just a few yards from the line of redcoats. [39]

At this point the Grenadiers were close to success. Now they should have charged the thin red line that stood before them, using the gradient to their advantage. But instead they stopped and began to fire. It would prove a fatal mistake.

'And now the battle for a moment hovered in the zenith of its glory,' wrote Blakeney. 'The contending foes were not above ten yards asunder, and scarcely were the enemy seen to move. Tenaciously maintaining their hold of the hill, they fought with desperation, defending every inch of ground; for the precipice was near. Their hardiest veterans stood firm; their bravest officers came forth displaying the banners of their nation.' [40]

At such close proximity almost every shot struck home and the slaughter on both sides was appalling. A French prisoner taken after the battle said that 'he expected to have seen our [the British] line turn every instant as he never saw men fall so fast.' [41] Here, wrote Charles O'Neil, 'the contest continued, with more bravery than before [and] the issue still remained quite doubtful.' [42] Victor could see that everything depended on which side could hold its ground. 'Conspicuous in the front the marshal was recognised by both armies waving his plume [hat] in circling motion high above his head, to fasten his troops to the hill.' Victor urged his men to make one final attack but they could not move forward against the rolling volleys of the British infantry. 'The execution was terrible,' continued

O'Neil. 'Again and again were they summoned to the attack; but the lines had hardly closed over their dying comrades, when another volley would again send confusion and death among the advancing ranks.'[43]

At this moment, Graham, sensing that the key moment had come, moved to the front of his own men, just 150 yards from the enemy. The taciturn Scot shouted a single word. But it was the word that changed the course of the Battle of Barrosa – 'Charge!'[44]

'Like electric fluid it shot from the centre of the British line to the extremities of its flanks, instantly followed by the well-known thundering British cheer, sure precursor of the rush of British bayonets.'[45]

Though moving uphill and against superior numbers, the line pushed back the heavy columns of the French infantry. To counter this Victor brought the two battalions of his left wing – the 2/9me *Léger* and the 1/96me *Ligne* – across in support. But the scattered remnants of Browne's provisional battalion, seeing the battle turn in Dilkes's favour, regrouped and began to advance up the hill once again. 'They darted from behind trees, briars, brakes, and out of hollows . . . . it was a magic effect,' Blakeney wrote of his men. 'We confidently advanced up the hill and, unlike most advances, in this one our numbers increased as we proceeded, soldiers of the flank battalion joining at every step.'[46] The attackers included Sergeant Cameron and seven men of the Royal Military Artificers. The blue coats of the Artificers were conspicuous amongst the red coats of the infantry and soon three of the men fell. Graham ordered them out of the fight 'as he might want them for other work.'[47]

The flank battalion, though now numbering less than 300 men, moved directly towards the 2/9me *Léger* and the 1/96me *Ligne*. Blakeney's small force could do little other than distract the two French battalions, but they delayed them just long enough for the Guards to break Ruffin's line. 'With loud and murmuring sounds', Blakeney recalled, 'Ruffin's whole division, together with Rousseau's chosen grenadiers, were instantly in whirling motion rolled down into the valley below. The battle was won; and the gallant Graham triumphantly stood on the bristling crest of Barrosa's blood-drenched hill.'[48]

The uphill fight had left Dilkes's men exhausted and there was no immediate pursuit. Together Dilkes's brigade and Browne's flank battalion had lost 603 men – approximately 30 percent of their combined force. Remarkably, French casualties were proportionately slightly less.[49] Browne's men took a French howitzer from the left of the French battery placed near the chapel on the summit and another gun was taken by the 1st Guards.

*

The rest of Graham's force was also heavily engaged beyond the woods below. Having been ordered to turn around upon themselves, the various battalions had become terribly mixed up, and when the first troops marched out of the wood at the foot of the *Cerro de Barrosa*, there was no longer any brigade formation. By some misunderstanding the rear companies of the 67th, which formed part of Wheatley's brigade, wheeled round and followed the men of Dilkes' brigade. However, this was balanced by the fact that two companies of the Coldstream Guards – which belonged to Dilkes – had been ordered to escort Duncan's guns and so they became embroiled in the fight against Leval's division.[50]

In the sudden turn round one of Duncan's artillery pieces became entangled with a pine tree. With the other guns racing away, there was no time to reverse the horse-team and disengage the piece. Instead, the drivers whipped the horses and drove forward, tearing the tree, complete with its roots, out of the ground![51] Graham had sent Barnard's flank battalion ahead of Wheatley's brigade to delay the French until the line infantry could get clear of the trees and deploy. Having reached the edge of the wood, Barnard's Rifles and the 20th Portuguese broke through the trees to find themselves facing Leval's entire division bearing down upon them barely 400 yards away, their drums beating the *pas de charge*. 'When we reached the plain, and perceived the enemy,' wrote one of the Riflemen, 'never did a finer sight present itself . . . The grenadiers had long waving red plumes in their caps, at least a foot in length; while the light infantry had feathers of the same length and make, but green with yellow tops. The whole of the French army had on their best or holiday suits of clothing, with their arms as bright as silver, and glancing in the sun as they moved in column, gave them really a noble and martial appearance.'[52]

The French were advancing in two columns of three battalions each, with the divisional artillery following towards the rear, entirely unaware that Graham's troops had turned back to fight. The right column was composed of the 1st and 2nd battalions of the 54me *Ligne* and the composite Grenadier battalion; the left hand column consisted of two battalions of the 8th *Ligne* and a single battalion of the 45me *Ligne*. Though Barnard and the Portuguese were unformed because of moving through the wood, they were at least prepared for battle and the Allied light infantry was able to open fire upon the two leading French battalions – one each of the 8me and 54me *Ligne* – before they could deploy.[53]

Thomas Bunbury was with the Portuguese who were slightly behind Barnard's 95th Rifles and he was also impressed with the fine appearance of the enemy: 'The advance of the French was a most imposing spectacle, and there was a much more ostentatious display of plumes and martial music than we could have shown under similar circumstances. The fire of their invisible enemies [the

Rifles] must, however, have proved very deadly, as it served to arrest their march and caused them to open a desultory fire from their whole line in return. This had considerably deranged their hitherto parade-like formation.'[54]

As the first Allied rounds punched into the packed French ranks, Wheatley's men emerged from the wood. The sudden appearance of the Rifles and the Portuguese had been a surprise to the French. They were even more shocked when a line of red-coated infantry appeared behind them, which was made worse when Duncan's ten guns rumbled through the trees and unlimbered by the edge of the wood. The position, Duncan later reported, could scarcely have been worse – it was confined, low and in the midst of high-standing gorse. Yet within minutes, the Royal Artillery was discharging its first rounds into the enemy at close range.

The French were stunned. Line after line of infantry was advancing upon them and two batteries of guns were belching fire. Believing that they were being attacked by a much superior force they began to panic. In the ensuing chaos, an order was given to the first battalion of the 54me *Ligne* to form square because they were being attacked by cavalry![55]

Before the French realised their mistake, Duncan's guns fired into their static formation with canister at what has been estimated was only 250 yards. Then, as this battalion of the 54me tried to deploy back into line, Barnard's riflemen swarmed around them. From comparatively short range the British light infantry poured hot lead into the helpless French battalion as it deployed. But Leval's men massively outnumbered the small British force ahead of the wood and as soon as the 54me *Ligne* was back in column it led the advance towards Barnard's thin line.

Once again the French moved forward in two lines with each battalion arrayed in column of double companies, which meant a depth of nine ranks with a frontage of about seventy men. Firing as they marched, the 8me *Ligne* shooting in volleys, the other battalions independently and indiscriminately, the French troops pushed the British and Portuguese light infantry back, which were now suffering heavy casualties.[56] Having done their job of holding up the French until Wheatley's brigade could deploy, the 95th withdrew. But Colonel Bushe of the Portuguese, being very short-sighted, was unable to assess the situation and he refused to retreat in the face of the enemy! Bunbury tried to explain that by remaining where they were the Portuguese were actually blocking the fire from Wheatley's line. Bushe replied by telling Bunbury to mind his own business! [57]

Bushe rode slowly backwards and forwards amongst his men, with his spectacles on, calling 'What beautiful music' as the musket balls whistled around his head. Bushe's confident attitude caused the French to hesitate. There was no apparent reason for the Portuguese to remain where they were and the French wondered what was happening. 'The French seemed suspicious of an ambuscade,' wrote Bunbury, 'halting, vacillating, and then marching again.' But, as he sat on his horse ahead of his men, Bushe was an easy target and, as the French started to move forward again, the Colonel was shot and mortally wouned.[58]

This prompted the senior captain of the Portuguese to order the detachment to retreat, shouting to his men, 'Boys, I always told you that these mad Englishmen would get us into some such scrape as this. Let us be off: what are we doing here?' But the French were now too close for the Portuguese to turn and run. Bunbury, who had earlier tried to persuade Bushe to withdraw, now urged the captain to stay and hold formation. 'I begged they would stay, as, if they attempted to move while the enemy was so near, they would be shot down like mosquitoes.'

The Portuguese would not listen to the young Bunbury and the captain turned and ran taking his own company and some of Bunbury's company with him. Bunbury tried to stop his men and he even seized one man as he ran by but the man was shot dead as Bunbury held him. As Bunbury had predicted, the French 'made dreadful havoc among them.' Barnard's battalion suffered 121 casualties, including both Bushe and Barnard. The latter was wounded twice, the second time being whilst the surgeon was dressing his earlier wound.[59]

Though the Allied skirmish line had been forced back upon itself it had delayed Leval just long enough for the rest of Wheatley's mixed force to form up on the edge of the wood beside Duncan's battery. 'The ground admitted of no manoeuvring', wrote Duncan, 'so that the action very quickly became general and I believe a warmer one never took place.' Duncan's gunners, operating at such close range and under fire the whole time from the French light troops and artillery, lost many men. One gun from Captain Gardiner's brigade lost so many men that the piece was kept in action by the efforts of a Sergeant of the Drivers who took over the duties of two gun numbers for much of the battle.[60]

Wheatley's battalions had experienced considerable difficulty trying to sort themselves out after their rush through the trees.[61] After some wrangling between the Guards and the 87th about which regiment should 'lead out', this body, including the remnants of the light battalion, formed a line of around 2,400 men, with all of Duncan's ten guns still operating.[62] The delay over which regiment should have precedence cost the 87th four officers and over fifty men who fell to the enemy guns.

Opposing them Leval's four leading battalions were still advancing in column, and still firing as they moved, with the other two battalions behind. The divisional artillery had already unlimbered and was engaged with Duncan's guns from a ridge about a mile to the north-east and at a range of some 1,300 yards. But Leval's artillery was out-numbered six to ten and it was not long before the French guns fell silent. 'Never,' Graham later wrote, 'was artillery better served.'[63]

Though deprived of artillery support the French columns pressed on. William Surtees of the 95th Rifles witnessed the French advance: 'their marauding columns came down upon us with an intrepidity seldom seen in the French army, and opening out their heavy and destructive fire.' This fight was a prime example of the line versus column duel for which the Peninsular War has become renowned. Leval's force numbered 3,800, whereas Wheatley commanded just 2,400 men. Yet the British line extended across the entire French front and partly overlapped the French flanks. Apart from the attempt by the 2nd Battalion of the 54me *Ligne* to deploy into line after mistakenly forming square, the French battalions remained in column of division. 'They never got into line,' wrote Surtees of the 95th, 'nor did they ever intend to do so, I believe, but advanced as a solid body, firing from their front.'[64] With the French unable to ascertain the depth of the long British line with its back to the wood, they thought themselves outnumbered.

Instead of waiting for the French columns to crash into his line, Wheatley ordered his men to charge the enemy as soon as the light infantry battalion had formed alongside his small force. 'In all my fighting', continued Surtees, 'I never was in an action where the chances of death were so numerous as in this.'[65]

The ground over which the opposing forces advanced towards each other was a practically level, open plain measuring about 1,000 yards across with nothing to impede movement. In the centre of the French formation was the 2/8me *Ligne* which, because of its greater discipline, was slightly ahead of the battalions on either side. Facing the 8me was the 87th Irish Regiment. Sergeant Peter Facey of the 28th Regiment wrote of the 8me that '1600 strong, when the action commenced, and justice I must allow them to be the finest regiment I ever beheld in the French service.'[66] Coincidentally, the 87th and the 8me regiments had met before – eighteen months earlier at the Battle of Talavera – and the French regiment had the better of the engagement.

The two battalions closed to less than sixty yards before Major Gough ordered the 87th to fire. The French responded with a single volley. But the front line of the 8me's column possessed a fraction of the firepower of the 87th's line and the French battalion simply fell apart.

To the left of the 87th were the Coldstream Guards, who had been joined by

Graham, whose horse had been shot under him, leading on foot in front. Some of the Guards opened fire, but Graham knocked up their muskets and shouted to them to 'Cease fire and charge.'[67]

With this the entire British line – the 87th leading with 'the most unearthly howl' – charged into the enemy ranks and then, wrote Wright Knox, 'commenced a scene of slaughter.' So awful was the bloodshed, Gough admitted, he found it intensely distressing. 'The French waited until we came within about 25 paces of them, before they broke, and as they were in columns when they did they could not get away. It was therefore a scene of most dreadful carnage, and I must own my weakness; as I was in front of the regiment I was in the very middle of them, and I could not cut down one, though I might have twenty, they seemed so confounded and so frightened.'[68] The fury of the 87th was later remarked on by the French, who recalled that if the Irish had broken their weapons they went on fighting with their fists! [69]

This was the start of the complete disintegration of Leval's Division. On the flank of the 2/8me was the 1/8me which, as it advanced, came under the fire of Duncan's artillery and the musketry of the British infantry. This massive volume of fire on its flank forced the 1/8me to move towards its right and into its sister battalion. As the 87th continued to push the French column backwards and the 67th to pour fire into its flank, Leval's force became condensed into a confused huddle.

Trapped against their own helpless countrymen, the French soldiers were being hacked and cut down in appalling numbers – the Irishmen, their blood up, revelling in the easy slaughter. Confusion in the French column rapidly turned into panic.

The 87th cut its way into the muddled ranks of the 1/8me *Ligne*, with the French Regiment's Imperial Eagle as its objective. The British Army had never captured a French eagle in a battle in the Peninsula, but now one was tantalisingly close.[70]

'Do you see that, Masterman?' called out Ensign Edward Keogh indicating the eagle to his sergeant.[71] The young officer and his sergeant pushed forward, shouting the Irish war-cry 'Faugh A Ballagh' – get out of the way – in their determination to reach the standard. Realising the danger, a number of French officers with some of their men tried to escape with the eagle. 'They were pursued by our men,' observed Wright Knox, 'here they made some resistance and every man of them was cut off.' A desperate fight then developed around the French standard. Keogh snatched the eagle from the standard-bearer *Sous-Lieutenant* Edmé Guillemin only to be bayoneted twice and killed by the colour-guard. Sergeant Patrick Masterson then drove his pike into the standard-bearer and the eagle was his.[72]

The 87th continued to drive the 8me backwards and into the reserve battalion, the 45me, which was at the rear of Leval's force behind the artillery. Leval had ordered the 45me forward to help the crumbling ranks of the 8me and it was still advancing as it met the 87th.

It was Graham himself, right in the thick of the action again, who saw the 45me bearing down on the 87th and he called out to Gough to try and bring his men back into some kind of order, as the 87th was exhausted and disorganised whilst the 45me was still fresh and composed. The French battalion should have been able to hold the 87th but, witnessing the other battalions disintegrating before them, the 45me hesitated. Gough had managed to bring approximately half of the 87th into line before the 45me came within musket range. 'After firing until we came within fifty paces of them', wrote Gough, 'they (for us fortunately) broke and fled, for had they done their duty, fatigued as my men were at the moment, they might have cut us to pieces.'[73]

On the French right, the two battalions of the 54me *Ligne* had met a similar fate. The leading battalion, the 1er, had swung further to the right, presumably to try and outflank the Allied line, whilst the 2me *Batallion* bore down on the 28th. Ignoring the threat to his left flank, or possibly expecting that the Portuguese and the 95th would deal with this problem, Colonel Belson led the 28th directly towards the 2/54me.

An officer of the 28th, Charles Cadell, takes up the story: 'We had formed line under cover of the 95th, and then advanced to meet their right wing, which was coming down in close column – a great advantage – and here the coolness of Colonel Belson was conspicuous: he moved us up without firing a shot, close to their right battalion, which had just then began to deploy. The Colonel then gave orders to fire by platoons from centre to flanks and low.'

Caught in the act of changing formation, the 2/54me was helpless. 'Fire at their legs', Belson bellowed, 'and spoil their dancing.' The volleys rolled out with 'dreadful' effect. Then the 28th lowered bayonets and charged, and charged again. 'But', continued Cadell, 'the enemy, being double our strength (since our flank companies were away), only retired a little on each occasion. Finally, giving three cheers, we charged a third time, and succeeded: the enemy gave way and fled in every direction.'[74]

The first battalion of the 54me *Ligne*, which had been sent through the wood in a bid to turn Graham's right, was held back by Barnard's riflemen who concentrated on their left flank. Failing to press home its attack, and seeing its sister battalion fall back, the 1/54me also withdrew. Leval had only one battalion in reserve, the composite Grenadier battalion, and this unit stepped forward and covered the retreat of the two battalions of the 54me as they joined in the general rout of Leval's shattered division.

During this bloody struggle Duncan had pushed his guns forward to a third position on a knoll on the summit of the Barrosa ridge from where he was able to sweep with his fire the open ground across which the French had fallen back.

The whole of Leval's division staggered back beyond the Laguna del Puerco to be joined by the remnants of Ruffin's division which had tumbled down from the Barrosa heights. Having driven the French from the hill, Dilkes halted his brigade on the summit to allow it to reform. He then resumed his forward movement; his men bringing up their right shoulders so as to edge Victor's battalions still further off their ground to the east.[75]

'It would be difficult to give a just idea of the impetuosity with which the common enemy was driven back from all the heights by the English bayonets; the same enemy who had charged us with such insolence and confidence as if he had already gained the victory,' wrote Whittingham. 'His force was double that of the English; but the victory, though costly, was complete, and decided by the point of the bayonet.'[76]

The final act, however, would be delivered with the sword, not the bayonet. Some of Victor's cavalry formed a hasty rearguard which Dilkes noticed as his men were moving down from the Barrosa heights. As the French horse, only 400 yards away, appeared to be poised to exploit any weakness in the Guards' formation, Dilkes called for the support of the German hussars. 'They arrived in good time', reported Dilkes, 'and immediately moved towards the enemy, who, after a slight resistance, advanced to the encounter: both parties meeting at a short gallop, they mixed, dispersed, and reformed, the enemy retiring and our hussars pursuing the stragglers: all this was clearly perceptible from the spot on which I stood.'[77]

Spurred on by a loud shout as they galloped past the British troops, the Hussars, having scattered the dragoons, rode on into the ranks of the French infantry and artillery, helping to capture two more field guns.[78] The French were already severely shaken after being repulsed by Graham's infantry and the charge of the KGL cavalry finally shattered their resolve. They still believed that they were greatly outnumbered by the British, the pine wood concealing the true size of Graham's small force and preventing them from seeing whether or not Graham had more troops in reserve, and it was difficult for them to believe that they had been attacked and driven back by inferior numbers. So when the Hussars got amongst them, the French broke and fled in a 'disordered mass' for Chiclana.

Graham's two brigades of infantry, no longer under immediate pressure, were at last able to form line in more-or-less regular order. Wheatley's brigade re-formed with its right flank in advance of Duncan's artillery and Dilkes's brigade came up on the right of the guns. Both Barnard's and Norcott's riflemen were pushed out in extended order. So for the first time in the day, Graham was able to form his entire force in battle order facing the enemy.[79] 'We collected on the top of the hill, from which we had beaten the enemy', wrote Cadell, 'and saw the French retreating in great confusion towards Chiclana, dismayed and crest-fallen – we gave them three hearty British cheers, at parting.'[80]

According to Blakeney a column of French infantry was seen approaching from the direction of Chiclana to also help cover the retreat. It was assumed that this was Villatte's division which had remained near the Almanza creek watching Zayas and keeping the Spanish troops on the Bermeja heights in check. As it transpired this column was in fact composed of the sick who had been marched out of the French hospitals of Chiclana. This supposed 'ruse' was designed to help deter any pursuit, but in reality the exhausted British were in no condition to follow up their victory and La Peña's Spaniards had no intention of leaving the security of the Torre Bermeja.[81]

Victor, by what Fortescue described as 'sheer personal ascendancy', was eventually able to steady his troops. The British followed up but only slowly. Though it seems that Browne sent some of his men out to skirmish with the retreating enemy, they were soon called off.[82]

The British troops collapsed exhausted upon the ground they had so dearly won. Around them, as Graham was later to write, the field was covered with the dead bodies and arms of the enemy.[83]

CHAPTER 7

'A Great and Glorious Triumph'

S ome of the French soldiers, which had become separated from the rest in the confusion of the retreat, sought refuge amongst the trees of the pine wood and it was at this point, with the battle already over, that the Spanish battalions of Cruz Murgeon returned to help their Allies, Beguines, with the baggage, having remained with La Peña. But as the Spaniards did not reappear until the fighting was over this aroused 'such disgust' amongst the British, Richard Henegan noticed, 'that notwithstanding the worn state of our men, they would willingly have stood up, to drive these fellows back to the hiding place of themselves and comrades.'[1]

Graham, possibly aware that these battalions had stood their ground at Casa de las Guardias, and had in fact been engaged during the battle, gave them at least some credit. In his report on the battle he wrote that: '. . . we were strengthened on our right by the return of the two Spanish battalions that had been attached before to my division . . . These battalions made every effort to come back in time, when it was known that we were engaged.' Graham also praised the two Spanish officers, captains Miranda and Naughton, attached to his staff who 'behaved with the utmost intrepidity.'[2] Lieutenant-Colonel Ponsonby also credited Cruz Murgeon's two battalions with 'moving forward rapidly [with] the greatest zeal' and when they reached the British positions the Spanish general put his men under Graham's orders.[3]

This, belated, assistance was the only help that the British received from any part of La Peña's command throughout the entire battle. All that stood between the Spanish General, with around 10,000 men under his command and the divisions attacking Barrosa, was Villatte, with around 2,500 men. If La Peña had marched between the divided French forces he could have cut Victor's army from its base at Chiclana. Yet he made no move either to support Graham directly or to move against the French rear. Even the French General Jean Sarrazin admitted that, if at that time of the battle La Peña had advanced, the French army would have been 'astonished at the boldness of this manoeuvre and at the intrepidity of the English, [and] would have immediately retreated, to avoid a destruction which must have been the inevitable consequence.'[4]

As Andrew Barnard of the Rifles also pointed out, one of the principal objectives of the entire enterprise was the destruction of the siege works which, during and immediately after the battle, were undefended. But, wrote Barnard, La Peña 'did not profit by the moment and get possession of the French lines, which were then deserted.'[5]

Verner of the Rifles considered La Peña's conduct as 'one of the most pitiable stories of the incapacity of the Spanish leaders in the whole Peninsular War.' It is said that La Peña fully expected Graham's tiny force to be destroyed, which is why he refused to send any of his troops to assist the British, and it was not until he actually saw the beaten French troops streaming through the pine wood that he accepted the reports that the British had won. Even then he refused to move his troops on the grounds that the men were tired and that 'enough had been done for one day'![6]

'Had the Spaniards moved towards Chiclana, the utter ruin of the French corps was certain,' wrote Graham's aide James Stanhope, '[yet] not one of whose officers thought it necessary even to see if we were cut to pieces, and that not one musket was fired in our aid, though numbers of their stragglers arrived, who murdered and stripped the wounded French and plundered indiscriminately the baggage of friend and foe. In every part of the field the wounded prisoners were crying out to be protected from their vengeance.'[7]

One of those Frenchmen, *Chef de Bataillon* Vigo Roussillon of the 2/8eme, who was amongst the dead and wounded left on the battlefield, found himself attacked by an Irish sergeant who was 'doing his best to transfix me with his pike.' Lieutenant Carroll of the 87th intervened and said to the French officer, 'You can no longer fight, Sir, you are alone, I beg you to surrender.' 'Willingly', said the Frenchman, 'and here is my sword; but please tell this devil of a fellow to leave me alone.' It was only then that the sergeant saw that the French officer was wounded and he apologised, calling some of his men to help carry him from the field. Roussillon's sword is now a prized trophy in the Royal Irish Regimental Museum.[8]

Victor had lost another of his senior officers – General Rousseau, who was found lying on the ground with his young Andalusian dog sat by his side. At first the dog refused to leave his master's side, but when Graham heard of this he had the dog brought to him and he took it into his care. Later he had the animal sent back to his estate at Bagowen in Scotland.[9]

Apart from the conduct of La Peña's Spaniards, the behaviour of the Allied cavalry under the command of Colonel Whittingham, an English officer, was also open to question. Whilst it is true that his force was engaged by the French dragoons during the early and main phases of the battle, during the closing stages he failed to take advantage of the disorder the French were in. Though the KGL Hussars had returned to help towards the end of the battle they had been led by Frederick Ponsonby not by Whittingham. This officer had not ordered his Spanish horse into action and was as guilty as La Peña in failing to pursue the retreating enemy. Whittingham commanded 800 cavalry, Victor had just 250. An opportunity to turn defeat into disaster had been thrown away. 'At this critical juncture', wrote Blakeney, 'every British soldier felt confident that a strong body of six hundred Spanish cavalry . . . would ride forward against the reeling columns of the retiring enemy, yet they never appeared. Abandoning their calling as soldiers they remained behind, mouthing the pebbles of the beach.'[10]

The original *History of the King's German Legion* was also highly critical of Whittingham's conduct. Aside from failing to utilise his Spanish cavalry, Whittingham's delay in releasing the two hussar squadrons also proved fatal: 'The arrival of this detachment of hussars ten minutes sooner', wrote Major Ludlow Beamish, 'would probably have led to the capture of the greater part of the French infantry, and the Allies had cause to complain of the misapplication of a force which, timely employed, would have crowned a victory which British bayonets had so nobly won.'[11] Stanhope made the same observation: 'if General Whittingham had chose to move his cavalry rapidly round their left to have profited by the victory, which our two squadrons of Germans, bravely as they conducted themselves, were not in numbers to effect, much more advantage might have been reaped.'[12]

*

When the last of the enemy had disappeared from view, the British troops were ordered to assemble on the battlefield. 'We collected there, and gazed around with saddened hearts,' recalled Charles O'Neil. 'I know of no sadder scene than a field of battle presents soon after the conflict, even though the glorious result may have filled our hearts with joy. When the roll is called, and name after name uttered without response, it cannot but awaken the deepest sensibility in the heart of the survivors.'[13] At last, though, the British troops could lie down and snatch a few moments rest. They had not eaten since the middle of the day before and they had to wait for another hour before any food could be found for them. This was because their muleteers had run away at the start of the fighting and the unguarded wagons had been plundered by the Spaniards. The troops remained for several hours on the battlefield, still hoping that the Spaniards 'would awake to the prospect of success and glory which the extreme valour of the British had opened', before Graham ordered his men to move closer to the Sancti Petri.

The British bivouacked in the fir woods near the Almanza creek, leaving the detachment of the 3rd Battalion of the 95th Regiment under Major Ross on the *Cerro del Puerco* to protect the wounded and to watch out for any renewed offensive by Victor.

La Peña, for his part, contented himself with sending a despatch into Cadiz. 'The allied army,' he wrote, 'had obtained a victory so much the more satisfactory as circumstances rendered it more difficult; but the valour of the British and Spanish troops, the military skill and genius of General Graham, and the gallantry of the commandant-general of the van-guard, D. Jose Lardizabal, had overcome all obstacles. I remain master of the enemy's position, which is so important to me for my subsequent operations.'[14]

Graham, however, had no interest in any subsequent operations with the Spaniards and he ordered his men to cross back to the Isla de Leon, sending James Stanhope to La Peña's headquarters to inform the Spanish general of his decision. This meeting was later recorded by Stanhope who arrived at La Peña's house close to the Sancti Petri at 0200 hours. The general was in bed: 'I was shown into the general's room, where in a few moments, were assembled General Lacy, Valcarel, and several other officers of the Estado Mayor.' When Stanhope told the gathered officers that the British troops intended to retire onto the Isla, La Peña declared, '*I cannot remain without the English*'! [Stanhope's italics].[15]

General Lacy then remarked that the British withdrawal was 'much to be regretted after such brilliant advantages had been gained.' Abandoning the Spaniards in such a manner, Lacy complained, made the result of the battle more like a defeat than a victory. Lacy then added that: 'There are no French in Chiclana; a single light battalion would take possession of it.'

La Peña was worried about his Spanish force being alone on the right bank of the Sancti Petri and he asked Stanhope if the British could wait for another day so that the Spaniards and their Allies could cross the river together. Of course it was far too late for this as the British were already starting to move back to the Isla and Stanhope scornfully replied that: 'I could not conceive His Excellency [La Peña] could be so much pressed . . . when by their own accounts there are no French in Chiclana'! This rebuke effectively ended the conversation.[16]

The weary British troops filed over the Sancti Petri and back to the Isla de Leon. When the 87th tramped back towards the bridge, they were met by Graham, who halted the regiment. Graham shook Gough's hand and thanked the Irishmen 'for deciding the fate of the day.'[17]

103

It was after dark when Ross' 95th had to walk back over the ground upon which they had fought to take up a new defensive position on the sand hills close to the shore. Quartermaster Surtees witnessed the sights and sounds of a battle so dearly won: 'I have never witnessed any field so thickly strewed with dead as this plain . . . my battalion retired over the field where the thickest of the dead and wounded were strewn, and many were the dying groans which struck upon our ears, as we traversed this bloody field; but, except these groans, no sound was heard where lately the din of arms had been loud and fierce, and where war had raged in all its fury . . . Never was victory so complete.'[18]

*

It was a truly remarkable victory. Barrosa was not a prepared Wellingtonian position where ground advantage benefited the British troops. On the contrary, every aspect of the engagement favoured the French – the British were taken by surprise whilst on the march, they were fighting uphill and they were heavily outnumbered. Yet in little more than one and a half hours Victor had lost 2,062 men, killed, wounded or taken prisoner, almost a third of his field force. He had also left behind six guns (two 7-inch howitzers, three heavy 8-pounders and one 4-pounder), an Imperial eagle and two wounded generals. Ten in every thirty-five Frenchmen involved in the action became casualties.[19] 'The real fact therefore stands thus,' wrote James Stanhope, 'that an English force only meant as a reserve, harassed with a night march and without food or rest, defeated completely an enemy double in numbers, fresh in their strength, collected in their front and formidable from their position.'[20]

Inevitably in such circumstances the British had suffered just as severely as the French. The 1st Guards lost 219 men out of 600, the Coldstream 58 out of 211, and the 3rd Guards 102 out of 320. Duncan had five men killed and forty-nine wounded, including eight, i.e. fifty per cent, of his officers. The two flank companies of the 28th Regiment suffered the severest casualties, with two-thirds of all their men and all the officers either killed or wounded. Total British killed and wounded amounted to 1,238. Thus for every minute of the battle thirty-six men were hit, or more than one every two seconds. Little wonder then that Napier described it as, 'Short, but most violent and bloody.' Wellington considered it to be 'the hardest action that has been fought yet.' John Burgoyne, later to become a Field Marshal, wrote that, 'Never did troops form under such disadvantages of ground and fire; never was a victory more decided.'[21]

As Verner has pointed out, this was an 'inspiring fight for Englishmen'. It demonstrated to the troops that they could beat the French without the unconquerable Wellington at their head. 'It taught them', Verner continued, 'that in the attack the British formation in line was able to overthrow Napoleon's redoubtable battalion-columns. Wellington's actions from Vimeiro onwards had shown how the greater volume of fire of the two-deep line used in defence invariably overwhelmed that of the French double-company column, but Barrosa demonstrated that it was equally deadly *in the attack.*'[22]

Verner also commented on the effectiveness of the Rifle companies. As they were able to move and deploy more quickly than the heavy infantry, the companies under Norcott and Barnard engaged and delayed the enemy whilst the line battalions formed up. Both the two companies of the 2/95th with Dilkes and the four companies of the 3/95th which supported Wheatley moved to the flanks of their respective main bodies where they were able to continue to fire upon the French columns. 'Never', wrote Verner, 'was the value of well-trained light infantry armed with rifles more clearly demonstrated . . . owing to Graham's soldier-like appreciation of their proper use they were employed in a manner which enabled full advantage to be taken of their armament and training.'[23]

In his despatch to the Earl of Liverpool Graham praised his troops with these words: 'No expressions of mine could do justice to the conduct of the troops throughout. Nothing less than the almost unparalleled exertions of every officer, the invincible bravery of every soldier, and the most determined devotion to the honour of His Majesty's arms in all, could have achieved this brilliant success against such a formidable enemy so posted . . . Where all have so distinguished themselves, it is scarcely possible to discriminate any as the most deserving of praise.'[24]

It is difficult to blame Victor for the defeat his troops suffered. His attack was, to quote Napier, 'well-judged, well-timed and vigorous'. With a few thousand more men he would have overwhelmed Graham and then turned upon the Spaniards who were trapped with the Sancti Petri at their backs. 'If Graham or his troops had given way, or even hesitated,' Napier wrote, 'the whole army must have been driven like sheep into an enclosure.'[25]

This statement is not mere conjecture as there was an incident during the battle which demonstrated how easily Victor could have cut the Allies off from the Isla de Leon if the British had been defeated. A small French detachment actually managed not only to cross the bridge over the Sancti Petri but also to seize and bring back prisoners! This clearly shows that if Graham had been beaten the Spanish force at Bermeja would have been unable to prevent the French from crossing the river. It was, without doubt, only that 'unconquerable spirit' of the British soldiers that prevented disaster.[26]

*

Though Graham had returned to the Isla de Leon the Spaniards had remained on the eastern bank. When Graham went back over the river to see what they were doing he found them 'all in alarm' because the British were no longer with them. Graham explained that his losses had been so great that his men had to recover. He also pointed out that the commissariat mules had been dispersed by the fighting and that his men could not remain beyond the Isla de Leon or they would starve. The truth was that, as Graham told Liverpool, he was 'fully determined never to expose my division to such management again.' Incredibly, the Spaniards tried several times throughout the next two days to persuade Graham to join them in another expedition, but the British general would have none of it.[27]

After the battle, Graham issued an Order of the Day, thanking his men. 'The disadvantages under which the battle of yesterday was begun are so striking that it is unnecessary the Lieutenant-general should state to the troops that he considered the safety of the whole of the allied army (circumstanced as it was at the time) depended on our defeating the enemy,' Graham wrote on 6 March. 'He [Graham] confided in the known valour of the British troops, and his expectations were completely fulfilled. The fatigue of a night's march of sixteen hours was forgotten by every man in the division. When such unusual praise is due to the incomparable behaviour of all, it is impossible to particularize by name those who distinguished themselves. *All did.*'[28]

Graham's most immediate concern was now with the wounded. Those that could not make their own way across the bridge were still on the eastern bank of the Sancti Petri and Graham needed to transport them back to the Isla. Graham ordered out a cavalry patrol along with 200 men of the 20th Portuguese to watch the movements of the enemy before the recovery of the wounded could be attempted. But, for no apparent reason, the Spanish troops still on the eastern bank were seized with panic, and the British patrol had difficulty getting across the river as the entire Spanish force was retreating over the bridge as fast as it could.

This amazed Graham as there was no sign of the French who were still beyond Chiclana recovering from the battle. Until that moment the Spaniards held all the ground from Bermeja to the Sancti Petri, and if the Spaniards had maintained their position and dug in on the Bermeja heights, as Graham had earlier suggested, the land blockade of Cadiz would have been broken. 'Why the Government, with this in view, gave up the position of Bermeja', Graham wrote on 19 March, 'must be a matter of astonishment to those who are unaccustomed to Spanish tactics.'[29]

The wounded were eventually transferred back to the Isla but it proved a slow and painful process. The heavy surf made it extremely difficult for the naval boats to be used for the badly wounded, so the artillery wagons were taken over the bridge to assist. Duncan was instructed to destroy all the reserve infantry ammunition and use the carts and wagons to help transport the casualties. But this proved very time-consuming as both the men and horses were so exhausted from the previous day's exertions, and it took many days to remove all the wounded and bury the dead, the last of the French casualties not being recovered until the evening of 8 March.[30]

*

Victor consolidated his forces after the battle with Cassagne's contingent marching back to Chiclana from Medina Sidonia. On the night of the 5th a council of war was held with Victor and his generals. Victor proposed another attack upon the Allies. The British had suffered severely in the battle and the Spaniards had shown no desire to fight. An attack upon the Allies, with their back to the river and only a narrow bridge between them and the Isla, might well induce an uncontrolled retreat resulting in complete disorder. The events of the 6th when the Spanish troops panicked and rushed across the bridge showed how correct Victor was in suggesting an attack. His proposal, however, was rejected by the others.[31] Instead the decision was taken that if the Allies followed up their success on the 6th, they would try and hold them off long enough for the forts to be blown up and the stores and flotilla to be destroyed. I Corps would then retreat upon Seville.[32]

As it happened this course of action was nearly implemented and Victor came close to abandoning the siege altogether. On the 6th, Admiral Keats made a series of raids against the French strongpoints across Cadiz Bay. The attacks were carried out by 200 marines of the British squadron and 80 Spanish marines, helped by around 300 seamen. They landed between Rota and Catalina, and between Catalina and Santa Maria. The marines stormed two redoubts and dismantled most of the defences that had been erected. This caused so much 'confusion and alarm' that Victor thought he was about to be attacked by the Allied field army.[33] Leaving strong garrisons in the largest of the armed camps he withdrew the remainder of his force beyond the Rio San Pedro. With the French siege lines devoid of the covering forces, this move by Victor had presented the Allies with a perfect opportunity to seize all the enemy's trenches and batteries. But La Peña had no interest in such a move and, rather than taking advantage of the French withdrawal, he himself withdrew, transferring almost all his remaining troops back to the Isla de Leon. When Victor sent out a reconnaissance party on the morning of the 7th he found only a small body of Allied soldiers east of the Sancti Petri. This small force – Beguines's three battalions – retired the next day to Medina Sidonia, later pursued by one of Victor's brigades. Observing no further movement by the Allies, Victor re-established the siege of Cadiz on the 8th.[34]

Though technically a defeat, Victor's daring attack upon the numerically superior enemy forces achieved its objective – that of preventing the Allies from raising the siege. Within a week Victor had concentrated his scattered forces and Cadiz was as securely blockaded as before. But the war in the Peninsula was indivisible and the main consequence of the battle was felt in Portugal rather than in Spain. Soult's expedition into Estremadura had been astonishingly successful. He had driven back Ballesteros' forces and captured the border fortress of Olivenza, taking more than 4,000 men prisoner. He then moved up to Badajoz. This mighty stronghold had a formidable garrison, 7,000 strong, which was aided by the Army of Estremadura, composed of 9,000 infantry and 3,000 cavalry. Soult should have been unable to mount a siege with such a force opposing him, but the Spanish Army was routed by Soult and the fortress was left to defend itself. The French settled down to begin formal siege operations, being constantly harassed by the garrison. But in one of the sorties the Governor, General Menancho, was killed and his successor, General José Imaz, meekly surrendered Badajoz after a breach had been blown in its walls.

In just fifty days Soult had destroyed the Army of Estremadura, taken 15,000 prisoners, and captured the most powerful fortress in Spain. But the Duke of Dalmatia did not have time to enjoy his success. Just three days after the fall of Badajoz, Soult was on the road again. He had learnt of the attack against Victor and, fearing for the safety of his Andalusia fiefdom, had handed over responsibility for Badajoz to General Armand Phillipon, and the Marshal marched back to Seville as quickly as he possibly could.

*

Despite the failure of the expedition, and the shocking losses his division had suffered, Graham remained convinced that he was correct in joining the operation. 'I am most thoroughly convinced that the results of the expedition could not have been any other than the raising of the blockade of Cadiz,' he told Wellington, 'had the management been in the hands of an officer who knew what to do.'[35]

Henry Wellesley agreed, telling his brother that since Graham's arrival at Cadiz various plans had been put before him for an attack upon the French, all of which he rejected as 'replete with danger and uncertainty'. But with Victor's forces having been considerably reduced the expedition on this occasion held out 'a fair prospect of success'.[36]

The days immediately following the battle proved difficult ones for Graham. His good relations with the Spaniards prevented him from making any official comment about the battle. 'I was aware from the beginning,' he told Lady Asgill, 'of the risk of placing myself in the hands of a weak and timid chief, but the circumstances imperiously called on me to incur it. I should have laid myself open to the imputation of disappointed ambition. Since I had agreed before to go out in the *command* of the expedition, it was impossible to retract when it was considered proper that a Spanish officer should go in the command. My reason for agreeing to go beyond my instructions (which really confine me to this place – Cadiz) was that I thought there was a favourable opportunity of raising this siege and forming an army in the country that would have relieved the pressure against Portugal . . . Now blame is attempted to be turned on me for having interrupted the progress of the plan by withdrawing my harassed and crippled people into the Isla, and for not having devoted them to certain destruction by continuing them in such unfit hands.'[37]

It was certainly true that La Peña had attempted to deflect blame from himself by claiming that the Spanish troops had remained on the eastern bank of the Sancti Petri and were therefore still engaged in the campaign, whilst the British division had abandoned the offensive by retreating back to the Isla de Leon. It was apparent, Henry Wellesley wrote in a private letter to Graham on the 6th, 'that it is the object of the Government to cover the misconduct of their General and troops, by making it appear that they had the principal share in the affair of yesterday, and that they were prevented from advancing to-day by your determination to cross the river.'[38]

General Cruz Murgeon fanned the flames of this fiery dispute by 'unblushingly' claiming in the Cadiz press that he took both guns and prisoners during the action. As all the captured artillery had already been accounted for, Colonel Ponsonby was able to refute this claim. According to Blakeney, Cruz Murgeon did indeed take four cannon after the battle – but they were his own guns on the very same spot that he had abandoned them earlier in the morning! As Blakeney was an eye witness to this event his statement was made public and the controversy ceased. In Blakeney's somewhat unfair words, Cruz Murgeon 'shrank from the paper warfare as disreputably as he had fled from the field.'[39]

At first, though, La Peña's and the other Spanish officers' accounts were believed in Cadiz and the British were subjected to abuse. 'If the misconduct of the Spanish general was flagrant, ten-fold more disgusting was the *ingratitude* and vanity of the whole population of Cadiz,' bemoaned Stanhope.[40] 'Scarcely a day passed without an attack upon us in the newspapers or in a pamphlet,' Henry Wellesley remarked, and in his determination to defend Graham he demanded a full inquiry by the Regency into the conduct of La Peña.[41] As it transpired, and much to his surprise, the Regency thanked Graham for 'the glorious victory' he had won. The Cortes then announced that Graham was to be offered the title of Duke and Grandee of the First Class, 'as a public and authentic testimony of their satisfaction, so due to his valour, military skill, and adherence to the cause of Spain.'[42]

Graham refused the honour, partly because he had heard that La Peña was also to be decorated for his contribution to the victory. This rumour proved to be false as, far from rewarding La Peña, the Cortes actually suspended him from his position pending a full investigation into his conduct during the battle. He was replaced by General Coupigny.

Graham felt vindicated in maintaining his silence over La Peña's cowardly actions but, predictably, this was not the end of the matter as far as La Peña was concerned. No sooner had La Peña been suspended than he issued a public statement claiming that, had it not been for the precipitous British withdrawal into Cadiz, then Victor's army would have been destroyed.

In the face of such accusations, Graham could no longer keep quiet and he finally wrote his report on the battle. 'The action at Barrosa was equally unseen and unheeded by the Spanish staff, within a quarter-of-an-hour's ride of the scene, and *nothing was done*; the British division, left alone, suffered the loss of more than one-fourth of its number and became unfit for further exertion. Need I say more to justify my determination to decline any further co-operation in the field . . . There is not a man in the division who would not gladly have relinquished his claim to glory, acquired by the action at Barrosa, to have shared with the Spaniards the ultimate success that was within our grasp.'[43]

Graham's report was translated into Spanish and a printed version was made available for the general public in Cadiz. No less than nine of Graham's senior officers also submitted reports detailing the battle from their various perspectives. Every one of these made it abundantly clear that the Spaniards had made not the slightest contribution to the fighting at Barrosa. The words of one of these, Cranley Onslow, who commanded the combined Coldstream and 3rd Guards, typify the sentiments expressed in the reports: 'I can take upon myself positively to say that during the battle in no one part of the field was there visible from the right of the British line any one or any part of a Spanish corps.' Likewise Captain Hamilton, Graham's Assistant-Quartermaster-

General, wrote: 'I am positive that at no one period of the action did any Spanish regiment or corps whatever engage the enemy.'[44]

Wellington also found time to support Graham in a letter which describes so accurately the problems of operating in the field with the Spanish armies: 'I congratulate you and the brave troops under your command on the signal victory which you gained on the 5th inst. I have no doubt whatever that their success would have had the effect of raising the siege of Cadiz if the Spanish corps had made any effort to assist them; and I am equally certain, from your account of the ground, that if you had not decided with the utmost promptitude to attack the enemy, and if your attack had not been a most vigorous one, the whole allied army would have been lost . . . The conduct of the Spaniards throughout this expedition is precisely the same as I have ever observed it to be. They march the troops night and day without provisions or rest, and abuse everybody who proposes a moment's delay to afford either to the famished and fatigued soldiers. They reach the enemy in such a state as to be unable to make any exertion, or to execute any plan, even if any plan had been formed; and then, when the moment of action arrives, they are totally incapable of any movement, and they stand by to see their Allies destroyed, and afterwards abuse them because they do not continue, unsupported, exertions to which human nature is not equal.

'I concur in the propriety of your withdrawing to the Isla on the 6th as much as I admire the promptitude and determination of your attack on the 5th; and I most sincerely congratulate you.'[45] This last statement was significant because Graham was worried that his decision to turn back and attack the French might be viewed as having been irresponsible. So concerned was Graham with this that in his report on the battle to Lord Liverpool he felt the need to explain 'the circumstances of peculiar disadvantage under which the action was begun, as to justify myself from the imputation of rashness.'[46]

Back in England Graham's victory was received with genuine excitement. Colonel Torrens, Dundas' Military Secretary, wrote: 'This action must be admitted as one of the greatest efforts of valour and discipline that ever distinguished our military annals, and I rejoice in the event which has so justly placed your merits in a point of view to attract the undisputed approbation of your country. Nothing was ever more general than the satisfaction expressed.'[47]

Graham was thanked by the House of Commons, with the Speaker ending the address with these words: 'Allow me to embrace the opportunity of expressing to you the cordial satisfaction with which I have witnessed the universal joy of all ranks of men, not only for this achievement – so brilliant in itself – but more especially that your name . . . will now stand recorded to the latest posterity upon the list of those great commanders who have been most renowned for advancing the military glory of their country.'[48]

Similarly, Lord Eldon, the Lord Chancellor, forwarded the thanks of the House of Lords: 'I believe I may with great truth state to you that I recollect no instance – great and glorious as the triumphs of British arms have been by sea and by land – in which the House of Lords ever manifested a more cordial unanimity than that which was displayed on this occasion.'[49]

The eagle of the 8me *Ligne* captured at Barrosa was taken back to London by Captain Hope and laid at the feet of the Prince Regent. The trophy was paraded through the city on 18 May 1811 and large crowds lined the streets to celebrate. Gold and silver medals were struck with the clasp inscribed 'Barrosa' and distributed to officers that had taken part in the battle. The 87th Regiment was granted the right to bear an eagle and laurel wreath above the harp on the regimental colours and appointments. The regiment was also granted 'royal' status, becoming the Prince of Wales's Own Irish Regiment. Sergeant Masterson, who had captured the eagle, was promoted to the position of Ensign. He eventually rose to the rank of Captain.[50]

Though it was the British that were receiving all the plaudits, the Spanish authorities could not allow it to be seen that their army had stood aside whilst their Allies faced the enemy alone. They therefore did nothing to suppress the claims of many of La Peña's officers that the Spaniards had contributed to the victory at Barrosa, and in June La Peña's Chief-of-Staff, General Lacy, published a book on the battle which included a number of passages that were insulting to Graham.

These remarks hurt Graham. He felt that his honour had been slighted and he sent a member of his staff, Colonel Frederick Ponsonby, to tell Lacy that he demanded 'satisfaction'. Lacy at once apologised and he assured Graham that the book would be withdrawn immediately. Graham believed that La Peña was instrumental in the production of the book so he told La Peña that either he should publicly denounce the book or permit Graham 'an early morning meeting'![51]

Faced with such a choice, La Peña backed down. He apologised to Graham and he gave his personal assurance that the relevant passages would be removed from Lacy's book.

The acrimony following Barrosa had soured relations between Graham and the Spaniards, as he explained to Lady Asgill: 'I begin to loathe this place . . . I don't know what I can do or say to get out of this odious prison and away from the still more odious people. Nothing is so mean or so corrupted as the upper classes – no wonder that things go ill with such management. I had no idea to what an extent of servile and contemptible falsehood they were capable of going. Many officers who could not possibly be *within reach of seeing* the enemy, publicly claim a great share in the success of the action, finding that the General and Government are anxious to have it believed that we were assisted by Spanish troops.'[52]

It must be observed, however, that there are some commentators who feel that some of the criticisms levelled at La Peña might have been unjust, and certainly there is a degree of confusion over the actions of the Spaniards and of Villate's division during the battle. Firstly, whilst it is frequently stated that the Spaniards were not engaged by the French, this is incorrect. Not only were Cruz Murgeon's battalions involved in the fighting with Whittingham, but the Spanish regiments that were on the *Cerro de Bermeja* also came under attack. It is said that when Victor attacked Barrosa, Villatte, who had received reinforcements from Chiclana, assaulted Bermeja. The Spaniards held their position until Victor called Villatte off when the rest of the French force retreated.

Secondly, La Peña had ordered Graham to join him and might, not unreasonably, have expected to see the British troops fighting their way towards Bermeja – not doing the exact opposite by marching back up Barrosa hill. 'Whatever error of judgement General La Peña might have committed,' wrote Robert Southey, 'the charges thus brought against him and his army were as ill-founded as they were intemperately urged. Instead of being cold-bloodied spectators of the battle, the main body of the Spaniards were four miles distant; there was a thick wood between them and the scene of action, and they were themselves actually engaged at the time . . . Marshal Victor affirmed in his official account, that when he determined to attack the heights [of Barrosa], the Spaniards under La Peña were at the time warmly engaged; the cannonade and the fire of the musketry were extremely brisk, he said.' This is supported to some extent by Sarrazin who recorded that the Spaniards lost 1,500 men during the day, though this includes those troops under Lardizabal that attacked Villatte earlier in the morning.[53]

The opposing view is that when La Peña was informed of the French attack upon Barrosa his first thought was to defend the line of retreat from Bermeja to the Sancti Petri. Consequently he drew up his battalions across this ground in a double or treble line, while Zayas with his force from Cadiz watched Villatte across the Almanza creek. According to Oman, Zayas repeatedly asked permission to attack Villatte but La Peña refused. Furthermore, when Leval's division was seen retreating past the head of the Almanza creek and it was obvious that Graham had somehow won the battle, Zayas urged his commander to allow him to join in the pursuit. La Peña's reply was that his men were tired and it was late in the day.[54]

It is difficult to reconcile these opposing views but the words of Colonel Lequetel, who was with Villatte's division, might hold the key: 'Hardly had the 3rd division [Villatte] arrived at Camp Saint Petri when it was assailed by a flock of sharpshooters by the heads of the columns which attacked by way of crossing the sand dunes bordering the same place. The Spanish Army at first was put in flight and cornered at the sea but so the English Army which was all in reserve presented itself in front of our lines and was beaten with all the fierceness of desperation. The Spanish rallied and we returned to the other side of the river. I, along with the brave General of Division, Villatte, were wounded.' From this we can glean that the Spaniards did indeed engage Villatte whilst the rest of I Corps attacked the British, but then Villatte pulled back across the Almanza. Villatte's withdrawal presented La Peña, who commanded around 10,000 men, with the opportunity to send part of his force to help the British. There was nothing to stop him from marching to help his Allies.[55] Yet he honestly believed that the British division would be beaten and saw no point in leaving his secure position and placing his men in danger. Worse still was his failure to take advantage of Graham's victory and pursue the French when it was evident that they were a beaten force. 'If Graham, instead of La Peña, had been the commanding general,' Sarrazin continued, 'the siege of Cadiz would have been raised, and marshal Victor, with half his army destroyed, would have been obliged to retire on Seville.'

Fuelled, therefore, by what was now seen as their embarrassing inaction at Barrosa, the Spaniards, in what can only be described as typical fashion, wanted to renew the attack upon Victor's positions. On 13 March Henry Wellesley informed Wellington that Zayas had been given command of 6,000–7,000 men with the intention of attacking the French across the Sancti Petri.

Zayas himself was opposed to the operation and Wellesley tried to dissuade the Cortes from ordering such a reckless scheme. The temporary bridge that had been thrown across the river had been damaged by gale-force winds coupled with a particularly high tide and the men could only cross the river by boats. If the Spaniards were routed, as was the most likely outcome of the escapade, they would have no means of retreat back to the Isla. 'I have done all in my power to stop this expedition', wrote Wellesley, 'which seems to be sent out with no other view than that it should be destroyed . . . ' Indeed, General Blake told Whittingham in full council that 'he did not wish a man of them to return if they did not succeed in raising the siege.' Whittingham was appalled at the mad scheme and he resigned command of the Allied cavalry in protest. Graham, equally, was amazed that the Spaniards believed they could succeed with such a force when almost twice that number had failed only days before![56]

Undaunted by Graham's opposition to a new offensive, General Coupigny pressed on with plans for Zayas's expedition. Though he knew that the British would not join in the operation, the new Spanish commander-in-chief asked Graham if he would at least help by mounting a feint attack to distract Victor. Instead Graham advised that they should start working on rebuilding the bridge over the Sancti Petri as this would appear to the French that the Allies were planning another attack across the river. But on 25 March the Spanish Government, 'after some uncertainty', finally gave up the scheme.

Instead, Zayas's corps of 6,000 infantry and 500 cavalry were despatched to Huelva near the Portuguese border to cooperate with Ballesteros's forces in Estremadura.[57]

Despite Wellesley's opposition, and even though Zayas himself had no confidence in the plan, the Regency demanded that the expedition went ahead.[58] As expected the operation failed with the loss of a number of men and horses. Graham had also predicted this disaster, blaming the Spanish Government, which he complained 'seem incapable of acting in a way to combine military operations and to give the Spanish troops a fair chance of success on any occasion.' So poor was the coordination between the Allies at this stage, that Zayas re-embarked his troops and set sail for Cadiz just as Beresford was crossing the Guadiana into Spanish Estremadura just a few miles away![59]

Another frustration felt by Graham over this abortive operation was that the absence from Cadiz of such a large body of men meant that there were not enough men left to continue work on the Cadiz defences. The recent bad weather had caused much damage to the works, particularly those at the point of Sancti Petri. This was especially galling to Graham as the positions abandoned by the Spaniards on the eastern bank were reoccupied by the French in force – thus every advantage gained by the victory at Barrosa had been thrown away.

A further problem for Graham following the battle was what to do with all the French prisoners. The Admiralty had issued strict instructions that no more prisoners were to be shipped back to Britain, but with Cadiz already over-full with Allied troops and refugees there was simply no suitable accommodation available. The locals were also unhappy at seeing paroled French officers freely walking around Cadiz. As the days passed more and more of the wounded French troops were recovering from their injuries and were ready to be discharged from the hospital. Altogether, around 300 men, including the severely wounded General Ruffin, were left waiting for a decision from London and subject to the abuse of the locals.[60]

A clear decision was eventually received, however, on the subject of any future requests from the Spaniards to participate in joint offensives. Graham was told categorically that 'you should decline placing yourself or the British forces entrusted to your charge under the command of a Spanish officer of any rank whatsoever.' This instruction was given to Graham in the form of an official despatch from the Prince Regent. At the same time Lord Liverpool wrote Graham a private letter explaining that Graham could still exercise his own judgement and cooperate with the Spaniards if he believed that doing so would 'be productive of decided benefit to the Allied cause'. But if he did not consider it wise to become involved in any operations with the Spaniards, he could simply show them the Prince Regent's instructions.[61]

A clearly relieved Graham replied that he was 'extremely happy now to be possessed of so positive and ostensible an order.' Further good news reached Graham. All the officers that Graham recommended for promotion following the battle received their reward. Remarkably, Major General Henry Torrens, the Military Secretary, even canvassed Graham's views on proposing to the Cortes that Graham should be made commander-in-chief of the Spanish Army! Graham, understandably, quickly dismissed this suggestion.[62]

It was not only the Spaniards who were pressing Graham to continue the offensive against Victor. Hoping that the victory at Barrosa would 'put life into the Spaniards', a friend of Graham's, the Duke of Atholl, wrote that he prayed 'that while Lord Wellington is destroying Massena, you may be able to drive the French from before Cadiz.'[63]

In reality, it was the French who displayed the most aggression. A new and 'considerable' construction was begun to the south of Chiclana which further consolidated Victor's hold upon all the territory around Cadiz. Observing this development, Graham quickly sought to dismiss any thoughts of renewing the offensive and he told Lord Liverpool that 'we are certainly no ways in a condition to attempt anything serious against any part of the [French] line now.'

Graham knew that the only important thing was the preservation of Cadiz and the independence of the Cortes. He was therefore willing to pay the Spaniards to work on the Cadiz defences from the British public coffers.

Fortunately for Graham all these frustrations were soon to be behind him as the orders he had so long anticipated finally arrived. He would shortly be off to Lisbon to join Wellington. Though Wellington had earlier told Graham that he might 'render the most important services there [at Cadiz]' and that 'to withdraw you from that place might shake the confidence and damp the spirits of the Spanish Government and of the people of the town', the breakdown in relations

The Cadiz mortar at Horse Guards Parade, London. Placed on an elaborate bed is the barrel of one of the Villoutreys mortars recovered from Victor's siege works. Its inscription reads: "To Commemorate the raising of the siege of Cadiz, in consequence of the Glorious Victory, gained by the Duke of Wellington over the French near Salamanca, on the XXII of July MDCCCXII. This Mortar, cast for the destruction of that great port, with powers surpassing all others, and abandoned by the Beseigers on their Retreat, was presented as a token of respect and gratitude by the Spanish Nation to His Royal Highness the Prince Regent."

The Guzman's Tower still dominates access to Tarifa beach and the little rocky island to which the defending Allied forces would have retreated if the town had been taken by the French in 1812.

The medieval walls still surround the old town of Tarifa. John Grehan is pointing to the plaque that marks the place where the breach was made in the walls during the siege of 1812. The gap in the walls on the right of the photo is where the portcullis used to be, under which the Retiro stream passed. The street opposite is named after the Spanish General Copons.

Part of the Battle of Barrosa monument on top of "El Puerco" Hill.

This inscription on the Barrosa monument is also inscribed in Spanish, French and German.

HILL "EL PUERCO"

ON THE 5th OF MARCH 1811 THE BATTLE OF CHICLANA WAS FOUGHT AT THIS PLACE DURING THE PENINSULAR WAR AGAINST NAPOLEON.
THOUSANDS OF BRITISH, FRENCH, SPANISH, PORTUGUESE, POLISH AND GERMAN SOLDIERS SHED THEIR BLOOD ON THIS HILL.
TODAY, IN A NEW MILLENIUM THE DESCENDENTS OF THOSE WHO FOUGHT HERE, ARE LIVING
TOGETHER IN A UNITED AND PEACEFUL EUROPE.
ON OCCASION OF THE VII CENTENARY OF THE TOWN OF CHICLANA DE LA FRONTERA
1303 – 2003

Looking across the top of Barrosa hill towards the north-west.

Looking up Barrosa hill in the direction that Dilkes' Brigade took in its advance against Ruffin's Division.

The Torre Barrosa, overlooking La Barrosa beach.

From the Torre Barrosa the beach runs around the bay to Bermeja which can be seen in the distance.

The monument at Bermeja to the Battle of Barrosa, or Chiclana as it is called by the Spaniards. The Torre Bermeja can be seen in the background.

The eagle of the French 8th Line Infantry Regiment captured at Barossa was deposited in the Royal Chelsea Hospital. There it remained until a thief broke through the tile roof, snapped the staff and took the eagle on 16 April 1852. Fortunately a good drawing of the eagle had been produced by a Lieutenant Pym from the 2nd Battalion of the 87th Regiment which enabled a replica to be made. The original was an eagle of the 1804 Model, which had a sheaf of rays that the eagle held in its right claw, and with the special peculiarity of having around its neck a gold laurel wreath with a blue enamelled bow, which had been granted on 22 September 1808 by the town of Paris to those regiments which had fought at Austerlitz.

This is the view that Laval's Division would have had of the pine forest on the edge of the plain. It was through these trees that the 95th and the 20th Portuguese, followed by Wheatley's brigade, burst upon the advancing French columns.

The 28th (North Gloucestershire) Regiment charges the French 54th Ligne at the Battle of Barrosa, 5 March 1811. Original painting by David Rowlands.

The main gateway into Cadiz, Las Puertas de Tierra, is always busy.

The walls of Cadiz facing Cadiz Bay.

Thomas Graham, Baron Lynedoch,
painting by Sir George Hayter.

Claude Victor-Perrin,
Duke of Belluno.

The Puente Zuazo over the Rio Sancti Petrie. At the time of the French siege of 1810-1812, it
was the only permanent link between the Isla de Leon and mainland Spain.

between Graham and the Spaniards meant that it was now 'advantageous to the public interests' for him to leave Cadiz.[64]

*

If the situation in Cadiz was less than harmonious, on the far bank of the Sancti Petri life for the French was even less pleasant. 'Our men were picked off by enemy fire, by illness, sometimes by suicide,' recalled one of the besiegers. 'Little by little, boredom – something that kills and stupefies just as surely as a narcotic – took control of the best soldiers . . . Meanwhile, the bitterness of our situation was increased still further by the sad fact that we almost never received any mail from our families . . . Nor did we know anything that was happening in France or the rest of Europe . . . Though free on the surface, in reality we were . . . poor exiles in a foreign land.'[65]

Captured French despatches also revealed the depressed state of the French forces blockading Cadiz. Colonel Juan, aide-de-camp to Napoleon's chief of staff, Marshal Berthier, was captured along with all his correspondence, which included a letter from the chief engineer of the besieging forces, Colonel Lequetel, who admitted that the bombardment of Cadiz was ineffectual. He also stated that the besiegers themselves were blockaded by the partisans who surrounded them and that they were engaged in an operation from which they could not recede 'without an irreparable loss of time and cannon or hope to prosecute with effect according to their present means.' Colonel Juan also spoke of Victor, saying that he 'is a good general, but is not happy here and sees things a little black.'[66]

CHAPTER 8

'That Terrible Day'

F ar to the north, Marshal Masséna, having received little help from Paris
and just limited assistance from Andalusia, had finally abandoned his
campaign in Portugal and had marched over the River Coa back into
Spain. Wellington, with only 36,000 men, had chased the French all the way.
The rest of the Anglo–Allied force had taken another route towards the Spanish
frontier – to the Guadiana. Badajoz, so recently won by Soult, was about to be
attacked.

The force allocated by Wellington to capture Badajoz was under the
command of Major General William Carr Beresford who, as Marshal General,
was also the commander-in-chief of the Portuguese Army. He had been
instructed to march upon Badajoz on 8 March. The very next day, however,
Wellington countermanded this order as he had been informed that Masséna
had concentrated his army and was preparing to stand and fight his pursuers. A
large part of Beresford's force was therefore sent to join Wellington, with the
remainder halting at Abrantes until the situation in the north was resolved. On
12 March it became clear that Masséna was not going to offer battle and the
troops taken from Beresford could be returned. Beresford's command was fully
restored by 22 March and the advance towards Badajoz resumed.

By this time Soult had learned of the Battle of Barrosa and he had scuttled
back to Andalusia, leaving Mortier with the unenviable job of trying to get
Badajoz into a satisfactory state of defence before the inevitable Allied counter-
attack. Whilst the walls of the fortress were hurriedly repaired Mortier was
busily securing his position on the border. On the very day that Soult marched
off back to Seville, Mortier moved against the small Portuguese border fortress
of Campo Mayor whilst Latour-Maubourg was sent to capture the neighbouring
Spanish fortress of Albuquerque.

The latter place was old and neglected but it possessed a citadel held by two
regular battalions built on a high crag, which dominated the town. With its lofty
position it was immune from attack by anything other than heavy ordnance and
could be expected to hold out for many days whilst the French engaged in formal
siege operations. Latour-Maubourg arrived before Albuquerque on 15 March
with just two cavalry regiments. In what was described as 'the most disgraceful

surrender made during the whole Peninsular War', the governor immediately opened negotiations with the French general and, when Latour-Maubourg told Major General José that infantry and guns were on their way, he simply surrendered.[1]

Campo Mayor, with its old walls defended by no more than 300 militia and, at best, another 500 poorly armed civilians with a single company of regular army gunners to man its guns, could not be expected to hold out for more than a day or so, especially if the example of Albuquerque was anything to go by. Against this small force Mortier was able to bring nine battalions of infantry, a brigade of cavalry and part of the siege-train which had helped to capture Badajoz.

Nevertheless, Major José Talaya, an old engineer officer who was in command of the fortress, resisted for almost a week, even beating off one attempt at storming the town. It was not until 20 March that a breach was blown in the walls, and the place rendered indefensible, that Talaya capitulated. The following day the French took possession of Campo Mayor and Major Talaya 'on account of his great age' was permitted to go proudly into retirement.[2]

The governor and people of Campo Mayor had occupied a corps of 7,000 men for six days and this had given Beresford the chance to move up to the Spanish border almost undetected. It was not until Beresford's force reached Arronches on 24 March that his cavalry encountered Latour-Maubourg's outposts, three miles outside Campo Mayor. The French had been sighting numbers of Portuguese cavalry on a regular basis since they reached the Badajoz area at the start of 1811, and so did not realise that these horsemen were the scouts of a major army.

At around 1030 hours on the morning of 25 March Beresford's force was seen approaching the French outposts. Latour-Maubourg happened to be visiting the outposts at the time, and so was amongst the first to realise that he was facing attack by a large body of men. He returned to Campo Mayor at high speed, and ordered his force to abandon the town and their baggage, and prepare to retreat back to Badajoz as fast as possible. By the time the first British troops reached the ridges overlooking the town, the French were already on the move.

Beresford sent his cavalry, under General Long, to cut off the French column. Though his men overtook Latour-Maubourg, and one of Long's regiments successfully charged the French 26th Dragoons, a disagreement between him and Beresford led to the rest of the French force escaping back to Badajoz unmolested.[3]

Beresford's objective was to recapture all the fortresses seized by Soult, drive Mortier's V Corps over the Sierra Morena and open up the road into Andalusia.

THE BATTLE OF BARROSA, 1811

His main task was to retake Badajoz for which he would need to concentrate all his resources. This meant that before he could mount such an operation he would have to ensure that the other fortresses occupied by the French were taken first. The French had abandoned Campo Mayor but Latour-Maubourg had garrisoned Olivenza and Beresford, with a siege train which he had put together with the aid of the Portuguese at Elvas, laid siege to the place on 9 April.

As it happened, Latour-Maubourg had placed just one battalion in Olivenza and, after bombarding the same section of the walls that Soult had a few weeks before, a practicable breach was formed. On 15 April the garrison of less than 400 men surrendered. Now nothing stood in Beresford's way and Badajoz was next.

The siege of the mightiest fortress in Spain was a major undertaking and, typically, Wellington wanted to make the arrangements for the siege himself. So, after shepherding Masséna back into Spain, Wellington rode south to discuss the operation against Badajoz with Beresford.

He arrived at the Portuguese frontier fortress of Elvas some twelve miles from Badajoz, which Beresford had adopted as his base of operations, on 20 April. After making a series of detailed reconnaissances with his chief engineer, Lieutenant Colonel Fletcher, he prepared a detailed plan for Beresford to follow. Wellington believed that Beresford would only have sixteen days at most to capture the fortress before Soult would be marching to relieve Badajoz, and his plan was based on this. Satisfied with his arrangements Wellington left Elvas on 25 April and Beresford moved forward to invest the fortress.[4]

*

Marshal Soult learnt of Latour-Maubourg's fortunate escape from Campo-Mayor on 30 March. He knew that the force he had left in Badajoz – some 3,000 men under the resolute General Phillipon – would be able to resist any attack for a considerable time, and he made no immediate move. By the end of April, however, he received reports that Beresford was about to invade Andalusia and he could delay no longer. Just eight weeks after leaving Estremadura, Soult had to march there again.[5]

Once more Soult had to strip his Andalusia garrisons to find a force large enough to face an Allied army in the field with some prospect of success. Napoleon, still trying to direct affairs from Paris, had anticipated a move by Wellington into Estremadura and, on 30 March, had advised Soult how to deal with this threat. Yet again, Napoleon underestimated the number of Allied troops that could oppose Soult: 'Wellington has only 32,000 British troops: he cannot make a detachment of more than 8,000 or 9,000 of them with 5,000 or 6,000 added. It is necessary to keep permanently about Badajoz the value of 15,000 men of all arms, in a good state and of the best regiments, so that at the least movement of the English on this side the Duke of Dalmatia, taking with him 8,000 or 10,000 men, should be able to concentrate in Estremadura a total force of from 25,000 to 30,000 men . . . But to arrive at this result it is necessary that the countryside should be entirely de-garrisoned, that all hospitals and magazines should be concentrated in Seville, and that Cadiz, Seville and Badajoz should be the only points to guard.'[6]

Napoleon also ordered Joseph to keep a division of 6,000 men between the Tagus and Badajoz which could join Soult if a large Allied force broke into Andalusia. The Emperor calculated that with the addition of a division from the Army of the Centre, Soult would be able to muster a force of between 30,000 and 35,000 men.

Soult had no wish to loosen his grip upon the Andalusia countryside in order to deal with the immediate threat upon Badajoz. Ignoring Napoleon's previous instruction to abandon all of Andalusia apart from Seville and the Cadiz Lines with just a corps of observation at Granada, Soult was able to raise a force of just 12,000 men. These men were taken predominantly from Cordoba, leaving Seville dangerously under-manned. After the near-disaster at Barrosa, Soult left Victor's corps virtually intact. The Cortes, the great symbol of Spanish independence, had to be kept contained. Even so, this left barely 20,000 men before Cadiz, including the sailors and the marines of the flotilla.

*

At midnight on 9/10 May, Soult marched from Seville. He hoped to surprise the Allies by the timing and speed of his advance. Moving as rapidly as he could, Soult made thirty miles in the first march. At the same time Latour-Maubourg, who had taken over command of V Corps from Mortier, who had been recalled to Paris, had moved towards the Guadalcanal. The two French corps joined forces at Fuente de Cantos on the 13th. Soult now had an army of around 25,000 men.[7]

Beresford had learnt of Soult's approach as early as the afternoon of 12 May. But by that time the French Marshal was already heading north across the Sierra Morena and was reported to be at Santa Ollala, scarcely eighty miles from Badajoz. When, on the following day, further reports indicated that Soult's force was still moving rapidly, Beresford called off the siege and by the night of the 13th his troops were marching to meet the enemy.[8]

Neither commander had an accurate estimate of the strength of their opponent but neither hesitated to commit their troops to battle. Beresford could have withdrawn from the frontier and waited until rejoined by Wellington, and Soult knew he was taking a terrible chance with his only field army.

The place chosen by Beresford to make his stand blocking the road to Badajoz was on a low, undulating ridge fourteen miles to the south-east of the fortress and just to the west of the River Albuera. At its highest point the ridge rose to about a hundred and fifty feet, and at its lowest just sixty. The bare eastern slopes of the ridge – the ones facing the approaching French force – inclined gently down to the narrow river. Neither the ridge nor the river could be considered difficult obstacles.

The backbone of Beresford's corps was William Stewart's 2nd Division, which formed three brigades with ten battalions of infantry and three rifle-armed companies of the 5/60th. The rest of his force was composed of the 4th Division, led by Lowry Cole, which consisted of just one brigade of Fusiliers and a composite brigade of light companies, plus an independent brigade of the King's German Legion. The bulk of his force, however, was Spanish, with both Blake's and Castanos' armies present. There was also a sizeable contingent of Portuguese. Under the command of Major General John Hamilton the Portuguese force numbered more than 10,000 men, including four regiments of cavalry and two batteries. Altogether, Beresford commanded 10,449 British, 10,201 Portuguese and 14,634 Spaniards – a total Allied force of 35,284 men. Soult was going to be overwhelmingly outnumbered.[9]

Soult's only advantage lay in surprise. Beresford was acutely conscience of this and he kept his cavalry forward in the hope that it could maintain contact with the advancing French columns. Nevertheless, when on the 15th Soult suddenly drove in the outposts on Beresford's left flank, it certainly came as a surprise. But there were no further developments that day and Beresford was able to concentrate a large part of his force on the Albuera heights unmolested. The next day the French attacked.

Beresford surmised that Soult would approach Badajoz along the high road and so he positioned his strongest unit, Stewart's 2nd Division, in line across the road. To strengthen this front still further he placed Alten's two battalions of the KGL in Albuera itself. To cover the left flank he posted the Portuguese and the right was allocated to the Spaniards. The Spanish did not begin to arrive until after nightfall and they were still taking up their positions at daybreak on the 16th. Cole's 4th Division, which also only reached Albuera during the course of the night, formed the reserve, stationed in the centre behind Stewart.

Beresford had made the best use of the few advantages the ground offered. But Soult, the master strategist, did even better.

Shortly after dawn a brigade of French infantry appeared, moving down the high road towards Albuera exactly as Beresford had anticipated. The French infantry crossed the Albuera stream and engaged Alten's two battalions. As the encounter developed, Berseford sent down the 1st Brigade of Stewart's division to support the Germans.

With everyone's attention focused upon the action in the village, Soult struck from an entirely different direction. Concealed by the woods that covered the eastern slopes of the Albuera valley, 8,400 infantry and Latour-Maubourg's cavalry had crept round the southern extremity of Beresford's position during the night. Turning in towards the right of the Allied line, this powerful force fell upon the unsuspecting Spaniards who were still forming up. Instead of facing the enemy, Blake's men found themselves being assailed from the flank.[10]

Four battalions under Zayas managed to change front and maintain formation. The rest of the poorly trained Spanish regiments fell apart as they attempted to wheel round to their right.

Realising that the frontal attack upon Albuera was merely a feint, Beresford ordered Stewart to take all three of his brigades and help Zayas, who was still valiantly holding his ground. Such was the urgency of the situation, Stewart did not wait to form his corps into line – he simply sent his brigades off in open column as they individually came about. Marching towards him was Girard's infantry of V Corps, which had been formed into two narrow, immensely long columns. Behind Girard were Latour-Maubourg's two cavalry brigades waiting for the opportunity to charge the Allied infantry.

As they advanced, the 3rd, 31st, 48th and 66th Foot of Colborne's brigade opened fire upon the flank of the great column stretching before them. They could hardly miss. Then, suddenly, a storm of rain and hail rolled across the battlefield. Visibility was reduced to little more than a few yards and muskets were rendered useless. At that very moment, a brigade of French cavalry dashed through the torrent and crashed into the flank of Stewart's men.

Led by a regiment of Polish lancers, the French cavalry cut, thrust and slashed its way through the ranks of the unprepared British infantry. Within just a few minutes, 1,300 out of 1,600 men had been killed, wounded or taken prisoner. Even Beresford and his staff had to draw swords to defend themselves. The cavalry then swung round and rode along the rear of Zayas's battalions. Incredibly, the Spaniards, with the French 5th Corps at its front and cavalry swarming all around them, stood firm.[11]

Despite Zayas's valiant stand all seemed lost, but then Stewart's 2nd Brigade appeared upon the battlefield. Passing through Zayas's depleted ranks, Houghton's men opened fire upon the French light cavalry, driving them from the top of the heights. Houghton's brigade breasted the ridge just as Girard's great column mounted the hill from the other side.

Though outnumbered by more than five to one, Houghton's three battalions opened fire on the French mass before them. Following behind was Abercromby's brigade which moved up the hill to the left and slightly below Houghton's line. These three battalions joined in the fire-fight and Girard's advance ground to a halt.

The rain lashed the troops as they exchanged volleys across the shallow depression in the ground that separated the two forces. 'There we unflinchingly stood', wrote an officer of the 29th Worcestershire Regiment, 'and there we unflinchingly fell.'[12] Then, gradually, the British line began to inch forward. Step by step, the thinning, shrinking red line moved closer to the bark blue mass until they were only twenty yards apart.

At such close range, the slaughter on both sides was appalling, but the proud regiments of France and Britain would not yield. It took the personal initiative of one of Beresford's officers to break the deadlock.

Without orders, Lowry Cole abandoned his reserve position behind Albuera and marched his division across the heights to help Stewart's outnumbered brigades. Deploying his Portuguese brigade as a flank guard against Latour-Maubourg's cavalry, he advanced up the hill with his Fusilier Brigade.[13]

Seeing the British reserves moving across the battlefield, Soult knew he had to respond and he threw his reserve – Welré's division – into the fray. The climax of the battle had now arrived.

The odds still favoured the French, but the advance of Cole's fusiliers proved unstoppable. 'Their dreadful volleys swept away the head of every formation,' ran William Napier's famous passage, 'In vain did the French reserves mix with the struggling multitude to sustain the fight, their efforts only increased the irremediable confusion, and the mighty mass, breaking off like a loosened cliff, went headlong down the steep: the rain flowed after in streams discoloured with blood, and fifteen hundred unwounded men, the remnant of six thousand unconquerable British soldiers, stood triumphant on that fatal hill.'[14]

The French had been repulsed and Soult could scarcely credit what he had witnessed. 'They could not be persuaded they were beaten,' he wrote in disbelief of the British infantry which now held the hill. 'They were completely beaten, the day was mine, and they did not know it and would not run.'[15]

There was no point in persisting with the battle against an enemy that refused to be beaten and, covered by his cavalry, Soult made his way back to Seville.

Beresford, who seems to have been just as shocked as Soult with the terrible carnage of the battle, was in no position to pursue the retreating French with any degree of vigour. Out of a total of 35,284 men, the Allies had lost almost 6,000. The British regiments had suffered the greatest and of the 6,500 who had been engaged less than 2,100 had survived unscathed. The Fusiliers had lost over half of their comrades, and of Colborne's brigade only a quarter remained with the colours.[16]

The French suffered equally severely. Of the 24,260 troops who had marched upon Albuera, nearly 7,000 had been lost. The battles of Barrosa and now Albuera had shown that even without Wellington at their head the British could not be beaten. 'The French,' observed one historian, 'gallant and experienced soldiers though they were, never wholly recovered from the effects of that terrible day. The memory of it haunted them thereafter in the presence of the British infantry.'[17]

Soult's battered battalions limped slowly back towards Seville. Beresford ordered a pursuit but it was only the Allied cavalry that made contact with the French rearguard. After a clash by the banks of the Usagre stream with Latour-Maubourg's dragoons, the pursuit was called off and the stream effectively became the line of demarcation. There was no further contact and with Soult seeking to re-establish his hold upon Andalusia, Berseford returned to his siege works before Badajoz.

*

As ever, with Soult's back turned, the opportunity presented itself for offensive action from Cadiz. Graham was asked to send troops to Tarragona to help raise and train a local force capable of defending that city which was besieged by the French. On 26 June a small flotilla arrived at Tarragona from Cadiz carrying the 2nd Battalion 47th Regiment, a detachment of the 3rd Battalion 95th Rifles, both of which had fought at Barrosa, and some additional flank companies sent from Gibraltar. The total of this little force was 1,147 men and they were under the command of Colonel Skerrett of the 47th.

When he landed, Skerrett found that the city walls were on the verge of being breached and that not only would there be insufficient time to train the locals but that the Spanish governor had decided to try and cut his way through the French lines rather than defend the place to the last. Skerrett judged that he would be placing his troops in great danger if they disembarked.[18]

On the 28th Skerrett sailed off and the following morning the French, under Marshal Suchet, stormed the breach.[19] Tarragona had been the centre of the

Spanish resistance in Catalonia for three years and its loss was a severe blow to the partisans. Predictably, Skerrett was blamed for failing to help the Spaniards. Whilst this was clearly unjust, Skerrett would soon become embroiled in yet more controversy over the defence of another Spanish town – when Soult ordered Victor to capture Tarifa.

Back in Cadiz, word that Beresford had been forced to raise the siege of Badajoz reached the city three days before the news of the Allied victory at Albuera. This caused widespread dismay and again raised fears that, if Soult was successful in Estremadura and he received the reinforcements that he had requested, the French would make a determined effort against Cadiz. 'A week ago', complained Graham, 'the people here who would not believe that the Allied army was not coming immediately to Seville, and to raise the blockade, are now as much discouraged.' Predictably, when the result of the Battle of Albuera was known, those same people were instantly demanding another offensive! 'They are always in extremes,' wrote a frustrated Graham.[20] Henry Wellesley groaned at the thought that if it was actually true that the Spanish troops did perform well at Albuera the authorities in Cadiz 'will be ten times prouder and more consequential than ever.'[21]

Soult, meanwhile, received a welcome reinforcement from France with the arrival at Seville of General Drouet's IX Corps on 13 June. This corps was composed of 4th battalions of regiments belonging to I Corps and V Corps and the 3rd and 4th squadrons of the dragoon regiments of the army in Andalusia. Instead of remaining as composite units many of the reinforcements were drafted into the regiments that had been so severely mauled at Albuera. The remainder were formed into a provisional division, 5,000 strong, which consisted of the 4th battalions of those regiments serving with Victor at Cadiz.[22]

Soult's failure to relieve Badajoz meant that Beresford was able to resume siege operations and on 19 May the fortress was reinvested. Wellington galloped down to Badajoz and, with Beresford still suffering from the terrible effects of the battle at Albuera, he took over command of the siege operation. As before, Wellington knew that he had only a limited amount of time before Soult, now reinforced, would intervene.[23]

Having seen how quickly Soult left Estremadura when he heard that Graham and La Peña had attacked Victor, Wellington hoped that the Cadiz forces might be able to create a diversion which would prevent Soult from marching to the relief of Badajoz. Wellington, in complete contrast to his beliefs before the Battle of Barrosa, asked Graham to consider conducting some kind of operation 'to alarm the enemy for his situation before Cadiz or for the security of Seville.'[24]

Soult, in fact, had anticipated being unable to lift the siege of Badajoz by himself and had written to Masséna to ask for his support. Masséna, however, being driven out of Portugal and then beaten by Wellington at the Battle of Fuentes d'Onoro, had been replaced by Marshal Marmont and it was to the latter that Soult's letter was delivered.

Marmont replied that he was well aware of the importance of Badajoz and that he was willing to send part of his new command south to assist Soult if required. Soult acknowledged Marmont's offer but asked him to join him with his entire force as it was only by combining the two armies together that they could hope to defeat Wellington. Marmont agreed and set off on 1 June to help Soult relieve Badajoz.

Together, the two marshals commanded a force of around 60,000 men and it was too much for Wellington. On 10 June Wellington issued instructions to withdraw the guns from the siege batteries and by the following morning the siege train was on the move back to Elvas.[25]

Eight days later Marmont and Soult met at Merida. Soult was hugely impressed with Marmont's 'unselfish' cooperation and, as he told Napoleon, he felt that together they could undertake any task. The combined force, amounting to 32,000 men of the Army of Portugal and 28,000 of the Army of the South, marched upon Badajoz via Albuera, arriving at the fortress on 20 June, the day the garrison ran out of food.

Wellington, after being so close to success, now found himself thrown onto the defensive. He had already ordered the rest of his army to march down from the north but even with all his forces concentrated Wellington could still only muster 54,000 men. He obviously could not retreat from the frontier and expose Portugal to another invasion, but neither could he risk an action against a numerically superior enemy. Therefore, he chose to position his troops along a ridge just ten miles from Badajoz, where he could protect the Portuguese fortress of Elvas which effectively barred the road to Lisbon. The ridge was steep and dominating and could not be outflanked. This was a typically cautious move by Wellington but it produced the desired effect. For a week the two marshals stared at the long line of hills. Unable to calculate Wellington's movements behind the crest of the ridge, and only able to guess at the numbers they faced, the French commanders were unwilling to risk an attack.

In the south rebellion had again broken out in Andalusia, so Soult turned his back on the Guadiana and once more sped down the highway to Seville, leaving just V Corps (now under Drouet) and most of his cavalry in Estremadura. Marmont stayed in the vicinity of Badajoz for another two weeks before a lack of food compelled him to leave the city to its fate and march back to the north.

It was during the siege of Badajoz that Graham, who had not been able to create the diversion Wellington had hoped for, finally received instructions to depart from Cadiz to join Wellington's army. Command at Cadiz was handed to Major General Disney. At the same time a detachment of the 3rd Battalion 95th Rifles and one squadron of the 2nd Hussars KGL were also ordered to sail from Cadiz to Lisbon. This was followed by Admiral Keats being relieved by Rear Admiral A. Legge, who assumed command of the squadron at Cadiz.[26]

The reason why Soult had to return rapidly to Andalusia was due to the activities of Blake and an uprising in the Ronda mountains. Soult had taken so many men from eastern Andalusia that there were barely 9,000 left in the whole of the province of Granada. This prompted Wellington to advise his brother Henry to urge the Spanish authorities to take action. 'In my opinion the most interesting points at present in Spain are the Sierra de Ronda and the Condado de Niebla. The former, if the Spaniards should be obliged to act alone, is the fittest scene of their operations, and they would always have a retreat upon Gibraltar . . . they could be supplied with facility from Cadiz, or they could be drawn thither if the enemy were to prepare for a serious attack upon that position. A corps of 10,000 or 12,000 men, well supplied, in the Sierra de Ronda, or the Condado de Niebla would be an effectual diversion for our operations.'[27]

Whilst all this was happening Soult was travelling back towards Seville escorted by two regiments of cavalry, with Conroux's and Godinot's infantry brigades following behind. As he rode back towards his capital he received the alarming news about Blake's uprising. At the head of 12,000 men he had done exactly what Wellington had recommended and had laid siege to the castle of Niebla which is only thirty miles, or two days' march, from Seville. Soult immediately ordered Conroux and Godinot to march southwards upon Niebla.

The castle was held by a polyglot 'Swiss' battalion of 600 men of all races from the Spanish and British armies that had deserted and sought service under King Joseph. Blake had no artillery with him and could do little more than blockade the place. So, whilst Ballesteros took up a covering position to the north, Blake invested the medieval castle with Zayas's division. Blake remained in front of Niebla from 30 June until, on 2 July, he heard that the French were moving towards him.

Blake did not hesitate for a moment. His army broke up and dispersed by road and by sea, Ballesteros disappearing into the hills to the north. The Spaniards fled so precipitously that it could be described as nothing short of panic. Blake himself, according to one source, made a 'ridiculous spectacle' of himself by wading a long way out to sea through shallow water to get out to a boat to escape even though there were no French troops within miles. Blake returned to Cadiz with some 7,000 men, followed a full six weeks later by Ballesteros with the rest of the army.[28]

Predictably disregarding the shameful scenes at Niebla, the Spanish involvement at Albuera, highly creditable though it was in some respects, led to exaggerated claims of a great Spanish success: 'The news of the victory in Extremadura', a despairing Graham had told Lord Liverpool, 'has filled the minds of the people [here] . . . with the most determined belief of the superiority of the Spanish army, which now in the public opinion neither admits of nor requires improvement, being already perfect . . . Without being a witness to this unfortunate national egoism . . . it is not to be believed, nor would anyone imagine it possible that people of all ranks should be so ready to deceive themselves and others.'[29]

The Spaniards in Cadiz, immune from the realities of the war within the secure confines of the city, could afford the luxury of complacency and throughout the Isla de Leon the same confusion of command and bitter personal rivalries which had led to so many disasters in the past still continued. When Soult marched into Estremadura he had taken with him four battalions of infantry and three regiments of cavalry from IV Corps. This left Leval (who had succeeded Sebastiani) in a weakened state which General Manuel Freire, commanding the Army of Murcia, had attempted to exploit.

Freire left Murcia and pushed into Andalusia, driving back Leval to Granada. But at this point Blake, having rested in Cadiz for only two weeks, gained permission from the Regency to take over command of the Murcian army and he sailed for Almeria at the end of July with more than 7,000 men to reinforce Freire.

Blake had also been made Captain-General of Murcia, Aragon and Valencia and, after handing over his troops to Freire, he travelled on around the coast to assess the military situation at Valencia. Freire now had the strength to attack Leval with some hope of a famous victory. But the Murcian general was now merely a subordinate to Blake and he refused to act.[30]

Once again the petty jealousies of the Spanish generals proved more destructive than the French armies they faced. Freire's failure to act gave Soult just enough time to march with a force to relieve Granada and save Leval. With just 6,000 infantry and 1,500 horse, Soult marched from Seville on the 8th. He arrived in front of Granada the following day, but after he assessed the strength and numbers of the Spaniards he decided to wait for the rest of his field army to join him before attacking.

Godinot, with some 4,600 men, was marching hard, with the objective of turning Freire's flank. He forced his way through the outlying Spanish posts as he rounded upon Granada.

Freire soon became aware of this new threat and he despatched O'Donnell's 4,000-strong division to block the French advance. Predictably, when the two forces met in front of the Guardal river, the Spanish were soundly beaten.

News of O'Donnell's defeat and the prospect of being enveloped by the French army was more than Freire could take. Under the cover of night, Freire abandoned his position in front of Granada and he ran for the hills.

When Blake returned from Valencia he found the Murcian command split in two. Soult could have taken advantage of this and marched upon the Murcian capital virtually unopposed, but it was a long march and Andalusia, his principle area of responsibility, was far from secure. He returned to Granada, sending his troops along the valley of the Guadalquivir and the passes of the Sierra Nevada to hunt down the many insurgents that had risked gathering together when Soult marched into Estremadura.

Soult had suppressed the uprisings that had developed during his Estremadurian expedition but the two parts of the Murcian army quickly formed together again and on 4 September another problem presented itself when Ballesteros landed at Algeciras with 3,000 men and started to rally the patriots in the Sierra de Ronda.

In order to protect the flanks of the besieging force in front of Cadiz, Soult placed one division to the west to watch the Spanish troops in the Condado de Niebla and another to guard the passes of the Ronda mountains to the south. The result was that Victor's corps was whittled down to what Oman described as an 'irreducible minimum'. Even taking into consideration the marines and the sailors of the flotilla, Victor could now scarcely count 20,000 men. Facing Victor across the Sancti Petri were at least as many Allied troops in the Cadiz garrison.

The weakness of the besieging forces was clearly evident to those within Cadiz. This was remarked upon by some British officers who had been absent from Cadiz for a period of time. This included a number of officers who had contracted the fever the previous year and had been shipped out of Cadiz to recuperate, amongst whom was Richard Henegan, who eventually became head of Wellington's Field Train Department. Henegan went to Lisbon to recover from the black vomit and when he returned to Cadiz he was surprised to see how much the place had changed in the intervening months: 'The city was no longer kept in a state of feverish excitement and alarm by the dropping shells from the enemy's batteries. Fort Puntales had ceased to dart its booming shot against the batteries of the Trocadero and Isla de Leon alone bore evidence of the proximity of the foe.'[31]

This mood was soon to change with the introduction of enormous guns which Soult had cast at the great arsenal of Seville. These Villoutreys mortars were able to fire their shot further than any artillery piece yet devised and were able to reach over the walls of Cadiz from the Trocadero. The first shells landed in the Barrio de Santa Maria district, but this was soon extended to other areas which meant that most areas of the city were under threat. At first the wealthier residents left their homes in the city and moved down to the Isla, pushing rents there to exorbitant levels. However, it was soon found that their discharges were intermittent and their bombs comparatively ineffective. The authorities also placed men with 'glasses' on the San Francisco and San Augustino towers to watch out for the approach of the shells, to warn the inhabitants with the ringing of an enormous bell. As the shells took almost a minute to reach the city, the civilians had plenty of time to find shelter.[32] Nevertheless, these truly remarkable weapons could throw their shells farther than any ordnance of their type previously constructed. The distance from the French batteries on the Trocadero to the nearest point of Cadiz was approximately 4,500 yards (a little more than two and a half miles) and many of the shells actually flew right over the city and fell into the sea beyond – a distance of at least 500 to 600 yards farther! The concussion from each discharge was so great that the mortar destroyed the bed in which it was fixed. So, to allow the gun to recoil without causing any damage, it was slung in the air in chains! At the same time, in order to carry so far, the projectiles had to be increased in weight and were consequently mostly made of lead with little internal space for powder. This meant that when they exploded they did little damage and, despite months of shelling, less than ten citizens had been killed or wounded by these missiles. The Spaniards had even devised a popular couplet deriding the mortars: 'The splinters of the bombs that the French threw served the ladies of Cadiz as weights to curl their hair.'[33]

But it was felt that if the French could find a weapon of such magnitude then so could the Brits. What was described as a 'double-fortified sea-mortar', which threw thirteen-inch shells, was shipped in from Gibraltar. The weapon was positioned in the rear of the town of Isla with the intention of showing the French gunners on the Trocadero that their enemy was not going to be out-done.

The first trial of the sea-mortar was conducted with an empty shell and a propellant charge of thirty-two pounds of powder. The violent explosion of such an enormous quantity of powder blew the shell to pieces. In the second attempt, the shell was filled with sand to give it greater weight and strength. This was a success, the shell landing on the mainland. But the gunners were not able to maintain any degree of accuracy over such long distances and the enterprise was eventually abandoned.

CHAPTER 9

A Confusion of Commands

Despite the previous failures of the insurgents across Andalusia, Ballesteros continued to harass the invaders. His force was shipped from Cadiz at Algeciras on 4 September 1811, and he then began a persistent guerrilla campaign from his base in the Sierra de Ronda. Limiting himself to attacking isolated posts or cutting off small detachments, Ballesteros evaded every effort by General Godinot's brigade to bring him to battle. With the mountains in front and the impregnable defences of Gibraltar on his right flank and the recently re-fortified town of Tarifa on his left, Ballesteros was in an extremely strong position. Even when a grand scheme was devised to trap Ballesteros using troops from Victor's force at Cadiz to support Godinot, the Spanish General merely retreated to Gibraltar and sat comfortably under the protection of the Rock's great guns.[1]

The French force of some 10,000 men could do nothing against Gibraltar so Godinot made a dash for the much-weaker walls of Tarifa in the hope of catching the place undefended. But as the French column made its way along the coast road from Gibraltar to Tarifa a squadron of the Royal Navy bombarded the exposed infantry, and Godinot was forced to march away inland and abandon the enterprise. His failure to defeat Ballesteros cost Godinot his life. After being severely reprimanded by Soult, a disgraced Godinot committed suicide.[2]

Almost as soon as the French turned away from Gibraltar, Ballesteros was harassing them again, even catching one of the columns returning to Cadiz and inflicting some 100 casualties, and forcing a battalion of Spanish troops in French pay to surrender.

Despite Ballesteros's successes, they were only fleeting victories and he would always be on the run – the French grip on all the major centres of population was as strong as ever. Tarifa was now the only secure base from which the insurgents could operate. It was also the fortress from which a small Anglo-Spanish field-force had been operating against the rear of the French lines before Cadiz. Soult decided that Tarifa must be taken.

Limiting the insurgents' freedom of movement was not the only reason why Soult wanted to take control of Tarifa. It had become, according to Colonel John Jones, 'the great point of assembly for supplies of every nature for Cadiz.' If the wind was unfavourable for shipping heading for Cadiz, the ships would put in at Tarifa and unload their cargoes, which would then be taken round in small boats to Cadiz. It was not uncommon for a shipment of as many as 2,000 head of cattle, sheep and pigs to be transported to Cadiz this way.[3] As well as disrupting supplies to Cadiz, Soult was hoping to obtain horses for his cavalry and oxen, which were needed by Victor's force in front of Cadiz, from the Moors in Tangier. Soult had sent a mission to the ruler of the Moors and had secured a promise that the supplies being sold to the Allies would, in future, be directed to the French. But Tarifa was also the home of privateers that prowled the Gibraltar Straits and unless they were driven from their safe haven there could be no communication with the Moroccan port. Once he had captured Tarifa, Soult's intention was to place a brigade in garrison there with a squadron of gunboats.[4]

When Soult first invaded Andalusia, Tarifa's defences had been unmanned. Tarifa remained undefended for months, until the Governor of Gibraltar, General Colin Campbell, placed a small body of picked troops into the fortress. This force comprised Browne's flank battalion with companies from the 9th, 28th, 39th and 47th Foot, along with two artillery pieces. This small force consisted of five captains, twelve subalterns, twenty sergeants, eight buglers and three hundred rank and file, plus one captain of the Royal Engineers and Lieutenant Mitchell with thirty gunners. In October 1811 this force was strengthened with the addition of the 2nd Battalions of the 47th and 87th regiments, a squadron of the 2nd Hussars KGL and Captain Jenkins's Company of the 95th Rifles, sent from Cadiz all under the command of Lieutenant Colonel John Byne Skerrett. This force was joined by Spanish troops also sent from Cadiz, a battalion each of the Irlanda and Cantabria regiments commanded by General Francisco Copons. The total force at Tarifa now amounted to some 1,750 British and 1,350 Spaniards.[5]

As mentioned above, it was from Tarifa that Skerrett mounted a number of raids upon French posts in the region. The most notable of these minor operations was against Vejer. The town is situated on a conical hill, along the base of which passed the road to Cadiz, which was separated from a range of hills by a deep stream. On these heights Skerrett's men placed a field gun from which they opened fire upon Vejer. Presuming this to be the onset of a large-scale attack, the French abandoned the place and retreated to Chiclana. Victor responded quickly and sent a large force to re-take the town, which Skerrett's force could not possibly hold, and the Allies had to conduct a fighting retreat back to Tarifa.[6]

Soult, therefore, had much to gain from taking Tarifa. This old town stands on a promontory which forms the southern extremity of mainland Europe, and was surrounded by a medieval (gothic) wall, eight feet thick and strengthened at intervals with square towers. Because the sea washed up to the southern and western walls, the only approach that an enemy could make was against the northern and eastern defences. However, there was no glacis and the walls were completely exposed to artillery, though they were too weak and narrow themselves to bear cannon. Worst still, its northern front was overlooked by a range of low hills just 300 yards away – a comfortable distance even for field guns. Tarifa did posses a citadel, but this also dated from the thirteenth century and was as vulnerable to bombardment as the town walls.[7]

Tarifa itself could not be expected to withstand a full-scale siege; however, half a mile out to sea there was a small, rocky island which was connected to the town by a narrow strip of sand. The island, which measures approximately 800 yards by 600 yards across, had been powerfully fortified with gun batteries and a strong redoubt – the Santa Catalina Redoubt – at the point where the sandy causeway joined the mainland. A huge old castle, the Guzman's Tower, dominated access along the beach towards the redoubt. If Tarifa fell, the garrison could retreat to the security of the island, where buildings had been erected for the troops, and a series of caves – *Cueva de los Moros* – had been converted into casemates and magazines. Apart from the level ground where the causeway joined the island, it was bounded by inaccessible cliffs.[8]

The island was clearly the real stronghold of Tarifa but some measures had been taken to stiffen the town's ancient defences. The convent of San Francisco, which was located seventy yards to the north of the town, had been converted into a redoubt with loopholes punched through its walls and entrenchments dug around its perimeter. A few of the towers on the main wall had also been reinforced to take artillery.

It was inevitable that any attack upon Tarifa would be delivered from the north. Not only would batteries on the northern hills overlook the town, they would also be immune from the guns of the Royal Navy in the bay. Once the San Francisco convent had been taken the walls of Tarifa would not withstand a bombardment for long, so some form of alternative defence had to be devised. This was found in the form of the town itself. The houses that backed onto the walls were barricaded and loopholed. The narrow streets were blocked with traverses and home-made *chevoux de frise* constructed from iron window-bars extracted from all the houses of the town.

The north-eastern front of Tarifa presented a particular problem for the defenders, as a ravine, the Retiro ravine, passed under the walls. The walls followed the contours of the ground and they dipped down to their lowest point where the Retiro passed under the walls and through a portcullis. This was clearly a very weak spot and to strengthen this sector palisades were planted around the outside of the portcullis. All the houses that overlooked the ravine were also loopholed and prepared for defence.[9]

Altogether there were twenty-six guns in Tarifa but fourteen of these were in the batteries on the island. On the town walls there were just four 6-pounder field guns and four mortars distributed across the various fronts, and a heavy gun in each of two towers on the northern sector.[10]

By contrast, Soult had at his disposal all the cannon that were sitting impotently before Cadiz – providing he could find transport for them. Soult's other great problem would be in finding enough food to sustain the besieging troops. The area around Tarifa was sparsely populated and would not be able to support a large body of men for any length of time. This would mean that the besiegers would have to carry all their provisions with them, which, in turn, would compound the transport problem.

Soult gave Victor the job of capturing Tarifa and a siege train of sixteen heavy guns was selected from the Cadiz lines. To help move all the guns, the ammunition and the essential engineers' stores, Victor took 500 horses from the artillery and the wagon train of I Corps.

All this preparation took time, which gave the troops in Tarifa the opportunity to further strengthen the town's defences. Skerrett and Copons first learnt of Soult's intention to attack Tarifa in November 1811, but the leading French troops did not arrive in front of the town until 20 December.

During this period Victor undertook a survey of the roads from Cadiz to Tarifa, the same roads that had caused La Peña and Graham such difficulty earlier in the year. With 2,000 men, the Duke of Belluno rode to Vejer, which is roughly half way between Cadiz and Tarifa. From Vejer, Victor sent heavily escorted patrols towards Tarifa to inspect the roads.

There were two routes which Victor could take. The shortest of the two roads descended from the hills to reach the sea at the Chapel of Virgen de la Luz, just three miles from Tarifa. The second route travelled further north before reaching the sea at Torre de la Peña. It then ran parallel, and close to, the sea for some distance. The route to Virgen de la Luz was little more than a track and was declared unsuitable for artillery by General Garbé, Victor's Chief Engineer. This left just the longer route but, in anticipation of a move against Tarifa, stretches of this road at Torre de la Peña closest to the sea had been destroyed by guns from the British and Spanish navies. Despite this, and even though Allied warships were always stationed off Tarifa, Garbé declared that this was the only road that was practicable for the vehicles of the siege train.

Garbé believed that the damaged sections of the road could be remade and that the British and Spanish frigates could be kept safely out of range by building batteries on the seashore.[11]

Wellington did not believe that Tarifa could survive an attack and he was very worried about the British troops in the place.[12] As early as 15 November he had written to General Cooke, who was now in command at Cadiz, advising him to withdraw the British contingent. 'The consequences of his [Skerrett's] remaining under existing circumstances, must be to involve him, and his detachment in the operations of General Ballesteros . . . but it was not my intention when I detached part of the army to Cadiz, nor is it the intention of the British Government, that any detachment of His Majesty's troops shall take part in those operations.'[13] The same day he wrote to his brother at Cadiz about withdrawing Skerrett's detachment: 'I know the Spaniards well, and particularly Ballesteros. They will never stop till they have lost that detachment.'[14]

*

In the first week of December, Victor's siege train left Chiclana and reached Vejer on the 8th of that month. The force under Victor's command totalled around 15,000 men, though only 10,000 of these troops actually took part in the attack upon Tarifa. On paper, Soult's Army of the South numbered 80,000 men, but the vast majority of these troops were fully occupied in manning the lines before Cadiz or garrisoning the principal towns and cities throughout Andalusia. This left Soult with little more than 10,000 or 12,000 men available to act as a mobile reserve. Consequently he could not afford to give Victor much help and the Duke of Belluno had to draw heavily upon his forces at Cadiz.

So from the Cadiz lines Victor drew eleven battalions, three from the 16me *Leger*, two from the 54me *Ligne* and the 63me *Ligne*, and one from each of the 27me *Leger*, 8me *Ligne*, 94me *Ligne* and the 95me *Ligne*. Six of these battalions were not coming directly from Chicalana but from the east. (This contingent, under General Barrois, had chased Ballesteros to Gibraltar, where the Spaniard had found sanctuary once more under the British guns.) Added to this were 3,000 men drawn from the garrisons of Grenada and Malaga, and a regiment – the 51me *Ligne* – from Cordoba. These three forces were to concentrate at Tarifa.

From the outset, Victor found himself hampered by the weather. The force from Malaga and Granada, under General Leval, reached the Ojen range of mountains, which separates Algeciras from Tarifa, when day after day of continual rains washed the road away and separated the column. This left a brigade under Cassagne stranded far in the rear and out of communication with Leval.

At this point Leval was joined by Barrois's force coming from the Gibraltar region. The two generals could do nothing but stay and wait for the weather to improve. Victor made three unsuccessful attempts to reach Cassagne, sending officers with strong escorts up the flooded road, and it was not until the 12th that a fourth patrol at last made contact with the isolated brigade.

Worse still was that Ballesteros had slipped out from Gibraltar and attacked Barrios's rearmost battalion with some 2,000 men. The French General detached a full brigade and turned upon the Spanish force, driving it back again towards Gibraltar.

At the same time that Ballesteros was assaulting the French rear, Skerrett, with his whole force and a small number of Spaniards, sallied from Tarifa and attacked the head of the French column. Skerrett's German hussars clashed with Leval's dragoons near the convent of Nuestra Senora, three miles from Tarifa. Skerrett held his ground overnight, but the following day some 4,000 French infantry marched up. After a prolonged skirmish, in which the Allies suffered around seventy casualties, Skerrett withdrew back to Tarifa.

Far to the west, the siege train was also experiencing considerable problems. The convoy came to a halt at La Janda where the lagoon had overflowed and inundated the road. The train was forced to cross the hills to reach the sea at Torre Peña, achieving just sixteen miles in four days. At Torre Peña the road runs very close to the sea, forcing the passage into a narrow defile. This was the most dangerous point in the entire journey for the French column but, as planned, Garbé's engineers had repaired the road and they had erected a battery of four 12-pounders and two howitzers facing the sea. Predictably, a number of Spanish and British gunboats, as well as the 64-gun line-of-battle ship HMS *Stately* and the frigate *Tuscan*, attempted to halt the siege train and the French march was temporarily delayed, but a strong westerly gale compelled the ships to seek shelter to the east of Tarifa and the smaller gunboats were successfully held off by the French artillery.[15]

On 20 December, with the siege train still in transit, Leval's and Barrios's forces invested Tarifa. Of the 10,000 men with Victor, 1,500 were used to secure the French lines of communications back to Cadiz, leaving just 8,500 to conduct the siege. The investment of the town can only be described as partial, at best. Tarifa was completely open to reinforcement and supply from the sea, and two Royal Navy frigates and a flotilla of gunboats in the bay kept the main besieging force behind the hills to the north, awaiting the arrival of the heavy artillery.

This loose investment prompted Skerrett to mount another sortie. He sent three companies to drive in the French pickets whilst the guns on the town walls dropped shells on the French encampment over the hill. The next day, with the besiegers still showing no signs of closing in upon the town, Skerrett attacked the French again. This time a larger force, supported by flanking fire from the gunboats in the bay, drove in the French pickets to the east of Tarifa. The real objective of the sortie was to demolish a house which was considered to be dangerously close to the Santa Catalina redoubt. This was achieved with the loss of just one man killed and five wounded.[16]

That night the siege train arrived. It had taken a full two weeks after the first columns began their march for the entire besieging force to concentrate in front of the town. At last, the long anticipated siege of Tarifa could begin.

The next morning Garbé's engineers surveyed the town's defences. Predictably, they recommended an attack upon the central section of the northern front. At this point, the ground from which the attack would be delivered was not exposed to fire from the gunboats in the bay and was directly opposed by only the guns on two of the town's towers.

This plan was accepted and that night – the 23rd – under the cover of darkness the first parallel was opened on the right side of the central hill, just 300 yards from the town walls. At daybreak the defending artillery shelled the French positions, but with little effect. The French continued to develop the parallel, suffering only seven casualties all day.[17]

The following day a second parallel was started on the hill to the east, approximately 250 yards from the walls. This was within range, but out of sight, of the gunboats lying inshore. Directed by signallers on the town walls, the gunboats tried to disrupt the digging but most of the shells failed to find a target. Meanwhile, over by the first parallel, the French sappers began a second trench along which a position was marked out for the first breaching battery.

Throughout the following two days the French continued to develop these two attacks. Both fronts were pushed closer to the walls, with a section of the second parallel on the central hill reaching down to just 180 yards from the town.[18]

The two Allied commanders had divided responsibility for manning Tarifa's defences equally, with each of them allocating two battalions to the defence of the town itself and both placing the rest of their troops on the island. The convent of San Francisco was held by a company of the 82nd Foot, and a company of the 11th Foot occupied the Santa Catalina Redoubt. Major Henry King's composite battalion (that previously led by Browne) was stationed on the island supported by seventy marines landed from the British warships and a battalion of Spanish *Cazadores*.

Despite their preparations, the defenders could do little to stop the French. Apart from the two 6-pounders on the Corchuela Tower and the indirect fire from the gunboats, the only other guns that could be brought to bear upon the enemy's works were the heavy 24-pounders situated on the island, which had to fire over the town, and the guns of the Royal Navy vessels. Even this limited effort was reduced when a severe south-east gale set in on the 26th, which compelled the Allied gunboats to abandon their station in the bay for fear of being driven against the shore. The boats sailed round to the west of the island and anchored in the lee of the great rock.

With the wind came the rain, and the weather began to favour the defenders. Work in the trenches became extremely difficult. The men slid around in ankle-deep mud and the wet earth would not bind to form parapets or banks. The workmen struggled on through an almost continuous downpour for the next two days, and by the 28th the parallels on the central hill had been completed and two batteries formed and the guns run in.

The purpose of the first battery was to silence the defending artillery, both on the walls and on the island. It was situated high on the hill and was armed with four howitzers and two 12-pounder cannon. The second battery was further down the hill, closer to the walls. It was armed with four 16-pounders and two 12-pounders. This was the battery that would breach the walls. The French also lined the lower parallel with sharpshooters to fire on the battlements.

At 1100 hours on the morning of 29 December, all twelve guns opened fire upon Tarifa.[19] The very first shot from the French artillery went straight through the old wall and buried itself in a house inside the town! Each successive shot crashed through the walls so that by nightfall a significant breach had been battered in the wall just to the south of the Retiro ravine, and the guns on the Jesus and Guzman's towers had been silenced.[20]

It was evident that nothing could prevent the French from widening the breach as far as they wished, or from mounting an assault whenever they chose. Skerrett and Copons had to decide what they were going to do next and they called together their officers for a council of war.

Skerrett had never considered the town capable of a prolonged defence and he proposed an immediate withdrawal to the island. Though this may have appeared an easy and obvious course of action, there were other factors to consider. The accommodation on the island for the troops, in the form of the recently erected barracks, was utterly insufficient for the 3,000 men of the garrison, and the *Cueva de los Moros* caves were already filled with civilians who had abandoned their homes in Tarifa. The island was little more than an exposed rock and the civilians who had escaped to the island and could find no room in the caves had suffered considerably during the recent storms. Though the island was virtually unassailable, the troops could not remain on the wind-swept rock indefinitely. Indeed, there would have been little point in holding the island as it could be easily isolated from the mainland by the French. There was no value in maintaining a presence on the island merely for the sake of holding the ground.

Skerrett was well-aware of all this and he had already received leave from General Cooke to abandon Tarifa entirely if he considered this course of action to be necessary. At the council of war Skerrett produced Cooke's letter to support his view that Tarifa should no longer be defended and that plans should be put in place to retire to the island from where the garrison could be taken away by sea to Cadiz. So certain was Skerrett that the place could not be defended, he ordered the 18-pounder cannon on the Guzman's Tower to be spiked.[21]

This incident caused a major row. The 18-pounder was an old piece and the spherical case shot supplied for it did not fit its bore closely. As a result one of the shells misfired and burst as it flew over the town, killing one person in the street. This naturally caused some alarm amongst the townsfolk, who complained to Skerrett. With what one person described as 'characteristic impetuosity' and another as 'with a rare activity', Skerrett ordered the gun to be spiked. The senior engineer, Captain Charles Smith RE, was angered by this as the problem of the excessive windage in barrel of the cannon could have been improved.[22] There was, as Skerrett's Brigade Major, Thomas Bunbury, noted, a great deal of divided authority amongst the officers of the garrison occasioning, as he put it, 'no little confusion and some mischief'.[23]

The complete abandonment of Tarifa, however, would have meant that the Allies had lost control of all of Andalusia except Cadiz. The political situation in the Cortes was hanging in the balance and the occupation of Tarifa by the French might just tip the scales in favour of those who were willing to reach an accommodation with King Joseph.

Skerrett was opposed by the senior British officers under his command. Major King, Colonel Gough and Captain Smith all believed that the island should form the basis of the defence of Tarifa with the town being held as an outwork. Smith said that he had already cut off the area behind the breach from the town by retrenchments and that the streets running from the northern walls had been blocked by barricades and the houses loopholed. Furthermore, at the point where the breach had been made, close to the Retiro ravine, the ground dropped away. Even if the French stormed the breach, they would find themselves facing a fourteen-foot drop to reach the ground. They would have to negotiate this drop under a heavy fire of musketry from the surrounding buildings. King then pointed out that, even if the attackers broke into the town, the garrison could retire to the castle which could be held until it too had been breached by the French artillery. At that point the garrison could still retreat safely back to the island.[24]

Major King further complicated the argument by reminding Skerrett that his battalion formed part of the Gibraltar garrison and was under General Campbell's command. Campbell had ordered King to hold Tarifa until the last possible moment, which King intended to do even if Skerrett evacuated his brigade. Copons also declared that his men would also stay and defend Tarifa to the end.

This bold opposition should have shamed Skerrett into a change of heart. Instead he told the officers that opposed him to put their views in writing. This, the three British officers did, and King sent a messenger by boat to Campbell to inform him of Skerrett's intention to abandon Tarifa without a fight. King also told Campbell that if the general could spare just a few more companies from the Gibraltar garrison he would try and hold Tarifa even if Skerrett took his brigade back to Cadiz.

Campbell was furious with Skerrett's pusillanimity and he sent a reply which forbade Tarifa to be abandoned without the approval of the senior officers of the artillery and engineers. King was also told to concentrate his Gibraltar battalion on the island so that the rock could be held even if the town itself fell to the French. Campbell's most effective move, however, was to order the transports back to Gibraltar. Without the ships to transport his men back to Cadiz, Skerrett would have no choice but to defend Tarifa!

To support King, Campbell sent two more flank companies from his Gibraltar force. But before these reinforcements reached Tarifa, the French had attacked the gaping breach in the northern wall.

*

The French batteries continued to pound the walls throughout the morning of the 30th, occasionally firing grape shot to deter the defenders from attempting to clear away the mounting pile of rubble.[25] By midday the breach was more than thirty feet wide and Leval summoned Tarifa to surrender: 'A breach has been opened since yesterday,' 'ran Leval's summons, 'and within a few hours it will be practicable; make then your choice, between an honourable capitulation and the horrors of an impending assault . . . Honour, which prompts you to resistance, at the same time imposes it as a duty upon you to spare the lives of a whole population, whose fate is in your hands, rather than see them buried amidst the ruins of their town.' Copons replied that he would meet Leval on the breach at the head of his troops ready to defend it.[26]

For the remainder of the day the French gunners concentrated on extending the breach. When the guns fell silent at dusk, there was a great hole, sixty feet across, beckoning the French to enter. Garbé's men examined the breach and declared it practicable for an assault. Tarifa would be stormed at dawn.

Shortly after nightfall, however, a torrential downpour swept across Tarifa. The violent storm drove the French from their trenches and demolished the ramparts of the batteries. There was no shelter anywhere for the attackers on the open hillside and conditions in the trenches were appalling.

Daylight the next morning revealed the sorry state of the siege works. The rain had washed away much of the lower works, and the parallels on the hill were clogged with mud and water. The wood from the roofs of all the houses in the neighbourhood for miles around had been removed to form the platforms of the breaching batteries, and the men were without shelter and were unable to light any fires. The besiegers were now desperate to capture the town as quickly as possible: 'The troops, unable to dry themselves, or to light fire to cook their rations, loudly cried for an assault', wrote one Frenchman, 'as the only thing that could put an end to their misery.'[27]

Yet during the hours of darkness, the garrison had cleared much of the rubble away from the foot of the breach, making the ascent to its summit difficult. Even those houses nowhere near the breach had been fortified so that the garrison could defend every house and every street.[28] Furthermore, the troops destined for the assault had escaped back to their camps to shelter from the storm and they had not reassembled at the front by the designated hour. So the attack had to be postponed until the troops were in position. Nevertheless, this gave the French artillery more time to batter the breach again, and render it practicable once more.

For the assault, the Grenadier and *Voltiguer* companies from every French battalion involved in the siege were drawn together – some 2,200 men. They were divided into two columns with the Grenadiers directed to assault the breach and the *Voltiguers* detailed to probe the Portcullis Tower to see if it had been sufficiently damaged to allow troops to penetrate through into the town. Diversionary attacks were also to be made on either side of Tarifa by Cassagne's and Pécheux's brigades.

The breach was held by a full Spanish battalion with the walls on either side occupied by Gough's battalion of the 87th, with two companies in reserve. On the Jesus Tower were posted 100 men of the 47th Regiment. The remainder of this battalion was placed at the south-facing front of the town.

The storming troops clambered out of the front trenches near the forward breaching battery at 0900 hours. The Grenadiers rushed towards the breach, with the *Voltiguers* running across to the eastern side of the Retiro ravine to fire upon the Portcullis Tower.

The rain had made the sides of the ravine wet and slippery and the Grenadiers slid down the bank into two feet of mud at the bottom. The attackers were fully exposed to gunfire from the walls and they were under a constant and heavy musketry. The sole surviving Allied cannon was situated on the Corchuela Tower and this was able to fire canister diagonally across the foot of the walls.

The fire poured down on the Grenadiers yet they persevered and reached the foot of the breach. But the attackers were now highly disordered and at the prospect of mounting the breach they wavered. Some began firing up at the defenders and a gallant few tried to climb up the rubble, dying in the attempt.

The mass of the attacking force veered away from the breach to the west to where the Portcullis Tower had been damaged by the breaching batteries, hoping to force up the gate. Thomas Bunbury watched the attack: 'A ploughed field of deep alluvial soil lay between us and their lines, and was almost impassable from continued rains. Their storming party plunged up to the knees at each step.'[29] The Grenadiers pulled down the palisades and clambered over the barricades. Together with some of the *Voltiguers* they broke through the temporary defences and reached the portcullis itself. The damage to the tower had been only hastily patched up but the repair was strong enough to keep out the attackers. The ground around the foot of the portcullis was swept by gunfire from the men of the 87th on the walls and the 47th on the Jesus Tower.[30] 'The fire of our people was galling in the extreme,' continued Bunbury, 'and did great execution. The French officers advanced in front and cheered their men on to imitate their example . . . At length they began to hesitate.'[31]

The French were unable to break into the town and, under the constant and heavy musketry, the attacking troops fell back. Many though, at the head of the column, had pushed right up to the wall and could not retire without being completely exposed to the fire of the defenders. Rather than face almost certain death, they chose to surrender. This number included the officer leading the Forlorn Hope, who handed his sword to Gough through the bars of the portcullis. The assault had failed.[32]

The official statement of French casualties from the assault is given as 48 killed and 159 wounded, though such low numbers have been called into question.[33] Of the defenders, the Spaniards had around twenty-one men killed or wounded and the British thirty-six.

The assault may have failed, but Victor was not about to give up.

Determination, however, was not enough. The rain continued to fall throughout the rest of the day and all night. By morning – on New Year's Day 1812 – the trenches, which were already waterlogged, were turned into lakes and the approach roads from Vejer and Fascinas became rivers. The powder in the main magazine of the breaching batteries was found to have been ruined by water and many of the musket cartridges were also discovered to be damp. Around one third of the transport horses had died because of the weather and the lack of suitable forage.

A breakdown in communications from the reserve depot had meant that the men had been on reduced rations for the previous three days. By 1 January, there was no food left. So the men went in search of something to eat. The French troops wandered as far as three miles from their camp in search of food – and better shelter than their hasty bivouacs.

The apparent lack of activity around the French siege works prompted Skerrett to order an investigation. A small party from the 47th crept out of the town and reached the foremost French trenches undetected. It found the works completely unmanned and full of water.

It had become apparent to all involved that the siege could not be continued. Leval told Victor – in writing – that the army would be destroyed if it remained where it was any longer.

Victor remained unwilling to accept defeat and by the night of 3rd/4th January the rain had eased, prompting the Marshal to order the parallels and batteries to be reoccupied. As a direct assault upon the walls had failed, an alternative strategy was decided upon. The new plan was to sap forward towards the Jesus Tower from the advanced trenches on the western side of the French works.

As soon as they were able, the French gunners brought their pieces into action once again, but only fifty rounds had been fired against Tarifa by nightfall. For a second day in succession the men had received no rations and the situation was becoming critical. When that evening the rain returned, Victor had to accept that he would not be able to keep his force together any longer. The besiegers were in such a poor state that when a British felucca from Tangier was driven ashore the French soldiers, despite fire from the walls of the town, swarmed down to pick up the shattered timbers for fuel and to take what food they could from the wreck.[34]

During the course of the night Victor ordered the guns to be removed from the batteries but the horses were so weak from hunger and the ground so heavy that only one 12-pounder and two howitzers could be extracted. Even when 200 infantry were pressed into helping move the guns, they could only drag them a few yards. So the guns were abandoned having been rendered unusable by having their trunnions broken off. The gunpowder in the batteries was also tipped out onto the wet earth. Any wagons that could not be removed were to be burnt, but the wood was damp and every attempt at setting them on fire was extinguished by the rain.

Leaving behind an enormous amount of equipment, Victor struck camp at 0300 hours on the 5th and marched for Vejer. The abortive siege resulted in the loss to the French of approximately 500 lives and at least 300 horses and mules, as well as nine guns and a great quantity of stores. Many of the men were in such a poor state of health from malnutrition and disease that the battalions which had taken part in the operation were not fit for active service for many weeks. All that the siege cost the defenders was a little under seventy men killed, wounded or missing.[35]

*

'Nothing more signal than this defeat of the French before Tarifa could have occurred,' wrote Bunbury. 'They were not only obliged to retire before a garrison too weak to pursue them, but also to sacrifice their heavy ordnance and military stores.'[36] It was certainly true that Allied success at Tarifa was quite unexpected, but because of the dispute between Skerrett and the other officers there was little celebration.[37] An angry General Campbell told Lord Liverpool that the garrison of the town was never in any danger of being cut off 'as their retreat would have been covered by the castle of Guzman's, the redoubt of Santa Catalina, and the island.' As far as Wellington was concerned, 'The island appears to be the principal point to defend, and the easiest to be defended at a small expense and risk of loss.' Yet many supported his view that the island could not be held for any length of time if the town fell to the enemy. One of the officers who took part in the defence of Tarifa gave this opinion: 'It was my impression then, and it amounts to conviction now, that the island, particularly during the winter, half-fortified as it was, and totally destitute of shelter from bombardment or from weather, could not have maintained against an enemy in possession of the town.'[38]

As we know, Wellington wanted the British troops out of Tarifa before the end of November and Major General Cooke, who now commanded at Cadiz, regarded Tarifa as indefensible against a serious enemy attack, and he had empowered Skerrett with the authority to withdraw the British troops if the town was taken by the French. In permitting Skerrett to abandon such an important post Cooke exceeded his own authority and he was admonished by

Wellington. It is the Secretary of State, Wellington told Cooke, 'with whom alone it rests to decide whether it was your duty to recall colonel Skerrett, and whether you performed that duty at a proper period, and under circumstances which render it expedient that you should give colonel Skerrett the orders in question.'[39]

Wellington was angry with Cooke because his instructions to Skerrett implied that Tarifa was not worth holding if it put the garrison at risk. Wellington was therefore supportive of Skerrett because he saw that Cooke's orders had placed him in an invidious position. 'We have a right to expect that his majesty's officers and troops will perform their duty on every occasion', he wrote on 1 February, 'but we have no right to expect that a comparatively small number would be able to hold the town of Tarifa, commanded as it is at short distances, and enfiladed in every direction, and unprovided with artillery and the walls scarcely cannon proof.' In his report on the siege to Lord Liverpool, Wellington applauded Skerrett: 'I cannot refrain from expressing my admiration for the conduct of Colonel Skerrett, and the brave troops under his command.'[40] So, despite the loud criticism of those such as King and Smith, Skerrett received no official admonishment for his conduct during the siege. Those who had served with him found him 'brave to rashness' as an individual but 'undecided, timid, and vacillating' when in command of others.[41] He went on to achieve the rank of Major General.

CHAPTER 10

'A Day of Unequalled Joy'

Victor's failure to capture Tarifa indicated just how weak Soult's position in Andalusia had become. Indeed, even as the assault against Tarifa was being repulsed, Soult learnt that General Hill, with a combined Anglo-Portuguese force, was moving into Estremadura and he was relieved to have Victor's troops available to meet this far greater threat.

Wellington had been made aware of Soult's intention to attack Tarifa so he sent Hill (who had effectively taken over Beresford's command) towards Andalusia in the hope that this diversion would force Soult to abandon the siege of the port. As it transpired, news of Hill's movements did not reach Seville until Victor was already committed to the siege.

On 23 October, Hill, with 12,000 men, made his move. Hill's objective was to surprise Girard's division which was isolated from the rest of Drouet's corps. It is understood that Girard was aware that an Anglo-Portuguese force had crossed the border and he moved towards Merida, though with no degree of urgency. But Hill marched his men hard and on the morning of the 28th was just five miles from the French camp at Arroyo dos Molinos, with Girard entirely unaware of the Allies' presence.

Marching through the dark, Hill fell upon Girard's division, which was caught entirely unprepared. The French division was all but destroyed. Some 1,300 men were taken prisoner and Girard escaped with only 400 or 500 men. Hill, however, did not risk advancing deep into Andalusia and his pursuit ended at Merida.[1]

As soon as he was informed of Hill's attack, Soult despatched 5,000 men to help Drouet. He also wrote to Victor to order him to abandon the siege of Tarifa but by this time the Duke of Belluno was already marching back to Chiclana. The lifting of the siege at Tarifa meant that Hill's expedition could no longer serve any immediate purpose and he returned to Portugal. Two of the regiments attacked at Arroyo dos Molinos were so depleted that they were ordered back to France, Soult having to replace them from his force in Andalusia, thus reducing his strength still further.

Though Soult's grip on the main urban centres of Andalusia remained unaffected by recent events, the French defeat at Tarifa should have prompted great rejoicing in Cadiz because, as one British officer observed, 'had the duke of Dalmatia once become possessor of the old walls of Tarifa, every city, village, fort, and watch-tower on the Andalusian coast, would soon have displayed the banner of king Joseph, and the struggle in the south of Spain was over.'[2]

Yet, if anything, Spain's future at the beginning of 1812 was looking increasingly bleak. Using their allegiance to Ferdinand VII as a pretext for disengaging with the Cortes, Spain's American colonies were set on obtaining independence from the mother country. Indeed, in Venezuela, Governor Miranda proclaimed the country as an independent republic in July 1811.

For more than 100 years, Spain's great wealth had been derived from the New World and to a very large degree the war against Napoleon was sustained by American gold. Without the treasure ships the Cortes would be unable to fund its operations or help to provide for their British Allies. Drastic measures were called for.

From Cadiz and Corunna ships left for the Americas with troops to suppress the rebellions. At a time when Spain was fighting for its very survival against France it was compelled to dispatch its soldiers to the other side of the world.

The fear of losing their American possessions led some Spaniards to consider approaching Napoleon with an offer of peace. If her armies could be released from fighting the French, then Spain could turn its full attention to restoring control of the disaffected colonialists. This would mean acknowledging the end of the Bourbon monarchy and the acceptance of Joseph Bonaparte as King of Spain. These were the very reasons that Spain had gone to war, yet some saw this as preferable to losing the colonies.

Such talk amongst the *Afrancesados* at Madrid prompted Joseph to attempt secret negotiations with the members of the Cortes. Napoleon told his brother that if the Cortes acknowledged Joseph as the legitimate king of Spain, then the French army would immediately withdraw back to France.

These proposals had to be relayed to the Cortes and Joseph sent an agent to Cadiz to sound out the Spanish politicians. This man was Cannon La Peña, who was a secret supporter of Joseph's regime; he was also the brother of the disgraced general who was at that moment being prosecuted for his shameful actions at Barrosa. The pretext he offered for travelling to Cadiz was that he wanted to help his brother during the period of the trial.

Cannon La Peña soon found that the mood in Cadiz was still staunchly opposed to any form of intervention by Napoleon in the affairs of Spain. What the Bonapartes may not have appreciated was that, for the Spaniards, peace with France meant war with Britain. This would have meant war with the most powerful maritime country in the world and a return to the blockade of the

Spanish fleet at Cadiz. This would most definitely have resulted in the loss of the rebellious American colonies, so war with Britain had to be avoided at all costs.

Britain had already tried to ferment rebellion in the Americas, albeit unsuccessfully, with General Whitlocke's assault upon Buenos Aries in 1807. But the situation had changed considerably since then. Britain was now seen by the colonies as a trading partner, opening up other markets that were previously denied to them by the mother country. A war with Britain would seriously affect trade across the Atlantic and, rather than risk losing their ships to the Royal Navy, the colonialists would simply trade their goods with Britain instead. The colonialists would have little reason to maintain their links with Spain and the independence movements across the Spanish Americas would be impossible to stop. So there was simply nothing to be gained by seeking an accommodation with France.

Cannon La Peña found that he dared not speak openly in Cadiz of an arrangement with France. Only in private meetings with selected members of the Cortes or of freemasons whose lodges in Madrid were under French influence could the Cannon put forward Joseph's proposals.

The Cannon was unable to garner much support for his proposals. Yet it would take many months, and a complete shift in military situation in the Peninsula, before he would abandon his futile efforts. He was encouraged by the fact that, whilst the majority of his countrymen would have nothing to do with the French, they were equally distrustful of the British. 'The spirit against us here appears to increase,' Henry Wellesley wrote to his brother at the beginning of August. 'We are accused of an intention of bringing reinforcements here for the purpose of getting possession of the place and keeping it. I am convinced that there are many spies in the town, but the majority of the people are with us, although every possible attempt is made to excite a spirit against us.' He also told Wellington that there was a widespread belief that Britain's policy was to weaken Spain by encouraging her to fight a ruinous war so that, if France should finally succeed, the country would be a burden upon Napoleon rather than a source of strength and power.[3]

In some respects, Canon La Peña could not have chosen a less receptive time for his intrigues in Cadiz than the early months of 1812. For even if this was a worrying period for Spain in the New World, it was a time when the members of the Cortes felt stronger, and therefore in less need of any association with Napoleon, than ever before.

1812 is one of the most notable years in Spanish political history. It marks the date of the first written constitution, a version of which still remains the cornerstone of Spain's legal and political system.

The principal aim of the constitution was the elimination of arbitrary and despotic monarchical rule. No longer would Spain suffer under a corrupt and ineffectual Bourbon king. In its place would be a 'constitutional' monarchy, with limited powers subject to parliament. New constituency areas and municipalities were formed to replace the historic provinces and there was no special provision for the Church or the nobility which had previously dominated all the positions of power and influence.

The Cortes attempted to incorporate many of the ideals of the French Revolution – equality for all before the law, the replacement of feudal privileges by freedom of contract, the recognitions of a landowner's right to dispose of his property as he saw fit, and a reform of the tax system to benefit the state not the nobility.

The right to vote, suffrage, was determined by property ownership. This, for the first time, favoured the commercial classes in parliament rather than the nobility and the clergy. However, the Church was protected in the constitution. Roman Catholicism was declared the official state religion and the practice of any other religion was expressly forbidden.

The fight against the French seemed to equate with the fight against the old order. It was a fight for freedom, no matter the enemy. One of the liberal newspapers, *Diario Redactor de Sevilla*, explained it in these words: 'The Spaniards are fighting to be independent, to be free. But will shedding their blood, facing death and exterminating the French be enough to achieve these two great objects? If we do not establish a system of government founded on just, wise and beneficent laws . . . will we truly be able to acclaim our victory? Will we really be safe from fresh attempts on the part of the usurper, or any other power that wishes to enslave us?'[4] A new liberal and democratic way of governing Spain had to be found.

Throughout the autumn of 1811 and the ensuing winter, the members of the Cortes had fiercely debated the clauses of the new constitution. Each section of the constitution was drafted individually and then scrutinised by the assembly. The *Liberals* and the *Serviles* fought each other over almost every clause, the result of which was an unsatisfactory, and in many respects unworkable, compromise. Of course, the great irony was that the main principles of the Constitution were little, if in fact any, different from those drafted by Napoleon in the Constitution of Bayonne which set his brother on the Spanish throne.

In terms of its effect upon the war, the constitution reinforced the belief that Spain was still a sovereign state with its own government. A government that could pass its laws and make its decrees as it saw fit, untroubled by concerns for other nations. But the muted applause for the constitution sounded the death-knell for the Regency. The regents acted for the monarch in his absence but, as the monarch's powers were severely curtailed by the new constitution, the Regency's authority was similarly restricted. It would be the Cortes, the elected parliament, which would now control the armies of the state.

It was against this backdrop that the Canon La Peña was trying to win support for his plan to subjugate Spain to the Napoleonic system. He was bound to fail. Why should the deputies, who had just voted themselves into a position of power in Spain, surrender that power to a French king?

*

Though few in Cadiz at this time would have recognised the fact, the war in the Peninsula had begun to turn against Napoleon. With the French forces driven out of Portugal, Wellington was set to move onto the offensive for the first time since his abortive campaign that ended with the retreat from Talavera. Yet the combined French forces in Spain were far too numerous for Wellington's small, though growing, army. Before he could risk another expedition across the border the military situation in Spain would have to change – and that is exactly what was about to happen.

Whilst Soult may have felt that his limited hold upon Andalusia had been restored, he, and the rest of the French commanders in Spain, were to receive a blow from which they would be unable to recover – Napoleon's invasion of Russia. In January 1812 the first troops were withdrawn from Spain to join the *Grande Armée* which was being assembled for Napoleon's great adventure in the East. Until this time reinforcements and replacements had poured southwards over the Pyrenees year after year to bolster the French armies in Spain. Throughout most of 1811 the French in Spain were on the defensive but most of the country was still undeniably under their control. In 1812 their grip was slowly prised apart as the Allies moved onto the offensive.

Now the French commanders in the Peninsula were expected to not merely manage with what they had got but also to send troops back to France. All the units of the Imperial Guard were withdrawn from Spain as well as the Polish regiments of the French Army. Altogether, this amounted to some 27,000 experienced men. For Soult it meant the loss of the 4th, 6th and 9th regiments of the Vistula Legion and the Polish lancers which had nearly turned the course of the battle at Albuera. In total, Soult lost 6,000 men, which he simply could not afford. Nor was this a phased withdrawal. Napoleon's dispatch of 27 January simply stated that the Marshal was to draft away these troops 'within twenty-four hours after the receipt of the order'!

Worse still was the fact that Napoleon turned his back on the Iberian Peninsula. He had found no cure for his Spanish 'ulcer' so now he would try and ignore it.

The first major event of 1812 in the Peninsula was Wellington's bold assault upon Ciudad Rodrigo. This, the most northerly of the two 'Gateways of Spain', was kicked open in mid winter in the most daring style. Wellington threw his men at the walls of the fortress only twelve days after it had been invested. It had taken the French more than forty days to capture Ciudad Rodrigo just a year earlier. Badajoz was next.

On 11 March Soult heard from Drouet that Allied forces were gathering at Elvas on the Portuguese border and nine days later the Marshal knew for certain that Wellington had advanced in considerable strength to invest Badajoz. This move was entirely predictable and Soult was not seriously troubled by it. French forces in Spain still outnumbered Wellington's, and provided that Marmont cooperated with Soult the two French commanders could bring together a field army strong enough to prevent Wellington from capturing Badajoz. 'As long as this communication shall exist', Soult wrote to Marmont on 7 February, 'the enemy will not dare make a push against Badajoz, because at his first movement we can join our forces and march against him for a battle . . . I am bound, therefore, to make a pressing demand that your left wing may be kept in a position which makes the communication between our armies sure, so that we may be able, by uniting our disposable forces, to go out against the enemy with the assurance of success.'[5]

Wellington, not the Spanish armies or the guerrillas, was now the greatest threat to the French in Spain yet it was really quite a simple task to keep him confined within Portugal. As long as Marmont and Soult acted in concert Wellington would not be able to capture Badajoz. This meant that the British general would never be able to mount anything other than hit-and-run raids into Spain through Ciudad Rodrigo, and Joseph's authority would not be seriously challenged. By contrast Wellington knew that if he was to capture Badajoz he would be able to extend his operations into the heart of Spain and this, he told his brother Henry, must result in Soult having to abandon the blockade of Cadiz.[6] Though there was pressure being brought to bear upon Wellington to relieve Cadiz and free the Cortes, he knew that the best way of achieving this was by taking Badajoz, and he asked for people in England to be patient about Cadiz, 'and allow us to do our work gradually.'[7]

On the day that he learnt of Wellington's move against Badajoz, 11 March, Soult sent a message to Marmont informing him that the expected attack upon the frontier fortress was now happening. The Duke of Dalmatia, fully anticipating that Marmont would immediately comply, started to pull together a force to relieve Badajoz. He could not risk removing any troops from in front of Cadiz – nothing was more important than containing the Spanish Government to the narrow limits of the country's south-western extremity – so he took just the 8,000 men of Barrois's division from Seville and a brigade of infantry and six regiments of cavalry from Leval in Granada.

With this force of around 13,000 men, Soult set off from Seville on 30 March. The Marshal met up with Drouet's corps at Llerena five days later. Soult now had 25,000 troops. Yet this was still half the number of men with which Wellington surrounded Badajoz. Soult had expected Marmont to make some effort to join him but Napoleon told Marmont that Badajoz was Soult's responsibility. Instead, Marmont was ordered to move against Ciudad Rodrigo, and threaten northern Portugal, as the Emperor believed that this would compel Wellington to abandon the siege and rush north.

Wellington sent a covering force of more than 30,000 men, led by Beresford and Graham, to Albuera to block Soult's advance. But there was no second Battle of Albuera. When Soult reached Villafranca on 7 April he learnt that Wellington had already assaulted and captured Badajoz. As there was no help to come from Marmont, Soult returned to his viceroyalty, declaring that he 'could not fight the whole British army' by himself.

Not only was Soult's latest expedition into Estremadura a waste of time and effort, it also allowed the insurgents in eastern Andalusia to stir up trouble once again in his absence. As soon as Soult's departure from Seville was certain, Ballesteros moved out from under the guns of Gibraltar, through the Ronda mountains, and arrived on 4 April in the plain of the Guadalquivir less than twenty miles from the Andalusian capital with some 10,000 men.

The main body of the Spanish Army of Estremadura, which amounted to little more than 4,000 troops under the Conde de Penne-Villemur, also moved towards Seville. Indeed, Penne-Villemur's cavalry pushed up to the very outskirts of the city and had to be driven off by the French artillery guarding the Triana Bridge over the Guadalquivir.

Seville was held by only about 3,000 men, including some 2,000 convalescents from the Cadiz Lines, many of whom were incapable of bearing arms. General Rihnoux, commanding in Seville, sent a desperate call out to Soult saying that he was surrounded by 14,000 Spanish troops and that he feared the Sevillians would rise up and open the gates of the city to let the enemy in.

Leaving two divisions with Drouet in Estremadura to watch Beresford and Graham, Soult hurried to save Seville with the rest of his field force. The Marshal reached Seville on the 11th after four days of forced marches only to find that Ballesteros had fled back into the mountains five days earlier under the false belief that a large force from Cadiz was marching to relieve Seville. Penne-Villemur had also retired on the 9th after learning that Badajoz had fallen, knowing that Soult would consequently soon be back in Andalusia.

The Spaniards had lost a great opportunity to seize Seville and present Soult with the daunting prospect of assaulting the city. Even so, Soult's brief absence allowed the *guerrilleros* to take control of large parts of Andalusia. Many of the smaller French posts had been surrounded and even the road to Madrid had been blocked, leaving Soult unable to communicate with Joseph at what was becoming a most vital time.

Soult was now faced with the task of reasserting control of his rebellious domain. With his ever-diminishing mobile force, he could no longer hope to re-conquer all the lost territory.

With the capture of Badajoz, there was almost no limit now to Wellington's freedom of action, apart from the usual logistical difficulties the British Army had always experienced in Spain. Portugal no longer trembled in fear of invasion and the Anglo-Portuguese Army could carry the war into Spain confident that its line of retreat, and its lines of communications, was secure.

Wellington was now able to consider his next move at leisure. Despite the fact that the various French armies still totalled approximately 230,000 men, they were scattered all over Spain. Reinforcements from England, plus a considerably reduced sick list, meant that Wellington was now able to put 60,000 men into the field. None of the French armies taken individually could stand before such a force, but their potential combined weight was still far in excess of anything Britain could hope to muster.

It was not until the beginning of June that Wellington felt that his troops had recovered sufficiently from the losses suffered at Badajoz to resume offensive operations. His objective was to crush the French forces in the centre of Spain. This would mean that Soult's position in the south of the country would be rendered untenable and he would be compelled to abandon Andalusia and withdraw northwards or face being cut off from the rest of Spain.

Wellington's first target was Marmont's 48,000 men posted around Salamanca. On 13 June Wellington crossed the River Agueda and made contact with Marmont's now inappropriately titled Army of Portugal, two days later. The opposing armies were numerically evenly matched and neither Marmont nor Wellington was prepared to risk an action unless presented with an extremely favourable situation.

For over four weeks the two armies marched and counter-marched in an attempt to out-manoeuvre their opponents, but neither side had been able to gain the upper hand. The decisive breakthrough came on 22 July. Marmont, whilst trying to race around Wellington's flank, over-extended his line. Wellington immediately took advantage of his opponent's error and, with the famous words addressed to the Spanish liaison officer on his staff, '*Marmont est perdu*', he attacked.

Wellington's timing was perfect and Marmont's army was cut in two. Marmont himself was wounded in the ensuing battle and his army was routed. General Clausel, Marmont's senior divisional officer, assumed command of the Army of Portugal and withdrew northwards towards Burgos. Wellington was tempted to pursue Clausel but this would have exposed his line of communication to an attack from Soult in the south. He chose instead to march on Madrid, entering the Spanish capital on 12 August. The intrusive king no longer had a capital.

Wellington's occupation of central Spain and his symbolic entry into Madrid meant that Soult's army in Andalusia was in danger of being cut off from all the other French forces in the Peninsular. Everyone on the Allied side believed that this would compel Soult to abandon Andalusia immediately.

Indeed, Joseph had already called on Soult in early July to send a large detachment north to assist Marmont but Soult had openly refused to send any troops at all to help his brother officer, as this would be tantamount to evacuating Andalusia. This case of blatant indiscipline had prompted Joseph to threaten to relieve Soult of his command.

Yet Soult remained convinced that Andalusia should not be abandoned and even offered an alternative strategy. He urged King Joseph to march south with all the strength he could gather – i.e. the Army of the Centre, the Army of Portugal and the Army of Aragon – to join forces with the Army of the South and hold Andalusia. This move would concentrate a sizable army in the country's richest province and the one where the Spanish Government could still be confined. 'Let your Majesty come to Andalusia in person, with every man that can be collected; if the number is large we can increase the expeditionary force in Estremadura to 25,000 or 30,000 men, and transfer the seat of war to the left bank of the Tagus. Army of Portugal, being relieved of pressure, will be able to come into line again. Whatever occurs, your Majesty will find yourself at the head of a splendid army, ready to deliver battle. If the worst came, and we were unlucky, there is always the resource of retiring on the Army of Aragon [in Valencia] and so keeping the field . . . I have the honour to repeat to your Majesty that I cannot send any detachments beyond the Sierra Morena or the Guadiana, save by evacuating all Andalusia and marching with my whole army. I must have a positive order from your Majesty to that effect.'[8]

When news of Marmont's defeat at Salamanca reached Seville on 12 August Soult still remained undismayed. 'The loss of a battle by Army of Portugal was nothing more than a great duel, which can be undone by another similar duel,' he told Joseph. 'But the loss of Andalusia and the raising of the siege of Cadiz would be events whose effects would be felt all round Europe and the New World . . . What does it matter if the enemy is left in possession of the whole space between Burgos and the Sierra Morena, until the moment when great reinforcements come from France, and the Emperor has been able to make his arrangements? But this sacrifice of Andalusia once made, there is no way of remedying it.' [9]

This move had much to recommend it and, even though Oman considered this proposal 'absolutely perverse and insane', Napier called it 'grand and vigorous'. It would bring together a force far greater than anything Wellington could possibly dare attack – a force which could hold out until Napoleon was able to send more armies across the Pyrenees – but, more importantly, it maintained the siege of Cadiz. As John Fortescue fully appreciated, the raising of the siege of Cadiz would be an event 'that would make itself felt all over Europe.'[10]

Joseph's response to Soult's persistent refusal to send any of his troops northwards was brief and to the point: 'You will see by my letter of the 29th July the errors that you have been labouring under as to Lord Wellington's real designs. Hasten, therefore, to carry out the orders which I give you – viz., to evacuate Andalusia and march with your whole army to Toledo.'

There was little that Soult could do in the face of such unambiguous instructions and slowly, reluctantly, he complied. Consequently, the siege of Cadiz was lifted on 25 August. Soult had already abandoned Niebla after blowing up the castle on 12 August, and a few days later the garrisons at Ronda and Medina Sidonia destroyed their fortifications and withdrew to Seville.[11]

Victor had the job of dismantling the siege works. After two years of occupation, this was a formidable task. The demolition was masked by a 'furious' bombardment of the city. 'Every piece of ordnance of whatever description was employed upon all points of the defences,' wrote one man, 'and the terror-striking mortars were incessantly vomiting forth the curses of France.'[12] With each salvo one or two of the siege guns were rendered unserviceable. This was accomplished by firing them at an angle against their muzzles which split them, or by intentionally over-loading them. Some, however, were simply spiked or thrown into the water or placed muzzle to muzzle and then ignited. The bombardment continued for two days at the end of which all the remaining ammunition was destroyed. All the huts and stores were burnt and the gunboats were sunk. The destruction continued throughout the 24th and that night the sky across the whole Bay of Cadiz glowed red from the fires.

Victor retreated in good order covered by his whole cavalry. At 0900 hours the Spanish troops of the garrison undertook a cautious sortie and occupied Porto-Real and Chiclana. They took possession of an enormous quantity of shot, stores and siege tools. They also seized 500 artillery pieces, many in a serviceable condition, and some thirty gun boats.[13] But there was no vigorous pursuit of the French. The Spaniards were so happy in being delivered, noted Sarrazin, 'that their joy absorbed all their faculties, and even paralyzed their desire of being revenged.'[14] Cadiz had endured the longest siege of the Napoleonic Wars and had earned for herself the distinction of being the only city in continental Europe to survive a siege by the forces of Napoleon.

Alcala Galiano remembered the day the siege was raised with obvious pleasure: 'The day this happened was one of unequalled joy,' he later wrote. 'The people rushed to embark in boats to visit the abandoned French encampment . . . There was a great desire to walk on the earth of the continent, to breath in fresh air . . . Accompanied by a numerous crowd we went round . . . the batteries which had contained the mortars whose effects we had been experiencing for such a long time. On the way back . . . all the boats carried a bunch of grass at their mastheads as a way of showing that they had completed a return trip that had been denied to the inhabitants . . . for more than thirty consecutive months.'[15] In what another described as 'the greatest fête in the year' every balcony was crowded with happy faces and the whole length of the *muralla* and *alameda* promenades were filled with more people than ever before.[16]

'It is impossible to describe the exhilaration of spirits which is excited by a sense of liberty after having been confined within a circle of fortified walls for many weary months,' wrote British Captain Alex R. C. Dallas. 'This was the state of the garrison at Cádiz when the retreat of the French left us free to leave our walls, and roam through the open country.'[17]

Rather than waste their energies on celebrations and roaming around, the French withdrawal should have sparked a furious assault by the Allies. No army is ever more vulnerable than when it is breaking camp and starting out upon a retreat. A week earlier Wellington had written to General Cooke, who was now in charge of the British contingent in the Isla de Leon, to fall upon the French in the lines as soon as the opportunity presented itself. When one considers how vehemently Wellington had previously opposed any offensive movement by the troops in Cadiz it demonstrates how much the war in the Peninsular had swung in favour of the Allies. Wellington proposed that Cook should cross the Sancti Petri and deliver a direct attack upon Chiclana.

But before this dispatch reached Cadiz, and before Victor had begun his destruction of the siege works, Cook had already embarked upon an operation in conjunction with the 4,000-strong Spanish division of General Cruz Murgeon. The British force amounted to just 1,600 men, representing the pick of the troops at Cadiz. These were six companies of Guards, six companies of the 2/87th Foot, two companies of the 2/95th Rifles, a contingent from the 20th Portuguese and the only cavalry available to him, which was a single squadron of the 2nd Hussars of the King's German Legion. This small force was placed under the command of none other than the man who had showed such trepidation at Tarifa, Colonel Skerrett.[18]

The two bodies of Allied troops were shipped to Huelva and together they advanced upon Seville. On 24 August, the day when they could have pursued the retreating I Cops had they remained at Cadiz, Skerrett and Cruz Murgeon drove in the French outposts at San Lucar la Mayor to the west of Seville. The Andalusia capital was Soult's concentration point and troops were filing into the city from all around the province. Aware of this Skerrett and Cruz Murgeon held their ground to await developments.

Their patience was rewarded when, on the night of 26/27 August, Soult moved out of Seville with the bulk of his force, leaving a small rearguard to man the city's defences. This rearguard was to be picked up by the troops from Chiclana, under Villatte, who were expected to reach Seville the next day.

With the departure of Soult, Skerrett and Cruz Murgeon launched an assault upon Seville. They stormed the suburb of Triana but the French had barricaded the bridge over the Guadalquivir, removed some of its planking and had sighted guns to sweep its length. Repeated attempts to rush the bridge were driven back and it was only when the Spaniards brought up a number of cannon, and blasted away the barricade, that the French abandoned the position and withdrew into the city.

After a running fight through the streets, in which some of the inhabitants took part, the French garrison fled the city, leaving behind some 200 men and a rich convoy of plunder which was to have been collected by Villatte. When the latter approached Seville later in the day and found it occupied by the enemy he bypassed the city and marched after Soult.[19]

Andalusia was free once more, and, to celebrate both the province's liberation and the nation's growing confidence in a brighter future no longer shackled by despotism, the Cadiz Constitution was proclaimed in Seville with great enthusiasm on 29 August.

Around Europe there was widespread appreciation of the determination shown by the people of Cadiz for 'the astonishing fortitude with which they have submitted to a blockade of two years and a half.' Yet as Thomas Sydenham complained, the editors of all the Cadiz newspapers 'seem to think that the war is at an end, and that nothing more is to be done.'[20] Nothing, of course, could be further from the truth.

*

Soult finally joined up with Joseph near Valencia around the middle of October. Together the King and the Marshal were able to muster 60,000 men in the east of Spain and, with the reinforced Army of Portugal totalling 50,000 men, they returned to the offensive, pressing upon Wellington from the north. Against such numbers the British commander had little choice but to withdraw his troops over the frontier back into the safety of Portugal.

For six months Wellington rested his troops and planned his next move, secure in the knowledge that the French dare not follow him into Portugal. Reinforcements received throughout the winter had brought Wellington's fighting force up to a total of 52,000 British and 29,000 Portuguese, to which he was able to add 21,000 Spaniards who had been placed under his direct command. With such a force, and support from the growing guerrilla movement, Wellington could adopt a far more ambitious strategy than had previously been possible. Until this time his offensive campaigns had been little more than extended raids into Spain, in which he never ventured far from his Portuguese base. With Andalusia abandoned by the French, and Madrid liberated, the rest of the war would be fought in the north, and every step that the Allies trod would take them ever further from Lisbon.

But now Wellington possessed the strength to match the combined armies of the enemy and to operate anywhere in the Peninsula. His new base was to be Santander in the extreme north of Spain and in the rear of Joseph's recently established positions on the Douro. Under the pretext of reinforcing the Spanish army of Galicia, Wellington assembled transport ships, guns and ammunition, at Corunna ready for the short journey along the Biscayan coast to Santander.

Joseph's headquarters, and therefore the headquarters of the French armies in Spain, were now at Vallodolid, with his forces distributed between the Tagus and the Douro. Wellington knew that, even though Joseph and Soult had only 60,000 men immediately at hand, he could call upon the Army of Portugal and the two divisions of Army of the North if Wellington advanced into Spain. He intended, therefore, to hold Joseph's attention with a show of force in front of the French forces on the Douro whilst the main body of the Anglo-Allied army would, in true Napoleonic fashion, cross the river further downstream and sweep round the enemy's flank.

On 22 May the advance began with six brigades of cavalry forming a dense screen to mask Wellington's movements. Behind this screen came only the Light Division, the 2nd Division, the Portuguese Division and two weak Spanish divisions.

The first contact with the French was on the outskirts of Salamanca. Immediately Joseph ordered the concentration of all his forces behind the Douro but a few days later the intrusive king realised that something had gone wrong with his plans. Six miles to the east of his concentration point, the British 1st, 3rd, 4th, 5th and 7th Divisions – a mass of almost 43,000 men – had crossed the Douro and were bearing down on his flank.

Joseph had to abandon his position and retreat. He decided to fall back as far as Burgos but the British divisions did not follow. Again Wellington marched around the French flank and again the French were compelled to withdraw. This time Joseph halted at Vitoria and he was determined to retreat no further. His men had been pushed back continuously for the previous month and morale was far from good. For his part Wellington, whose force now outnumbered his opponent's, was happy to accept battle. On 21 June 1813, the two armies clashed in the plain outside Vitoria. The result was a resounding victory for the Allies. There was no orderly withdrawal by the French this time. Utterly routed, they fled back into France.

The Allied army followed the French as far as the Pyrenees and occupied the mountain passes. The port of Santander, which is less than 100 miles from the French frontier, was established as the new operational base from which Wellington planned to invade France. The French forces, all of which were now commanded by Soult, did force their way through the Pyrenean passes in an attempt to relieve the beleaguered French garrison in the fortified town of Pamplona, but without success.

For the rest of the war the French were on the defensive, gradually being pushed deeper into France. Finally, on 12 April 1814, shortly after driving the French out of Toulouse, Wellington was brought the news of Napoleon's abdication. The Peninsular War was over.

CHAPTER 11

Long Shadows

'The brilliant success gained on the heights of Barrosa was but the prelude to other victories,' wrote one of the officers that had fought with Graham that day. 'The star of Napoleon, so long in the ascendant, had begun to decline in the horizon.'[1] Few people would have realized this in 1811 and the Battle of Barrosa's place in history has never been fully understood. In particular, just how close the Spanish Government came to being captured has not been appreciated. It may be recalled that during the battle a small French force crossed the bridge over the Sancti Petri, took some prisoners and returned safely. With Zayas's force on the mainland there were very few troops left on the Isla de Leon, which meant that there was almost nothing to stop Victor from breaking into Cadiz and seizing the Regents and the members of the Cortes. It is hard to imagine organised Spanish resistance continuing after such a catastrophe. To state, therefore, that the Battle of Barrosa was one of the most important battles of the Peninsular War, is no exaggeration. Yet in most books on the Peninsular War it receives little more attention than a brief sentence or two. Some historians have written entire books on the Peninsular War and related topics without mentioning the battle at all.[2]

The reasons for this are not hard to discern. From the Spanish perspective, no historian is likely to devote much attention to an event which cast the Spanish Army in such a poor light. Whilst the defence of Cadiz, the formation of the Cortes and the Constitution of 1812 are justifiably revered in Spain to this day, the Battle of Barrosa and La Peña's shameful conduct, both during and after the engagement are, quite understandably, less well remembered – though on 3 February 1815 a cross of honour was issued to all those who 'attended' the battle.

The French, for their part, were able to view the Battle of Barrosa (or to both the Spaniards and the French the Battle of Chiclana) as nothing more than a sortie from the besieged city that was driven off, albeit with heavy casualties. The Allies had failed in their bid to break the siege and Victor was quickly able to re-establish his land blockade of Cadiz. So the defeat at Barrosa is easily dismissed as a minor reverse in a protracted campaign which only ended when the French themselves decided to abandon the siege and consolidate their strength elsewhere. The official French account of the battle, as published in *Le*

161

Moniteur, was that Victor was hopelessly outnumbered and that his troops were called upon to try and achieve the impossible.[3]

Baron Lejuene went even further in the defence of his countrymen: 'On their side the French, weakened by the vast extent of the coastline they had to defend, taken by surprise by this attack on the scattered outposts of their rear, and arriving as they did in small detachments on the battlefield, might with equal justice look upon the issue of the struggle as a brilliant victory, in which, their courage making up for the absence of any settled plan, they baffled the schemes of their enemies, and compelled them to retreat.'[4]

The famous French historian Adolphe Thiers declared that Victor, with his 5,000 men 'had no hesitation taking the offensive' against 8,000 or 9,000 English and 12,000 Spaniards. He wrote that: 'When the attack commenced, the impetuosity of our men obtained some temporary success, but there was no probability that 5,000 men could vanquish 20,000, especially when 9,000 were English.' Rather than actually admit that the French had been beaten and retreated, he then states that 'Marshal Victor therefore took up a position somewhat withdrawn, and then awaited General Villatte.' This is all he has to say about the Battle of Barrosa in his massive twenty-volume history of France under Napoleon.[5]

By contrast, Barrosa was seen in Britain as an astonishing victory at the time, and Graham was showered with honours. Poems were written and songs were composed. Lord Byron waxed lyrically about the 'marvels of Barrosa's fight'. William Glen glorified 'gallant' Graham, who had 'rushed to battle, and therefore won his fame – thy name shall never die,' he declared; and Robert Southey wrote, 'Though the four quarters of the world have seen the British valour proved triumphantly upon the French, in many a field far famed. Yet may the noble island in her rolls of glory write Barrosa's name.'[6] Even the French General Jean Sarrazin admitted that 'the victory of Barrosa, gained by the English general, Graham, over Marshal Victor, afforded [the British] the most sanguine hopes as to the speedy deliverance of the peninsula.'[7] Colonel William Light, who fought at Barrosa as a junior officer, named a region in South Australia after the battle when he became the colony's Surveyor-General. The wines produced in the Barossa Valley have attained international recognition and have become as famous as the battle itself.

Yet Barrosa was soon to be overshadowed in scale by Wellington's great victories in the north of Spain. In order to narrate the story of Wellington's campaigns few writers divert from the actions of the army under his direct command. Yet Wellington's operations, until the latter stages of the Peninsular War, were just one aspect of a multi-faceted conflict. The largest French army that Wellington faced in the Peninsula – Masséna's Army of Portugal in 1810 – numbered little more than 70,000 effective men, yet at that time the total of the French forces in Spain amounted to 360,000. Thus Wellington's operations occupied only one-fifth of the French army in the Peninsula.

Just to emphasize this point, one only need look at the respective number of troops involved in the invasion of Portugal and the invasion of Andalusia. Whilst any casual student of the Peninsular War would be forgiven for believing that Masséna's campaign in Portugal involved the largest number of troops during the period that Oman called 'the central crisis of the whole war', it was in fact the Andalusia campaign which tied up at least as many French troops – and for a considerably longer period.[8] This was stressed by Adolphe Theirs who wrote that Soult's Army of Andalusia, almost 80,000 strong, was composed of the best French troops in Spain and had 'no rival but the corps of Marshal Davout in Hanover'.[9]

There has been an attempt in recent years to address this imbalance by highlighting the efforts of the Spanish regular and irregular forces. Laudable though those efforts have been, none have appreciated the fact that if the Spanish Government had been captured, or driven from Cadiz, Spanish resistance, lacking coordination, would have gradually petered out.

This, though, was fully appreciated at the time. General Jean Sarrazin, a Commander of the *Legion d'honneur*, published his *History of the War in Spain and Portugal from 1807 to 1814* in 1815. He was unequivocal in his belief that if Cadiz would have been seized the war in Spain would have been all but won for Napoleon. Soult's failure to capture Cadiz when the opportunity presented itself in January 1810 was, Sarrazin wrote, 'justly considered as the first cause of the disasters experienced by the French in the peninsula.'[10] The war really did hang in the balance at this stage. Joseph believed that the occupation of Seville and the dissolution of the Supreme Junta 'would be deemed misfortunes of such magnitude that all resistance would cease.' Such was Joseph's confidence that the war had turned so decidedly in his favour, on 12 February 1810 he summoned all principle strongholds still in Spanish hands throughout the entire country to surrender to his authority.[11]

Another contemporary writer, William Napier, supports this view 'the capture of Cadiz,' he states, 'would have been a fatal blow to the Peninsula.' Equally, Joseph's failure to seize Cadiz ultimately cost him his crown.[12] To Sir John Fortescue, Joseph was guilty 'of a great and fatal military blunder'.[13] From the moment that Albuquerque established himself behind the Sancti Petri, 'the operations of the French were permanently distracted and weakened by the detention before Cadiz of a considerable force, which could not without peril be withdrawn.'[14] To James Herson, 'Cadiz, along with Andalusia, served as a source of strategic consumption of the French Army in the Peninsula, and contributed directly, to the loss of Spain for the French.'[15]

Sarrazin claims that: 'At this period the whole population [of Cadiz] was in favour of the French . . . The English were distrusted, and their good faith suspected. Had Victor arrived before the duke of Albuquerque, he would have been received with the greatest enthusiasm.' As evidence to support this claim, Sarrazin points to the treatment Albuquerque received at the hands of the Cadiz authorities – the 'galling vexations' to use Sarrazin's words, 'with which the partisans of the French overwhelmed that unfortunate nobleman.' This is supported by James Stanhope who pointed out that Albuquerque had disobeyed orders in marching to save Cadiz and this did not go down well with the Cadiz authorities who 'feared' him. Albuquerque died broken-hearted at London, from having met with so much 'vulgar bitterness of mercantile insolence and ingratitude' on the part of his fellow citizens.[16]

Remarkable though it may seem, so strong was the pro-Joseph movement in Cadiz it was even thought that it would be necessary to ask the Army of Estremadura under the Marquis de la Romana to transfer his soldiers to Cadiz for the purpose 'of controlling the Cortes by an armed force.' It was also thought, as revealed in one of Henry Wellesley's despatches, that if the Marquis' army did enter Cadiz it might be able to 'compel them [the inhabitants of Cadiz] to work at the fortifications.' Even a brigadier-general in the Spanish Army told Wellesley at the beginning of March 1810 that 'Spain cannot be saved.'[17]

This shows how perilously close Cadiz came to succumbing to the French, and how the inhabitants probably would have opened the city's gates to the French if it had not been for the presence of the English army.[18] Such was the expectation that Cadiz would fall to the French, the Regency actually made plans to evacuate to the Balearic Isles, Majorca or Minorca.[19]

As Charles Esdaile has made clear, across Spain at this time the struggle against the French was being lost.[20] It would not have taken much for the leading Spaniards to realise that it would be in their interests to make peace with King Joseph, particularly if this meant that in doing so they could regain their estates and retain their positions. If Spain had been brought to heel in this way the British forces could not have remained in the Peninsula. With Iberia subdued Napoleon could have turned the full weight of his empire's resources upon Russia, and the Napoleonic Wars might have had a far different conclusion. 'Cadiz,' Robert Southey remarked, 'was the point whereon all eyes were at this time turned,' and M. de Rocca declared that 'the siege of that city was then the only military event worthy of attention [and] Spain had been in a manner reduced to Cadiz.'[21]

We may recall that the British Government understood the importance of Cadiz and placed a 'higher value' on it than Lisbon, and, even though Wellington refused to give up Portugal, Lord Liverpool made it clear to Wellington that he was far from happy with the General's decision. This was relayed to Wellington on 17 February 1810: 'Considering the various essential objects connected with the security of Cadiz, and the means of defence which that place affords compared with any other in the Peninsula, it is His Majesty's pleasure that you should have your attention invariably fixed on this object, and that you should afford every assistance which may be necessary for its preservation.'[22]

Wellington, nevertheless, was well aware that the continuation of the siege of Cadiz benefitted his position in Portugal because it tied up a very large body of French troops in the far south of Spain a long way from the main theatre of operations. La Peña's sortie from Cadiz was the last thing Wellington wanted as it risked destabilising the entire strategic balance. A decisive victory by the Anglo–Spanish Cadiz force was potentially as disastrous to Wellington in Portugal as a comprehensive defeat. 'If these facts are applied to this intended operation,' he wrote in June 1810 when an attack upon Victor's corps was first discussed, 'it will appear, that whether successful or otherwise, it will probably have the effect of increasing the force to be employed against us [in Portugal]. If it should be successful, the force now employed upon the useless blockade of Cadiz will be thrown upon our right through Estremadura. The French will evacuate Andalusia probably, and hold the left of their army in the Sierra Morena, covering their operations upon us. But the raising of the siege or blockade of Cadiz, which would set at liberty a certain force of the Allies now in [the Cadiz] garrison, would not give us the advantage of the operations of this force, as an army in the field, on account of the total want of cavalry, and deficiency of field artillery; and I much doubt whether the force could leave Cadiz at all.'[23]

At the time when Wellington was facing the might of Masséna's Army of Portugal, and the outcome of the war hung perilously in the balance, nothing could have been more dangerous for his position at Lisbon than if Soult's Army of the South was freed from the siege of Cadiz and able to throw its weight behind the invasion of Portugal. These thoughts were on his mind as early as 20 May 1810, when he actually predicted the possibility of an action similar to the Battle of Barrosa: 'I think the French will soon discover that they have not a force sufficiently large to blockade Cadiz, and attack us in Portugal at the same time; and if we begin to make sorties from Cadiz, they will remove their force from thence to throw it upon this country [Portugal].' Soult did indeed move a large part of his force in Andalusia to support the invasion of Portugal and it did lead to a sortie from Cadiz just as Wellington had foreseen.

In considering the consequences that might have followed the successful raising of the siege of Cadiz, Professor Oman agreed with Wellington, 'what would have followed that success no man can say, for it would have brought about such a convulsion in Andalusia, and such a concentration of the French troops, that the whole of the conditions of the war in the south would have been altered.'[24]

Wellington continued to worry about the consequences of the lifting of the siege, as he told Charles Stuart on 11 September 1810: 'I can only tell you that of which I am the most apprehensive, is that the enemy will raise the blockade of Cadiz. Unless Heaven will perform a miracle, and give the Spaniards an army, arms, and equipments, we should be ruined by this measure, and then the cause is gone.'[25] When Wellington learned of the departure from Cadiz of Graham's and La Peña's force the following February he was so worried that he put all his plans on hold until the result of the operation against Victor was known.[26]

This gives some indication of just how significant Joseph's failure to capture Cadiz really was. When Napoleon sent tens of thousands of reinforcements into Spain over the course of the winter of 1809/10 the French commanders in the Peninsula had a real opportunity to push the British out of Portugal. Even though such an opportunity was lost when Joseph invaded Andalusia, if the 'Intrusive' king had captured Cadiz and in doing so brought the campaign to a speedy conclusion, it might still have been possible to concentrate an overwhelming force against Wellington and drive him from the Lines of Torres Vedras.

Apart from the above, and the fact that Joseph's failure to capture Cadiz meant the Spanish Government could continue to challenge the legitimacy of his rule, there were other consequences which had a profound effect upon the course of the war. The first was that Cadiz acted as the catalyst for the insurgency throughout Andalusia. The benefits of maintaining the siege of Cadiz whilst fostering rebellion in Andalusia became apparent to Wellington after the Battle of Barrosa. Before the Barrosa campaign Wellington, as we have seen, was opposed to any large-scale enterprise by the Cadiz forces, but after Barrosa his attitude changed completely and he began to positively encourage operations in Andalusia to help keep Soult from interfering with the Anglo-Portuguese siege of Badajoz. After initially agreeing with Graham not to have anything further to do with joint ventures with the Spaniards, by July 1811 he was recommending to Henry Wellesley that they 'combine their operations with ours'.[27] Such was the effect of the victory at Barrosa, Soult could never risk exposing Victor's besieging force to another defeat of that magnitude. As a result Wellington was able to capture Badajoz untroubled by Soult and in doing so shifted the strategic balance of the war in the Peninsular.

The second was that the siege of Cadiz required a vast amount of ordnance. Many of the guns taken down to Andalusia for this purpose were sorely needed by Masséna in his siege of Ciudad Rodrigo. It was stated by a French officer on Masséna's staff that the siege of Cadiz 'had absorbed all the personnel and material brought into or found in Spain.' The considerable delay in capturing Ciudad Rodrigo which this shortage caused gave Wellington vital weeks in which the Lines of Torres Vedras grew to the formidable fortifications that Masséna dared not assault.[28]

Just as significant was Cadiz's importance as the principal port for the importation of specie from Spain's colonies. Gold and silver from the New World had been vital to Spain's economy for almost 200 years and in turn had greatly increased the circulation of specie around Europe as a whole. Because of the war the amount of gold and silver reaching Europe had reduced considerably and if Cadiz would have fallen to the French the further loss of specie would have proven to be disastrous. From the very beginning of Britain's involvement in the Peninsula, George Canning, the then Foreign Secretary, had made it clear to the Spaniards that Britain's ability to aid the Spaniards would be contingent upon gaining access to American silver.[29] Wellington reiterated this to his brother Henry in April 1810, and it was a subject he returned to many times over the subsequent months: 'You are aware of the great difficulties existing in England for procuring specie. We are in the greatest distress for money in this country; and if we should lose the supplies of money which we receive from Gibraltar and Cadiz, we should very soon be obliged to quit the Peninsula for want of money to subsist in it.'[30] As Aspinall–Oglander has written, this was no idle threat from Wellington and, regardless of other military considerations, Britain could not have continued to maintain an army in Iberia without the local currency the British authorities could obtain there against bills drawn on London.[31]

*

There are many other questions concerning the war in Andalusia. There can be little doubt that it was one of the most crucial episodes in the Peninsular War. Joseph Bonaparte knew this and when he entered Seville he believed that the subjugation of Spain was all but complete. Victor had been sent to seize Cadiz, which should have completed the campaign. As Joseph told Napoleon, Cadiz would be taken '*sans coup férir*' – 'without firing a shot'.[32] But something went wrong.

There are conflicting opinions about this. Surprising though it may seem, many blame Victor, a subordinate general, for failing to capture Cadiz and an officer on Soult's staff wrote that 'Victor might have made a more rapid advance.' Further criticisms were also leveled by William Napier: '. . . it is generally supposed, that he [Victor] might have rendered himself master of [the Isla de] Leon, for the defensive works at Cadiz and the Isla were in no way improved, but rather deteriorated . . . The bridge of Zuarzo was indeed broken, and the canal of Sancti Petri a great obstacle; but Albuquerque's troops were harassed, dispirited, ill clothed, badly armed, and in every way inefficient; the people of Cadiz were apathetic, and the authorities, as usual, occupied with intrigues and private interests. In this state, eight thousand Spanish soldiers could scarcely have defended a line of ten miles against twenty-five thousand French.' Victor's failure to make an attempt upon Cadiz at this, its most vulnerable time, was, Napier states, because he was 'deceived as to its real strength'.[33]

Even when Cadiz had been rendered more secure with the arrival of the British land and sea forces, there was still a chance of its weak defences being stormed by Victor's army. Wellington certainly believed that this would happen: 'The Spaniards and us would deceive ourselves', he informed General Stewart on 27 February 1810, 'if we should suppose that a most serious attack will not sooner or later be made upon this island [the Isla de Leon], or upon the communications between the island and Cadiz.' At that stage of the conflict Wellington could only guess at the future direction of the war yet he knew that nothing was more important than defending the seat of the Spanish Government: 'It is impossible to say whether the enemy will begin by making his great attack upon Cadiz, or will turn their attention to our situation in Portugal; but sooner or later all that force and art can do to obtain possession of the Isla de Leon will be done.'[34]

Wellington was convinced that the French would make every effort to capture Cadiz. Because of its importance he believed that 'the serious attack which will certainly be made upon it' and that this assault would be 'directed and assisted by all the resources which art can furnish, and made by all the French troops which can be assembled from all parts of the Peninsula.'[35]

Wellington understood the war in the Peninsula better than any other and he fully appreciated the consequences of allowing Cadiz to fall to the enemy: '. . . every man who knows anything of the state of Spain, and of the sentiments of the people of the country, must be certain that if Cadiz should hold out, and the

Mediterranean islands continue in the possession of the patriots, and the colonies continue true to the cause, the Bonapartes may have the military possession of the country, but sooner or later they must lose it.'

Yet, in early 1810, there was every possibility that the war in Spain would be lost to the French and, with it, the vital trade with Spanish colonies. British commerce had been badly affected by the loss of European markets because of the war with France. New markets were needed elsewhere and the emerging countries in the New World were ripe for development. This prompted Henry Wellesley to make a most remarkable suggestion. 'I have sometimes thought,' he wrote on 12 March 1810, 'that in the event of the conquest of the rest of Spain, Cadiz might be induced to declare itself a free port under the protection of the English, and that its connection with South America might facilitate any arrangements we might wish to make in that quarter.'[36]

Knowing, therefore, the importance of Cadiz and the value which the British Government placed upon its alliance with Spain compared with its much smaller neighbor Portugal, Wellington was concerned that resources would be diverted to Cadiz at the expense of Lisbon. Consequently, he repeatedly stressed that 'the British army in the Peninsula cannot be better employed, even with a view to prevent the enemy from obtaining possession of Cadiz, than in Portugal' and that the 'British army would do better to carry on its operations through Portugal and make Lisbon the point of its communications through the south of Spain, communicating with Cadiz.'

Just to emphasize the point, Wellington presented it from another perspective: 'If we should withdraw from Portugal', he told Lord Liverpool, 'Cadiz would then be attacked by the whole French army . . . In a view, then, to the continuation of the contest at Cadiz, as well as in every other view that I have ever taken on the subject, I consider it highly desirable that we should maintain ourselves in Portugal as long as possible.'[37]

It must be remembered that the general opinion, both in Portugal and Britain, was that Wellington would not be able to defend Portugal against the large army that was being assembled under Masséna. So seemingly inevitable was the evacuation of Portugal, it was referred to in correspondence between Lord Liverpool and Wellington as if it was a foregone conclusion: 'It may be depended upon that *when* the British troops shall have evacuated Portugal', appeared in one dispatch, followed by 'would it not be better, *after the evacuation of Portugal* . . .' In this light it can be seen just how important the security of Cadiz was to the Allied cause in the Peninsula. Whatever the result of the contest in Portugal, the war against Napoleon would not end providing Cadiz remained in the hands of the Allies.[38]

Indeed, all the preparations necessary were made by Wellington for an evacuation to Cadiz. This included a fortified embarkation point on the Tagus at Lisbon (St Julien) and the preparation of defences for a small rearguard to be held as the last troops took to the boats. Wellington also arranged for Graham to send him 'vessels of any description capable of transporting troops to the Tagus.'[39]

Yet the retention by the French of such a large force in Andalusia meant that Wellington was able to operate in central Spain with a freedom that would not have been possible if the I, IV and V Corps would have remained around Madrid. Indeed, as we have seen, Wellington was unable to attack Badajoz when Soult and Marmont combined in early 1812. In such circumstances it is unlikely that Wellington could have done more than simply defend Portugal. Even when Napoleon drew forces from the Peninsula for his Russian expedition, the combined disposable force available to Joseph matched that of Wellington.

Soult, therefore, must bear much of the blame for the loss of Spain. When Wellington had broken out into central Spain there was still a chance for the French armies to concentrate and drive the Anglo-Portuguese forces back in Portugal. But Soult repeatedly refused to abandon Andalusia until it was too late. 'Summing up the events of June-July-August 1812 in southern Spain,' wrote Oman, 'it is impossible to avoid the conclusion that Soult's personal interests wrecked any chance the French might have had of retaining their dominant position in the Peninusla.'[40]

The fact that the Battle of Barrosa failed to achieve any decisive shift in the situation was, in fact, the best possible outcome for the Allies. As Sir John Fortescue has explained, 'it allowed the French to persist in their grand error, the siege of Cadiz, with little inconvenience even for the moment to the Allies, but with lasting and ruinous damage to themselves.'[41] Even Napoleon was later forced to admit that the protracted struggle in the Iberian Peninsula cost him his empire: 'That unfortunate war destroyed me; it divided my forces, multiplied my obligations, undermined my morale. All the circumstances of my disasters are bound up in that fatal knot.'[42]

*

Barrosa may have saved Spain from Napoleon but it could not save Spain from herself. Though the Peninsular War had ended and peace was soon to reign over most of Europe, the fighting in Spain was far from over. King Ferdinand VII was released from captivity by Napoleon and, on 24 March 1814, a representative of the Regency met the King on the French border. The young king would be allowed to return to his country providing upon his return to Madrid he complied with the terms of the Constitution. Though his reply was evasive, Ferdinand was not prevented from entering Spain as it was expected that he would have little choice but to accept the changed circumstances.

This was a time of great optimism in Spain. Gone was the old despotic regime with its archaic systems of taxation and conscription, its hereditary town councils and its nepotism. Gone too was censorship and for the first time Spain could boast a free press. Every man was now equal before the law and even the Church had seen its authority curtailed.

Spain now was ruled not by a monarch and his arbitrarily selected advisors but by a democratically elected government. There was a place in the new Spain for Ferdinand, but only if he abided by the principles of the Cadiz Constitution, which severely limited the authority of the monarchy.[43] Ferdinand would have none of it.

Supported by many of the generals and a large part of the army, Ferdinand repudiated not only the Constitution but also the body that had promulgated it. On 4 May 1814, he issued the following Proclamation: 'I declare that my royal intention is not only not to swear or agree to the said Constitution or any decree of the general and extraordinary Cortes and of the ordinary Cortes now in session . . . but to declare that Constitution and those decrees nul and of no validity or effect, now or at any time, as if those acts had never been passed and are now obliterated.'[44]

To the surprise of many, riots broke out in Madrid in support of Ferdinand, led in numerous cases by the clergy, who stood to lose much if the Constitution was upheld. The politicians, as is so often the case, had failed to appreciate the mood of the people who had little interest in the lofty ideals of the liberals. 'From ignorance of human nature, or from too strong democratic notions, they absolutely courted the opposition of the upper classes by wanton changes, and a total disregard of their feelings and prejudices,' observed Colonel John Jones, 'so that the constitution, the fruits of their labour, whilst it abased the kingly power, degraded the nobles, robbed the church, and limited the authority of the military.'[45] With such powerful figures encouraging the mob, the hall of the Cortes in Cadiz was sacked and a stone inscribed with the Constitution smashed.

A week later, a division of the Second Army marched into Madrid, dissolved the Cortes and arrested as many of its members that it could catch. Six years after the departure of the Spanish Royal Family which had provoked the riots that marked the beginning of the great struggle against French occupation, the Bourbons were once again in their capital, and back in power. Ferdinand was warmly received by the Madrilènes. Absolute rule had returned to Spain.[46]

It is interesting that even as early as November 1810 Wellington had predicted this course of events: 'The nature of all popular assemblies, of the Spanish Cortes among others,' he told his brother Henry, 'is to adopt democratic principles and vest all the powers of the state in their own body; and this assembly must take care that they do not run in this tempting course, as the wishes of the nation are decidedly for a monarchy: by a monarchy alone can it be governed.'[47] It is remarkable how prescient Wellington, a foreigner, was all those years earlier.

Though it may well have been the case that Spain in the early nineteenth century could only be ruled by a monarchy, a return to the *ancien regime* meant a return to the inefficiency and ineffectiveness of the past and the reintroduction of the hated *Inquisition*. Ferdinand proved to be even more despotic than his forebears and his failure to recognise the changed situation in Spain's colonies and grant them the political and commercial freedom they demanded led to a complete breach. The loss of the South American colonies was a ruinous blow to the Spanish economy and to the Spanish court. Ferdinand was soon bankrupt.

He responded, not by allowing more free enterprise and liberalism, but with further regressive and oppressive methods. Minister after minister was sacked as the country continued its rapid decline.

Yet war creates change and the Peninsular War changed the political landscape of Spain forever. The principles of liberalism were never entirely eradicated from the hearts and minds of many Spaniards. That particular genie was out of the bottle. The actions of Ferdinand, and the state to which the country had deteriorated since his resumption of power, only further reinforced the views of the radicals – and soon Spain was at war with itself.

The former guerrilla leaders, General Espoz y Mina and Colonel Portlier, took up arms again. Though the uprising was suppressed, the desire for change could not be stopped. In January 1820, some 10,000 troops who had assembled at Cadiz for an expedition to South America mutinied. Led by the liberal agitator, Rafael del Riego y Nuez, the soldiers marched upon Madrid and compelled Ferdinand to swear allegiance to the Constitution he so detested.

Not that things ended there. As one historian eloquently explained, the Peninsular War 'cast forward long shadows across the Spanish history of the nineteenth century.'[48] The situation in which Ferdinand now found himself threatened the monarchies of the other great countries of Europe. If liberal and democratic movements could overwhelm conservative Spain then what could happen in the traditionally volatile nations such as France or Russia? Such movements had to be eradicated before they spread.

So, two years after Ferdinand had signed the Cadiz Constitution, the plenipotentiaries of Russia, Prussia, Austria and France decided that liberalism had gone too far in Spain. At the Congress of Verona in October 1822, the Quadruple Alliance of Britain, France, Holland and Austria gave France a mandate to intervene and restore the Spanish monarchy. So, in a strange twist of fate, a French army once again invaded Spain, though this time the French troops entered Madrid not to depose the Bourbon monarchy but to re-establish its authority!

The French army drove the constitutionalists south to Seville and then Cadiz. Just as had happened a decade before, the Spanish Government sought refuge in Cadiz, this time taking a captive Ferdinand with them. Once again French troops occupied Andalusia and laid siege to the Isla de Leon.

On 31 August the French launched a surprise bayonet attack against Fort San Luis from the sea-side during low tide. For the cost of thirty-five killed and 110 wounded (as opposed to 150 dead, 300 wounded and 1,100 captured on the part of the garrison) they successfully stormed this key fortification. The French were now able to turn the fort's powerful guns towards Cadiz.

On 20 September fort Sancti-Petri also fell to the attackers in a combined amphibious operation. Three days later the guns of the Sancti Petri and San Luis forts, along with those of the small French fleet, bombarded the town and on the 28th the constitutionalists adjudged the town lost. On 30 September Cadiz surrendered. The great Spanish port which had withstood the longest siege of the Napoleonic Wars had succumbed after just one month.

The Cortes decided to dissolve itself, give back absolute power to Ferdinand VII and hand him over to the French. Ferdinand returned to Madrid and his despotic regime was restored.

Until his death eleven years later, Ferdinand's authority remained absolute, but the country continued in a state of ferment and the Spanish liberals fought on. 'Spain is a bottle of beer and I am the cork,' Ferdinand so accurately perceived. 'Without me it would all go off in a froth.' And it did.

On 29 September 1833, Ferdinand died. He had no male heir and the struggle for the Spanish throne split the country along the lines of 1812. Once again liberals fought reactionaries in what became known as the First Carlist War.

The Carlist Wars tore Spain apart for most of the nineteenth century. Though the Third and last Carlist War ended in 1876 many consider the Spanish Civil War of 1936–1939, which again saw republicans fighting monarchists, as a continuation of that same conflict. In fact it was not until the mid 1970s, that Spain finally settled on the road to democracy and Juan Carlos I became the country's constitutional monarch. Long shadows indeed.

The Battlefields of the Barrosa Campaign – A Visitors' Guide

Cadiz, Tarifa, Chiclana and Barossa are easily accessible from Gibraltar, the great British stronghold. Gibraltar played an important part in the Andalusia campaign as a sanctuary for the Spanish forces operating behind the French lines. Though most of the thirty-four miles of military tunnels that have been carved out of the limestone rock are not assessable to the public, a number of the galleries, bastions and gun batteries can be visited, giving some indication just how formidable Gibraltar's defences really were.

Across the border is La Linea de la Concepción. From here the N351/CA34 travels out of the town to the A-7, which skirts around the bay to Algiceras where Graham's division disembarked before marching along the coast to Tarifa. The A-7 integrates with the N340 as it leaves Algeciras, the latter continuing on to Tarifa.

Now a popular windsurfing resort, aspects of the siege of Tarifa are still present in the form of Guzman's Tower (the *Castillo Guzmán el Bueno*) which is open to the public (though at the time of writing it is closed for renovation). The importance of its position, dominating the beach and overlooking the island, is easily understood. Considerable sections of the town's old walls are still standing and the point where the walls were breached by the French is identified by a plaque which reads '*Hanc partem muri a gallis obsidentibus dirutam, britanni defensores construxerunt 1812*'. The part of the wall where the portcullis had been placed to allow the Retiro to pass through has gone, though the spot can be identified by following the line of the Retiro as it drops down to pass under the streets of the town.

From Tarifa the N340 continues westwards. After a little more than five miles the road travels close to the sea before diverting inland. This point is at Torre de la Peña. It was here that the frigates HMS *Stately* and *Tuscan* destroyed the road to try and prevent the French from moving their siege train from Cadiz to Tarifa in the winter of 1811. The French engineers rebuilt the road and then erected batteries on the shore to keep the Allied ships at bay.

The N340 then passes through Ventas de Facinas, just beyond which there is a right turn onto a smaller road, the CA-7201, which runs to Facinas. This is the point where the old roads divide and it is where La Peña decided to turn inland towards Medina Sidonia. From Facinas a small track leads across the area of the Laguna de la Janda to Casa-Viejer, now known as Benalup-Casas Viejas. The Laguna is not the obstacle it was in Napoleonic times. The area has been drained to provide excellent agricultural land. During heavy rains, however, the Janda still floods and the great extent of the lagoon is briefly revealed. It is famous for the wide variety of migratory birds that can be seen wintering in this, the most southerly part of mainland Europe. The old convent, or *casa* (i.e. house), which was attacked and taken by the Allied army, is no longer identifiable.

Medina Sidonia is situated on a dominating hilltop and had been an important strategic fortification since medieval times (it was Admiral Alonso Pérez de Guzmán 7th Duke of Medina Sidonia who led the Spanish Armada against England in 1588). Its fortifications are still impressive and La Peña's decision not to spend time trying to capture it was quite understandable, even though in doing so it would have brought Victor out of Chiclana, which was the main objective of the expedition.

At Casa-Viejer, La Peña changed his mind about marching upon Medina Sidonia and he took instead the road down to Vejer, now the A-2228 to Vejer de la Frontera. This road crosses the Barbate where the Allied army experienced such difficulty negotiating the passage of the river.

From Vejer the N340 continues for some fifteen miles through Conil to a turning for Playa La Barrosa. Here the CA-9001 runs towards the coast and climbs up to the summit of Barrosa hill (now known as the Loma de Sancti Petri), before which can be seen what remains of the wood through which the British troops were marching as Victor's men attacked. Described by Graham as 'a great pine forest [which] skirts the plain and circles round the height' most of it has disappeared. There are, however, still a considerable number of the low pines which are quite different from the pines encountered in the UK, and it is easy to understand why the French were unable to see if the British had reserve forces in the wood. The description of the ground as being a plain is quite accurate, as the land is very flat.

The top of Barrosa hill is marked by a monument to the battle (at 36° 20. 13'N, 06° 09. 23'W). Erected in 2003, its inscription reads, (in Spanish, English, French and German), "El Puerco' Hill. On the 5th March 1811 the Barrosa or Chiclana battle was fought around this place, during the Peninsular War against Napoleon, thousands of British, French, Spanish, Portuguese, Polish and German soldiers shed their blood on this hill . . . '

Though the top of the hill is still open ground and some is covered in gorse, much of the battlefield is now occupied by hotels and villas and the ground up which Dilkes advanced is now covered in part by a golf course. The most surprising aspect of the battlefield of Barrosa is how low the Barrosa 'heights' actually are, and how gentle are their slopes. The impression one gets from reading the accounts of the battle is of steep undulating terrain. Nevertheless, it is easy to appreciate Graham's reluctance to abandon his position on the hill as it completely dominates the ground towards Cadiz to the north.

At the southern end of the road that crosses the battlefield, Barrosa's old watchtower still stands guard over the beach. The coastal path that Whittingham's force took ran just north of the tower and is now difficult to distinguish. From the tower the beach curves round towards the Torre Bermeja. This can be reached by travelling along the CA-9001 until the Avenue de la Barrosa is reached, which runs directly to Bermeja.

Looking back along the beach from Bermeja towards Barrosa it is remarkable to see just how close the Spaniards were to the fighting and how easily they could have intervened. At Bermeja is a monument to *la Batalla de Chiclana* where La Peña was stationed during the battle (36° 22. 29'N, 06° 11. 23'W). There is also a bust on a plinth dedicated to General Graham. It can be found in Les Jardines del General Graham at the Casa del Coto (on the Calle Viña del Mar) by a roundabout on the road leading from the Torre Bermeja to Chiclana.

Continuing on to Chiclana de la Frontera, the Casa del Coto, a nineteenth century mansion, which allegedly served as a French command post during the battle still stands, and is now the home of the Coast Interpretation Centre and Tourist Office (*Centro de Interpretación del Litoral, Chichanero y Oficina de Turismo*). For some years the main street in Chiclana was named the Calle 5 de marzo de 1811 and a section in the Chiclana Museum is dedicated to the battle. The museum is at Casa de los Briones on the Playa Mayor. It is open from Tuesday to Saturday, 10.00 to 14.00 and 18.00 to 21.00. The exhibits include a diorama of the battle, and copies of a few paintings. Of greater interest is a map of the battlefield compiled by the Quartermaster General's Department dated 1812 and a plan of the gun batteries both in Cadiz and along the French siege works during the siege.

Returning to the N340 and then onto the A-48, it is a short drive across the salt-marshes to the bridge over the Sancti Petri. The modern bridge to San Fernando and the Isla de Leon runs close to the old bridge but the latter forms part of a one-way system and can only be crossed when returning back to the mainland. Next to the old Puente Zuazo, which was broken by the Duke of Albuquerque as he retreated onto the Isla de Leon in February 1810, is an old redoubt that defended the passage of the river. There are also another couple of redoubts which are currently in the process of being restored.

The A-48 becomes the CA-33 as it travels through San Fernando and across the narrow isthmus of the Cortadura. The road passes through the Cortadura fortifications (or the Battery of San Fernando) that flank the road as it approaches Cadiz.

Reputedly the oldest city in Europe, and once the most important port in Spain, Cadiz suffered a long period of decline after the Peninsular War due to the loss of trade with the American colonies when they gained independence. The old city is situated towards the north-western end of the Isla de Leon, the eighteenth century Puerta de Tierra (Land Gate) marking its eastern boundary. The CA-33 passes through the gate's main arches.

It is still possible to walk along sections of the great walls that surrounded the magnificent city of Cadiz. The city itself, with its congestion of narrow streets, is difficult to navigate by car and street parking is virtually impossible. There are, however, a number of underground car parks which enable the city to be explored on foot.

El Real Teatro (the Royal Theatre) where the Cortes sat, is a surprisingly insignificant-looking building. It is now the Museo de las Cortes de Cadiz. After the Peninsular War its importance declined and it was not until 1995 that restoration work was begun to save the building. There is a large monument to the 1812 Constitution in the Plaza de Espana.

Across the bay the Trocadero is now heavily industrialised and Fort Matagorda has disappeared under docks and warehouses. Fort San Luis lies neglected in ruins. The distance across the bay to the mainland is considerable and one cannot help but admire the builders of the Villoutreys mortars.

Of the Cadiz forts in use during the siege only Fort Puntales remains a military establishment, its fortifications having been considerably modernised in 1863 and then, in 1923, it was transferred to the Spanish Navy. It is still in naval hands and is also a base for the Naval Maritime Service of the *Guardia Civil*. Naval vessels can usually be seen berthed there.

Returning back across the old Puente Zuazo, it is worth stopping by the bridge to look at the inscription it carries: 'This was the limit of free Spain. In this historic bridge, the artillery and infantry brigades, Royal Navy and Army and naval forces under the command of Captain Don Diego de Alvear y Pone de Leon, his heroism and courage, rejecting the attacks of the French army since February 10, 1810 to August 25, 1812 made these venerable stones the last bastion of Spanish independence.' Not one word about the British.

Appendices

I

Force under Major General John Randall Mackenzie directed to Cadiz, February 1809

2nd Battalion 9th Foot	630
3rd Battalion 27th Foot	793
29th Foot	634
Bredin's Company, Royal Artillery	101
4th Company, KGL Artillery (No data)	

II

The army under Captain General the Duke of Albuquerque, Isla de Leon, 24 February 1810

Cavalry	1,710 (having 1,050 horses unfit for service)
Artillery	300
Vanguard	2,757
First Division	2,839
Second Division	2,430
Independent battalions	2,740
Total 12,776	

III

Allotment of the troops under Lieutenant General Graham, Isla de Leon, 30 July 1810

	At Isla			
	Officers	Sergeants	Drummers	Rank & File
Cavalry	15	20	5	391
Royal Engineers	8	2	0	48
Royal Artillery	20	8	4	363
Royal Artillery Drivers	1	3	1	51
1st Brigade (Brig. Gen.Dilkes)	39	62	18	1,192
2nd Brigade (Maj. Gen. Fergusson)	140	165	77	2,890

3rd Brigade (Brig. Gen. Sontag)	84	104	40	1,813
Company Royal Staff Corps	3	1	1	50
Total	**310**	**365**	**146**	**6,798**

At Cadiz

Royal Artillery	10	7	3	240
4th Brigade (Brig. Gen. Houghton)	74	102	54	1,490
Total	**84**	**109**	**57**	**1,730**

IV

THE BATTLE OF BAROSSA, 5 March 1811
Order of Battle

British forces:
Officer Commanding: Lieutenant General Thomas Graham

Cavalry:
2nd Hussars King's German Legion — 206

Brigadier-General William Dilkes' Brigade:
1st Guards, 2nd Battalion — 611
Coldstream Guards, 2nd Battalion (2 companies) — 211
3rd Guards, 2nd Battalion (3 companies) — 322
2nd Battalion 95th Rifles (2 companies) — 217
Brigade total — 1361

Colonel Sir Henry Wheatley's Brigade:
1st Battalion 28th Foot (8 companies) — 457
2nd Battalion 67th Foot — 527
2nd Battalion 87th Foot — 696
Brigade total — 1680

Lieutenant Colonel John Browne's Flank Battalion:
9th Foot, 1st Battalion (2 companies); 28th Foot, 1st Battalion (2 companies);
82nd Foot, 2nd Battalion (2 companies) — 536
Lieutenant Colonel Andrew Barnard's Flank Battalion:
95th Rifles, 3rd Battalion (4 companies); 47th Regiment, 2nd Battalion (2 companies) — 644
20th Portuguese Regiment (2 companies) — 332

Royal Artillery (Major Alexander Duncan) — 362
Royal Engineers — 59
Royal Staff Corps — 37
Army total — 5217

THE BATTLE OF BARROSA, 1811

Spanish forces:
Officer Commanding: General Manuel La Peña

1st Division – General Fran isco Lardizabal
Regiments, Campomayor, Carmona, Murcia (2 battalions), Canaris

2nd Division – Prince d'Anglona
Regiments, Africa (2 battalions), Siguenza, Cantabria (2 battalions), Voluntarios de Valencia
Artillery – 14 guns
Cavalry – Four squadrons under the command of Colonel Samuel Whittingham

Approximate total 6,800

Approximate Allied Grand Total = 12,017

French forces:
Officer Commanding: Marshal Claude Victor-Perrin, Duke of Belluno.

A – troops engaged against the British

1st Dragoons	398
Artillery (2 batteries)	169

1st Division, General of Division Fran ois Amable Ruffin:

2/9me *Léger*	596
1/24me & 2/24me *Ligne*	1193
1/96me *Ligne*	764

2 provisional battalions of Grenadiers/Carabiniers formed from the 1st and 2nd Battalions of the 9me and 16me *Léger*, 24me, 96me, 8me, 45me, and 54me *Ligne* (numbers present included in their respective battalions)

Total 2553

2nd Division, General of Division Ann Gilbert Laval:

1/8me and 2/8me *Ligne*	1468
1/45me *Ligne*	710
1/54me and 2/54me *Ligne*	1323

Provisional battalion of Grenadiers/Carabiniers formed from the 3rd Battalions of the 9me *Léger*, and the 8me, 45me, 54me, 24me, and 96me *Ligne* 549

Total 4050

B – troops engaged against the Spanish forces under
Generals Zayas and Lardizabal in the combat by the Torre Bermeja

3rd Division, General of Division Eugene-Casimir Villatte:

1/27me & 3/27me *Léger*	1025
1/94me *Ligne*	550

2/95me & 3/95me *Ligne*		1056
2nd *Dragons*		289
Artillery (one battery)		78
	Total	2998

Grand total   101,68

French forces at Medina Sidonia
Commanding Officer – General of Division Louis Victorin Cassagne
5th *Chasseurs à Cheval*
2/27me *Léger*, 3/94me *Ligne*, 2/96me *Ligne*, 1/95me *Ligne*.
Composite light battalion comprising the *voltigeur* companies from the 3rd battalions of the 8me, 24me, 45me, 96me *Ligne* and the 6me *Léger*

French forces in garrison in the Cadiz Lines
1/9me *Léger*, 2/45me and 2/94me *Ligne*.

With Soult in Estremadura
V Corps – Marshal Édouard Adolphe Casimir Joseph Mortier
  1st Division, General of Division Jean-Baptiste Girard

34me, 40me, 88me *Ligne* (three battalions each)	5,835
2nd Division, General of Division Honoré Théodore Maxim Gazan:	
21me and 28me *Léger*, 100me and 103me *Ligne* (three battalions each)	5,775
Cavalry Corps, General of Brigade André-Louis-Elizabeth-Marie Briche:	
21st Chasseurs and 10th Hussars	971

From I Corps

63me *Ligne* (three battalions)	1,450
4th, 14th and 26th Dragoons	1,332
2nd Hussars	405

From IV Corps

27th Chasseurs á Cheval	990

Artillery and Train	1,261
Engineers and Sappers	698
4th Spanish Chasseurs à Cheval	246
Gendarmerie	25
Ètat-Major-General	22

Total   19,010

V

Graham's Barrosa Dispatch

Isla de Leon, March 6, 1811

My Lord,

Captain Hope, my first aide-de-camp, will have the honour of delivering this dispatch, to inform your lordship of the glorious issue of an action fought yesterday by the division under my command, against the army commanded by Marshal Victor, composed of the two divisions Ruffin and Laval.

The circumstances were such as compelled me to attack this very superior force. In order as well to explain to your lordship the circumstances of peculiar disadvantage under which the action was began, as to justify myself from the imputation or rashness in the attempt, I must state to your lordship, that the allied army, after a night-march of sixteen hours from the camp near Veger, arrived in the morning of the 5th on the low ridge of Barrosa, about four miles to the southward of the mouth of the Sancti Petri river. This height extends inland about a mile and a half, continuing on the north of the extensive heathy plain of Chiclana. A great pine forest skirts the plain, and circles round the height at some distance, terminating down to Sancti Petri; the intermediate space between the north side of the height and the forest being uneven and broken.

A well-conducted and successful attack on the rear of the enemy's lines near Sancti Petri, by the van-guard of the Spanish army, under Brigadier-general Lardizabal, having opened the communication with the Isla de Leon, I received General La Pena's directions to move down from the position of Barossa to that of the Torre de Bermeja, about half way to the Sancti Petri river, in order to secure the communication across the river, over which a bridge had been lately established. This latter position occupies a narrow woody ridge, the right on the sea-cliff, the left falling down to the Almanza creek, on the edge of the marsh. A hard sandy beach gives an easy communication between the western points of these two positions.

My division being halted on the eastern slope of the Barrosa height, was marched about 12 o'clock through the wood towards the Bermeja, (cavalry patrols having previously been sent towards Chiclana, without meeting with the enemy). On the march I received notice that the enemy had appeared in force on the plain, and was advancing towards the height of Barrosa.

As I considered that position as the key of that of Sancti Petri, I immediately counter-marched, in order to support the troops left for its defence; and the alacrity with which this manoeuvre was executed served as a favourable omen. It was however impossible, in such intricate and difficult ground, to preserve order in the columns, and there never was time to restore it entirely.

But before we could get ourselves quite disentangled from the wood, the troops on the Barrosa hill were seen returning from it, while the enemy's left wing was rapidly ascending. At the same time his right wing stood on the plain, on the edge of the wood, within cannon-shot. A retreat in the face of such an enemy, already within reach of the easy communication by the sea-beach, must have involved the whole allied army in all the danger of being attacked during the unavoidable confusion of the different corps arriving on the narrow ridge of Bermeja nearly at the same time.

Trusting to the known heroism of British troops, regardless of the numbers and position of their enemy, an immediate attack was determined on. Major Duncan soon opened a powerful battery of ten guns in the centre. Brigadier-general Dilkes, with the brigade of guards, Lieutenant-colonel Browne's (of the 28th) flank battalion, Lieutenant-colonel Norcott's two companies of the 2nd rifle corps, and Major Acheson, with a part of the 67th foot, (separated from the regiment in the wood) formed on the right.

Colonel Wheatley's brigade, with three companies of the Coldstream Guards, under Lieutenant-colonel Jackson (separated likewise from his battalion in the wood), and Lieutenant-colonel Barnard's flank battalion, formed on the left.

As soon as the infantry was this hastily got together, the guns advanced to a more favourable position, and kept up a most destructive fire.

The right wing proceeded to the attack of General Ruffin's division on the hill, while Lieutenant-colonel Barnard's battalion and Lieutenant-colonel Bushe's detachment of the 20th Portuguese, were warmly engaged with the enemy's tirailleurs on our left.

General Laval's division, notwithstanding the havoc made by Major Duncan's battery, continued to advance in very imposing masses, opening his fire of musketry, and was only checked by that of the left wing. The left wing now advanced, firing; a most determined charge, by the three companies of the guards, and the 67th regiment, supported by all the remainder of the wing, decided the defeat of General Laval's division.

The eagle of the 8th regiment of light infantry, which suffered immensely, and a howitzer, rewarded this charge, and remained in possession of Major Gough, of the 87th regiment. These attacks were zealously supported by Colonel Belsen with the 28th regiment, and Lieutenant-colonel Prevost with a part of the 67th.

A reserve formed beyond the narrow valley, across which the enemy was closely pursued, next shared the same fate, and was routed by the same means.

Meanwhile the right wing was not less successful; the enemy confident of success, met General Dilkes on the ascent of the hill, and the contest was sanguinary, but the undaunted perseverance of the brigade of guards, of Lieutenant-colonel's Browne's battalion, and of Lieutenant-colonel Norcott's and Major Acheson's detachment, overcame every obstacle, and General Ruffin's division was driven from the heights in confusion; leaving two pieces of cannon.

No expression of mine could do justice to the conduct of the troops throughout. Nothing less than the almost unparalleled exertions of every officer, the invincible bravery of every soldier, and the most determined devotion of the honour of his majesty's arms in all, could have achieved this brilliant success, against such a formidable enemy, so posted.

In less than an hour and a half from the commencement of the action, the enemy was in full retreat. The retiring divisions met, halted, and seemed inclined to form: a new and more advanced position of our artillery quickly dispersed them.

The exhausted state of our troops made pursuit impossible. A position was taken on the eastern side of the hill; and we were strengthened on our right by the return of the two Spanish battalions that had been attached before to my division, but which I had left on the hill, and which had been ordered to retire.

These battalions (Walloon Guards and Ciudad Real) made every effort to come back in time, when it was known that we were engaged.

I understand, too, from General Whittingham, that the three squadrons of cavalry he kept in check a corps of infantry and cavalry that attempted to turn the Barossa height by the sea. One squadron of the 2nd Hussars, King's German Legion, under Captain Busche, and directed by Lieutenant-colonel Ponsonby, (both had been attached to the Spanish cavalry), joined in time to make a brilliant and most successful charge against a squadron of French dragoons, which was entirely routed.

An eagle, six pieces of cannon, the general of brigade, Rosseau, wounded and taken, chief of the staff General Bellegrade, an aide-de-camp of Marshal Victor, and the colonel of the 8th regiment, with many other officers, killed, and several wounded and taken prisoners; the field covered with the dead bodies and arms of the enemy, attest that my confidence in this division was nobly repaid.

Where all have so distinguished themselves, it is scarcely possible to discriminate any as the most deserving of praise. Your lordship will, however, observe how gloriously the brigade of guards, under Brigadier-general Dilkes, with the commanders of the battalions Lieutenant-colonel the Hon. C. Onslow, and the Lieutenant-colonel Sebright wounded, as well as the three separated companies under Lieutenant-colonel Jackson, maintained the high character of his majesty's household troops. Lieutenant-colonel Browne, with his flank battalion, Lieutenant-colonel Norcott, and Major Acheson, deserve equal praise.

And I must equally recommend to your lordship's notice Colonel Wheatley, with Colonel Belson, Lieutenant-colonel Prevost, and Major Gough, and the officers of the respective corps composing his brigade.

The animated charges of the 87th regiment were conspicuous; Lieutenant-colonel Barnard (twice wounded), and the officers of his flank battalion, executed the duty of skirmishing in advance with the enemy in a masterly manner, and were ably seconded by Lieutenant-colonel Busche, of the 20th Portuguese, who (likewise twice wounded), fell into the enemy's hands, but was afterwards rescued. The detachment of this Portuguese regiment behaved admirably throughout the whole affair.

I owe too much to Major Duncan, and the officers and corps of the royal artillery, not to mention them in the highest approbation; never was artillery better served.

The assistance I received from the unwearied exertions of Lieutenant-colonel Macdonald, and the officers of the adjutant-general's department, of Lieutenant-colonel the Hon. C. Cathcart, and the officers of the quarter-master-general's department, of Captain Birch and Captain Nicholas, and the officers of the royal engineers, of Captain Hope, and the officers of my personal staff (all animating by their example) will ever be most gratefully remembered. Our loss has been severe: as soon as it can be ascertained by the proper return, I shall have the honour of transmitting it; but much as it is to be lamented, I trust it will be considered as a necessary sacrifice, for the safety of the whole allied army.

APPENDICES

Having remained some hours on the Barossa heights, without being able to procure any supplies for the exhausted troops, the commissariat mules having been dispersed on the enemy's first attack of the hill, I left Major Ross, with the detachment of the 3rd battalion of the 95th, and withdrew the rest of the division, which crossed the Sancti Petri river early the next morning.

I confidently trust that the bearer of this dispatch, Captain Hope, (to whom I refer your lordship for further details) will be promoted, on being permitted to lay the eagle at his majesty's feet.

I have the honour to be, etc.
THOMAS GRAHAM, Lieutenant-general

P.S. I beg leave to add, that two Spanish officers, Captain Miranda and Naughton, attached to my staff, behaved with the utmost intrepidity.

VI

OPPOSING FORCES AT THE SIEGE OF TARIFA

Anglo-Spanish Garrison of Tarifa, 20 December 1811

British contingent under Colonel John Skerrett

2/47th Foot Regiment	570
2/87th Foot Regiment	560
Converged Flank Company Battalion	400
95th Foot Regiment (1 coy)	75
2nd KGL Hussar Regiment (1 troop)	70
Hughes Battery, RA	83

Spanish contingent under General Fran isco Copons

Cantabria Infantry Regiment	450
Irlandia Infantry Regiment	357
Cazadores	333
Artillery	106
Sappers	83
Cavalry	17
Allied Total = 3104	

DISPOSITION OF THE ARTILLERY
In the town
4 x British 6-pounders on the N E and N W towers
2 Spanish 12-pounders on the Eastern Tower
2 Coehorn mortars on the front attacked, moved according to circumstances

On the island
2 x 24-pounders on traversing platforms
2 x 24-pounder carronades in the flanks
4 x 12-pounders in battery
2 x 10-inch mortars in battery
1 Spanish 12-pounder
1 Spanish 70-inch howitzer .

St Catalina
1 Spanish 12-pounder

In addition to the above, one iron 18-pounder was landed from HMS *Stately* and mounted on the Guzmans' Tower and a brass 5.5-inch howitzer was placed on the Retiro. There were also two light 6-pounders kept in reserve for sorties by the garrison which were in a fleche constructed outside the sea gate.

French forces at the Siege of Tarifa, December 1811 – January 1812

Det. Division: Leval
43rd Line Regiment
7th Polish Line Regiment
9th Polish Line Regiment
Total   **3,600**

Det. Division: Barrois
16th Legere Regiment
51st Line Regiment
54th Line Regiment
Total   **4,200**

Det. Division: Villatte
27th Legere Regiment
94th Line Regiment
95th Line Regiment
Total   **1,800**

Cavalry:
16th Dragoon Regiment   500
21st Dragoon Regiment   85

Artillery:
7/1st Foot Artillery   46
19/6th Foot Artillery   69
21/6th Foot Artillery   21
Det/8th Artillery Artisian Company   17
Det/2nd Principal Train Battalion   245
Det/2nd Principal Equippage Train Battalion   70

French Total = 106,53

APPENDICES

VII

Composition of the British forces at Cadiz, 25 August 1811 (effective strength/total strength)

Commanding the Force: Major General George Cooke

First Brigade: Lieutenant Colonel William Prevost

2nd Battalion 67th Foot	465/521
2nd Battalion 87th Foot	627/669
Battalion of Foreign Recruits	686/742
Brigade total	**1778/1932**

Second Brigade: Colonel John Skerrett

2nd Battalion 47th Foot	679/749
20th Regiment Portuguese Infantry, two battalions	1250/1331
Brigade total	**1929/2080**

Reserve Colonel John Lambert

3rd Battalion. 1st Footguards	1148/1214
Detachment 2nd Battalion 95th Rifles	164/181
Detachment 2nd KGL Hussars	141/158
Brigade total	**1453/1553**

Royal Artillery	595/632
Royal Artillery Drivers	170/187
Royal Engineers	74/98
Royal Staff Corps	36/39
Wagon Train	11/12
Force Total:	**6046/6533**

Notes and References

Chapter 1. SAVING SPAIN

1. Jan Read, *War in the Peninsular*, p.47.
2. Jan Read, *Ibid*, p.47.
3. *La Correspondance de Napoleon 1er*, vol. XVII, No.14242, p.427.
4. Dumas Count M., *Souvenirs* (Paris 1839), pp.321–2, quoted in D. Chandler, *The Campaigns of Napoleon*, p.620.
5. J. North, *In the Legions of Napoleon*, p.78
6. Canning to Frere, Jan 14 1809, The National Archive quoted C. Oman, *History of the Peninsular War*, vol. II, pp.25–6.
7. Ron McGuigan, 'The Origins of Wellington's Peninsular Army, June 1808–April 1809', in Rory Muir *et al*, *Inside Wellington's Peninsular Army 1808-1814*, p.64; strengths from the return of British forces in Portugal, 1 March 1809, in TNA, WO17/2464. The composition of this force can be found in Appendix I.
8. *Wellington's Supplementary Despatches*, vol.VI, p.210.
9. *Wellington's Despatches*, vol.5, pp.50-1, 90 & 94.
10. He visited Seville between 2 and 4 November 1809, and Cadiz on 6 and 7 November, returning to Seville for one night on the 9th. The Ambassador was his eldest brother, the Marquis Wellesley, who was shortly to return to Britain to take up the position of Foreign Secretary, Oman, *op. cit.*, vol.III, p.107.
11. C. Esdaile, *Napoleon's Wars*, pp.370–2, says that for the first two years of the war Cadiz was the 'chief territorial point of friction' between the British and the Spaniards'.
12. W. Walton, *The Revolutions of Spain*, vol. I, p.141.
13. Oman, *op. cit.*, vol.III, p.122; J. Fortescue, *History of the British Army*, vol. VII, p.360.
14. J. Pelet, *The French Campaign in Portugal*, p.157.
15. Wellington gives a figure of 24,000, see *Wellington's Despatches*, vol.7, p.292.
16. Fortescue, *op. cit.*, pp.360–1.
17. *Wellington's Despatches*, vol.7, p.294.
18. W. Napier, *History of the War in the Peninsula*, vol. III, p.104.
19. Oman, *op. cit.*, vol. III, p.138.
20. A. Bigarré, *Mémoires du Général Bigarré, Aide de Camp du Roi Joseph, 1773–1813* (Paris, 1903), p.270, quoted by C. Esdaille, *The Peninsular War*, p.233.
21. Esdaile, *The Peninsular War*, p.222.
22. Fortescue, *op cit.*, p.361.
23. Oman, *op. cit.*, Preface to Vol. IV.
24. J. Sarrazin, *History of the War in Spain and Portugal*, p. 89.
25. According to James Stanhope, the British offered to remove all the cannon from the Seville arsenal to Cadiz so that they would not fall into enemy hands. The Spaniards rejected the offer and 150 mortars, 300 siege guns and clothing for 30,000 men (which had been supplied by Britain) were seized by the French when they occupied the city; see G. Glover (ed.), *Eyewitness to the Peninsular War*, p.21.
26. Fortescue, *op cit.*, p.364.

27. See the summary of the various arguments over who was responsible for failing to march directly upon Cadiz, in Oman, *op. cit.*, vol.III, p.135.

Chapter 2. ENTER THE LION
1. Fortescue, *op. cit.*, vol. VII, p.366
2. Fortescue, *op. cit.*, vol. VII, p.367; C. Aspinall-Oglander, *Freshly Remembered*, p.206.
3. Sarrazin, *op. cit.*, p.90.
4. Aspinall-Oglander, *Freshly Remembered*, p.206.
5. Fortescue, *op. cit.*, vol.VII, p.366.
6. Oman, *op. cit.*, vol. III, p.201; Fortescue, *op. cit.*, vol. VII, p.373.
7. A captured despatch which came into the hands of the authorities in Cadiz in the second week of March indicated that Victor had only 18,992 men, and a total of just 27,006 for all the French troops in Andalusia. This does not seem to be correct and may refer to Victor's I Corps only see G. Glover (ed) *Eyewitness to the Peninsular War*, pp.21–2.
8. *Wellington's Supplementary Despatches*, vol.6, p.484.
9. *Wellington's Despatches*, vol.5, p.522. This was a recurrent theme of Wellington's, as he emphasized to his brother Henry on 27 March, 'If I should go from this country [Portugal], Cadiz would not hold a month, even if I were to take there a great part of the British army. The French might, and could collect there, their whole force; and then the serious attack would be made, and the place would really be in danger' (*Wellington's Despatches*, vol.5, p.581).
10. *Ibid*, p.523.
11. Fortescue, *op. cit.*, vol.VII, p.368; *Wellington's Despatches*, vol.5, pp.508–9.
12. *Cumloden Papers*, Wellington to Stewart, 5 February 1810.
13. W. Knox, *At Barossa with the 87th*, p.17.
14. J. Donaldson, *Recollections of Eventful Life of a Soldier*, p.60; W. Surtees, *Twenty Five Years in the Rifle Brigade*, p. 101.
15. Knox, *op. cit.*, pp.17–18. The exact numbers are as follows shown as effective strength/total strength, taken from 'Journal of the proceedings of the British Army serving at Cadiz and the I. of Leon', February 6th 1810, in TNA WO28/339:
    1/79th (Cameron Highlanders) (872/925)
    2/87th (Prince of Wales's Irish) (462/667)
    94th (Scotch Brigade) (596/662)
    Royal Artillery, 270.
16. T. Bunbury, *Reminiscences of a Veteran*, vol.I, p.58; *Cumloden Papers*, Stewart to Wellington, 11 March, 1810. Stewart told Wellington that all he needed now to make his division complete was a squadron of dragoons.
17. The Spanish and Portuguese were still the bitterest of enemies at this time and there was much apprehension about how they would be treated at Cadiz. As it happened they were surprisingly well received, but when Lieutenant General Graham arrived at Cadiz to take over from Stewart he was told that he could send the Portuguese back to Lisbon if their presence proved problematical; *Wellington's Despatches*, vol.6, pp. 25–6.
18. J. Brown, *England's Artillerymen*, p.155.
19. *Wellington's Despatches*, vol.5, p.508.
20. *Ibid*, p.512.
21. Napier, *op. cit.*, vol. III, pp.173–5.
22. R. Southey, *History of the Peninsular War*, vol. IV, p.398.

23. Malaga was provided with 148 artillery pieces of various calibres in addition to twenty-three field guns destined for the army of Catalonia, J. Sarrazin, *History of the War in Spain and Portugal*, pp.92–3.

24. *Wellington's Despatches*, vol.5, p. 511.

25. *Ibid*, pp.510–12

26. Napier, *op cit.*, vol. III, p.174.

27. A. Delavoye, *Life of Thomas Graham*, p.302; shortly after Graham's arrival Stewart requested a transfer to join Wellington's army in Portugal, *Wellington's Despatches*, vol.6, pp. 115 & 202.

28. *Wellington's Despatches*, vol. 5, p.540 and vol.6, p.15.

29. *Wellington's Despatches*, vol. 5, pp.583–4.

30. F. Wellesley, *The Diary and Correspondence of Henry Wellesley*, p.53.

31. Wellesley, *op. cit.*, p.54.

32. *Ibid*.

33. Wellesley, *op cit.*, pp.54–5.

34. *Wellington's Supplementary Despatches*, vol.6, p.491–2.

35. Oman, *op. cit.*, vol.III, p.325.

36. *Wellington's Supplementary Despatches*, vol. 6, pp.493–4.

37. *Wellington's Supplementary Despatches*, vol.6, p.495.

38. T. A. Heathcote, *Wellington's Peninsular War Generals & Their Battles*, pp.55–8; R. Southey, *History of the Peninsular War* (1932 edition), vol. III, pp.157–8.

39. Delavoye, *op. cit.*, p.302.

40. Delavoye, *op. cit.*, p.309.

41. Napier, *op. cit.*, vol.III, p.180.

42. Delavoy, *op. cit.*, p.309.

43. Delavoye, *op. cit.*, pp.315–7.

44. *Wellington's Despatches*, vol.6, pp.83–5; Delavoye, *op. cit.*, p.355.

45. Delavoye, *op. cit.*, pp.302–3.

46. Delavoye, *op. cit.*, pp.313–4.

47. Delavoye, *op. cit.*, p.316.

48. *Ibid*.

49. Delavoye, *op. cit.*, p.317.

50. Delavoye, *op. cit.*, pp.324–5.

51. *Wellington's Despatches*, vol.6, pp.37–9.

52. Delavoye, *op. cit.*, pp. 316–7.

53. Delavoye, *op. cit.*, pp.320–1.

54. Delavoye, *op. cit.*, p.364.

55. Fortescue, *op cit.*, vol. VII, pp.394–5

Chapter 3. A COMMON CAUSE

1. The Allied forces on the Isla de Leon had worked out a system of signals to communicate to each other. During the day a series of flags, riders and cannon shot could relay quickly to the main garrison in the city proper if the French were attempting a crossing or some other offensive operation against the Isla. At night, different coloured rockets, red for the British and green and blue for the Spanish, served the purpose; James P. Herson Jr., *'For the Cause' Cadiz and the Peninsular War*, p.103.

NOTES AND REFERENCES

2. Oddly, Oman, *op. cit.*, vol. III, p.321–2, gets his dates mixed up at this point and he has the storm of 6–9 March *after* the British lost Matagorda ; see also *Wellington's Despatches*, vol. 5, p.567.

3. Donaldson, *op. cit.*, p.65.

4. Surtees, *op. cit.*, p.94; Oman, *op. cit.*, vol.III, p.319.

5. Donaldson, *op. cit.*, pp.71–3.

6. Donaldson, *op. cit.*, pp.74–5.

7. Napier, *op. cit.*, vol. III, p.181.

8. J. Brown, *England's Artillerymen*, p.156.

9. R. Henegan, *Seven Years Campaigning in the Peninsula*, pp.155–7.

10. C. O'Neil, *The Military Adventures of Charles O'Neil*, p.121.

11. Napier, *op. cit.*, vol. III, pp.183 & 591; Delavoye, *op. cit.*, pp.356 & 359.

12. Sarrazin, *op. cit.*, p.97.

13. *The Military Adventures of Charles O'Neil*, p.121. The Spaniards regarded the French prisoners as 'out of the pale of humanity' and were not prepared to risk their lives in the rough seas to help them; R. Southey, *History of the Peninsular War*, p.399.

14. Baron Lejeune, *Memoirs*, pp.60–4, spoke to one of the escapees who relates the story in detail. In it he states that the two ships escaped together, but this is not supported by others, particularly Napier, *op. cit.*, vol. III, p.591. The total number who escaped from the two ships amounted to around 1,500 but it is not known how many of these were killed in the escape.

15. J. Sarrazin, *op. cit.*, pp.99 & 114.

16. Delavoye, *op. cit.*, p.360.

17. Delavoye, *op. cit.*, pp.342–3.

18. Delavoye, *op. cit.*, pp.367–8.

19. Bunbury, *Reminiscences of a Veteran*, vol.1, p.69.

20. Delavoye, *op. cit.*, pp.357 & 362.

21. *Wellington's Despatches*, vol.6, p.106.

22. Delavoye, *op. cit.*, p.362.

23. Delavoye, *op. cit.*, p.393.

24. Delavoye, *op. cit.*, p.394.

25. Delavoye, *op. cit.*, p.398–9.

26. John Grehan, *Lines of Torres Vedras*, pp. 7–8.

27. Oman, *op. cit.*, vol. III, p.272.

28. *Wellington's Supplementary Despatches*, vol. 6, pp.567–70.

29. *Wellington's Despatches*, vol.6, p.359; Delavoye, *op. cit.*, p.404.

30. *Wellington's Despatches*, vol. 6, p.158.

31. *Wellington's Despatches*, vol. 6, p.158 & pp.258–9.

32. Wellington continued to be worried about this. On 14 July he again wrote to Lord Liverpool, following a rebuke from the minister: 'The object of my letter of the 30th of May was not to induce his Majesty's Government to refrain from reinforcing Cadiz to any extent that might be deemed advisable to provide for the permanent defence of that important post, but to dispose of the troops after they should have evacuated Portugal, in such a manner as that it would be easy to reinforce Cadiz, if that measure was necessary; and that if the reinforcements were sent they should be well received by the inhabitants of Cadiz.', *Wellington's Despatches*, vol.6, pp.257–8. See also vol.6, pp.552–5.

33. Wellington first got wind of a proposed sortie from Cadiz towards the end of June: 'I

find there are some thought of making a sortie from Cadiz, which I think must fail. Whether it fails or succeeds, it will affect our situation in this country, I fear, injuriously', *Wellington's Despatches*, vol.6, p.200.

34. *Wellington's Despatches*, vol.6, p.203.
35. Delavoye, *op. cit.*, p.395–6.
36. Delavoye, *op. cit.*, p.379.
37. *Wellington's Despatches*, vol.6, pp.203–4.
38. Delavoye, *op. cit.*, p.387.
39. *Wellington's Despatches*, 6, 224.
40. Delavoye, *op. cit.*, p.403.
41. Delavoye, *op. cit.*, p.395–6.
42. Delavoye, *op. cit.*, p. 403.
43. Aspinall-Oglander, *Freshly Remembered*, p.213.
44. *Wellington's Despatches*, vol. 6, pp. 324–5; Delavoye, *op. cit.*, pp.405–6. The regiments withdrawn from Cadiz were the 79th and 88th Foot, 100 men of the 95th Rifles in addition to the 13th Light Dragoons, *Wellington's Despatches*, vol.6, p.359. The 94th Foot was shipped to Lisbon later, *Wellington's Despatches*, vol.6, p.368.
45. Aspinall-Oglander, *op. cit.*, p.209.
46. Delavoye, *op. cit.*, p.411.
47. Delavoye, *op. cit.*, p.406; C. Esdaille, *The Peninsular War*, p.282.
48. Delavoye, *op. cit.*, p.418.
49. *Wellington's Despatches*, vol.6, p.607.
50. Delavoye, *op. cit.*, pp.353–5; Aspinall-Oglander, *op. cit.*, pp.210–11; *Wellington's Despatches*, vol.6, pp.83–5.
51. Aspinall-Oglander, *op. cit.*, p.211.
52. *Wellington's Despatches*, vol.5, pp.116–7 & 454

Chapter 4. A CONSIDERABLE RISK

1. Oman, *op. cit.*, vol. 3, p.511.
2. Oman, *op cit.*, p.512.
3. Delavoye, *op. cit.*, pp.420–1.
4. Aspinall-Oglander, *op. cit.*, p. 217.
5. Henegan, *op. cit.*, pp.160–1.
6. Henegan, *op. cit.*, pp.161–2.
7. Esdaile, *The Peninsular War*, p.283.
8. Henegan, *op. cit.*, pp.220–1.
9. Aspinall-Oglander, *op. cit.*, p.216.
10. Sarrazin, *op. cit.*, p.114.
11. Knox, *op. cit.*, p.23.
12. G. Glover, *Eyewitness to the Peninsular War*, pp.25–6.
13. Delavoye, *op. cit.*, p.419; Surtees, *op. cit.*, pp.97–8.
14. Delavoye, *op. cit.*, p.421. Wellington wished to have Graham join him but did not have the authority to remove him from his position at Cadiz, *Wellington's Despatches*, vol.6, p.558.
15. Delavoye, *op. cit.*, p.431.
16. *Wellington's Supplementary Despatches* vol.7, pp.10–11.
17. Delavoye, *op. cit.*, pp. 439 & 441.

18. Delavoye, *op. cit.*, pp. 432–3.
19. Delavoye, *op. cit.*, p.424.
20. Delavoye, *op. cit.*, p.438.
21. Delavoye, *op. cit.*, p.425.
22. Delavoye, *op. cit.*, p.434.
23. *Wellington's Despatches*, vol.7, p.26.
24. Delavoye, *op. cit.*, p.442.
25. See TNA, WO17/2486.
26. Delavoye, *op. cit.*, p.445.
27. Those sources were in fact the reports of a 'confidential agent' who was employed by the Spanish Government. He was on the French side of Cadiz Bay but was able to cross between the two opposing lines. He stated, on 29 December, that 5,000 men had been detached from Victor's force and he reported that it was generally assumed that these troops were to be part of a force which was destined under Soult for Badajoz, see *Wellington's Supplementary Despatches*, vol.7, p.10.
28. *Wellington's Despatches*, vol.7, pp.89 & 92–3.
29. Delavoye, *op. cit.*, pp.447–8; *Wellington's Despatches*, pp.98 & 112. Fortescue, *op. cit.*, vol.VIII, p.40 says that Graham first learned that Victor's force in front of Cadiz was being reduced on 22 December. The Chasseurs Britanniques sailed on 19 January.
30. 'Memorandum of Operations in 1811' in *Wellington's Despatches*, vol.8, pp.494–5.
31. Oman, *op. cit.*, vol.III, p.458 & vol. IV, pp.26–7.
32. Oman, *op. cit.*, vol. IV, p.24.
33. Oman, *op. cit.*, vol. IV, pp.30 & 93.
34. Aspinall-Oglander, *op. cit.*, p.217.
35. Oman, *op. cit.*, vol.IV, pp.94–5.
36. N. Ludlow Beamish, *History of the King's German Legion*, vol.I, p.306.
37. Delavoye, *op. cit.*, p.448.
38. J. Sturgis, *A Boy in the Peninsular War*, p.154.
39. Sturgis, *op. cit.*, pp.154–5.
40. Sturgis, *op. cit.*, p.155 says that Browne commanded 470 men plus the artillery.
41. Sturgis, *op. cit.*, pp.155–6.
42. Sturgis, *op. cit.*, pp.158–61.
43. Sturgis, *op. cit.*, pp.164–66.
44. Delavoye, *op. cit.*, pp.450–1.
45. Delavoye, *op. cit.*, p.451;Fortescue, *op. cit.*, vol. VIII, p.40, called the handling of the boats 'injudicious'.
46. G. Glover, *Eyewitness to the Peninsular War*, p.45.
47. Delavoye, *op. cit.*, pp.450–1.
48. Delavoye, *op. cit.*, p.452.
49. *Wellington's Despatches*, vol. 7, pp.65–6.

Chapter 5. MANOUEVRES IN THE DARK
1. Delavoye, *op. cit.*, p.455.
2. Delavoye, *op. cit.*, pp.457–9.
3. Oman, *op. cit.*, vol. IV, pp.99–100.
4. Henry Wellesley to Marquis Wellesley, 10 March 1811, in *Wellington's Supplementary Despatches*, vol.7, p.77.

5. Aspinall-Oglander, *op. cit.*, pp.218 & 220. He told Lady Asgill that 'We shall give an honest assistance; and I trust that whatever may be the result, I shall be considered as acting on the principle I have ever professed – an anxious wish to be useful without any selfish view or personal ambition actuating me.'
6. O'Neil, *op. cit.*, p.127.
7. Sebastiani, uncertain as to how the situation would develop in Soult's absence, concentrated a column at Estipona from where he could easily march either to the coast or to the Ronda mountains, Napier, *op. cit.*, vol.III, p.442.
8. R. Southey, *History of the Peninsular War,* vol. III (1832 edition), p.159.
9. Oman, *op. cit.*, vol. IV, pp.95–6.
10. Ludlow Beamish, *op. cit.*, p.306.
11. *Wellington's Supplementary Despatches*, vol.7, p.74.
12. Fortescue, *op. cit.*, vol. VIII, p.41.
13. Major Duncan's Despatch, TNA WO 55/1195.
14. G. Glover, *Eyewitness to the Peninsular War*, p.45; Beamish, *op cit.*, p.306.
15. Aspinall-Oglander, *op. cit.*, pp.220–1.
16. Delavoye, *op. cit.*, pp.460–61.
17. G. Glover, *op cit.*, p.45.
18. Delavoye, *op. cit.*, pp.462–3.
19. Oman, *op. cit.*, vol. IV, p.98; Bunbury, *op. cit.*, vol. I, pp.71–2. Fortescue, *op. cit.*, vol.VIII, p.41, gives a total of 5,100 for Graham's force. See Appendices for further details.
20. M. E. S. Laws, 'The Royal Artillery at Barrosa 1811', *Journal of the Royal Artillery*, vol. LXXVIII, pp.198–9.
21. Delavoye, *op. cit.*, p.463.
22. Sturgis, *op. cit.*, pp.170–2.
23. O'Neil, *op. cit.*, p.125; Sturgis, *op. cit.*, p.175.
24. Oman, *op. cit.*, vol. IV, p.99.
25. R. Southey, *History of the Peninsular War,* vol. III (1832 edition), p.160.
26. O'Neil, *op. cit.*, p.128.
27. Sturgis, *op. cit.*, p.177; G. Glover, *op cit.*, pp.45–6.
28. Oman, *op cit.*, vol. IV, pp.99–100; W. Verner, *History & Campaigns of the Rifle Brigade*, Vol.2, p.190.
29. Southey, *History of the Peninsular War*, vol.III (1832 edition), p.159.
30. Verner, *op cit.*, p.191; Oman, *op. cit.*, vol. IV, p.99, says that the force halted at the 'village of Bolonia'. This is incorrect. The village of Bolonia lies on the shore of the Atlantic over four miles away.
31. Southey, *History of the Peninsular War* vol. III (1832 edition), pp.159–60.
32. Delavoye, *op. cit.*, p.463.
33. G. Glover, *op. cit.*, p.6.
34. C. Oman, *op. cit.*, vol. IV, p.101.
35. Sturgis, *op. cit.*, p. 178.
36. Sturgis, *op. cit.*, pp.178–9.
37. O'Neil, *op. cit.*, p.125; Oman, *op. cit.*, p.103.
38. Fortescue, *op. cit.*, vol.VIII, pp.42–3; Aspinall-Oglander, *op. cit.*, p.221.
39. Aspinall-Oglander, *op. cit.*, p.221.
40. R. Southey, *History of the Peninsular War* vol. III (1832 edition), pp.162–3.

41. Beamish, *op. cit.*, vol.I, p.308.
42. Bunbury, *op. cit.*, vol. I, p.73.
43. Stanhope says that it was Graham who managed to persuade Le Peña not to march until the following morning, G. Glover, *op cit.*, pp.45–6.
44. Verner, *op. cit.*, p.193.
45. The exact numbers of the Spanish are hard to calculate. This is especially so with Southey, *History of the Peninsular War* vol. III (1832 edition), p.163.,who, whilst giving a total of 12,000, breaks it down as 2,100 in the van, 6,000 in the centre with 5,100 in the rear under Graham and 800 cavalry under Graham. This gives a total of 14,000!
46. G. Glover, *op cit.*, pp.46–7.
47. G. Glover, *ibid*, pp46–7.
48. G. Glover, *op cit.*, p.47.
49. Surtees, *op. cit.*, p.101.
50. G. Glover, *op cit.*, p.47, stated that at one point one of the artillery guns became stuck in a deep part of the river and that it was moved by Graham and his staff. This, though, may be the same incident as what is otherwise referred to as a cart.
51. Fortescue, *op. cit.*, vol. VIII, p.45.
52. Sturgis, *op. cit.*, 179–80.
53. Sturgis, *op. cit.*, p.180.
54. G. Glover, *op cit.*, p.47.
55. Fortescue, *op. cit.*, Vol. VIII, p.45.
56. Delavoye, *op. cit.*, p.464.
57. Beamish, *op. cit.*, vol. I, p.309.
58. G. Glover, *op cit.*, p.47.
59. Oman, *op cit.*, vol. IV, p.103; R. Southey, *History of the Peninsular War*, vol.III (1832 edition), pp.158 and 163; G. Glover, *op cit.*, p.47.
60. Aspinall-Oglander, *op. cit.*, p.222.
61. Lequetal to Victor, 7 March 1811, TNA WO 1/402.
62. Oman, *op. cit.*, vol. IV, p.103; Sturgis, *op. cit.*, p.181.
63. Sturgis, *ibid*.
64. Verner, *op. cit.*, p.196.
65. Oman, *op cit.*, vol. IV, p.105.
66. G. Glover, *op cit.*, p.47; Verner, *op. cit.*, p.197.
67. Delavoye, *op. cit.*, p.465.
68. G. Glover, *op cit.*, p.47.
69. Fortescue, *op. cit.*, vol. VIII, p.47.
70. Verner, *op. cit.*, pp.197–8.
71. P. Facey, *Diary of a Veteran*, p.19; Verner, *ibid*.
72. Napier, *op. cit.*, vol.III, p.443.
73. Oman, *op. cit.*, vol. III, p.107; James Stanhope, in G. Glover, *op cit.*, pp.47–8, puts a slightly different slant on this affair. He claims that an intercepted letter from Ledentil, *Chef des Genie*, to General Lery at Seville, revealed that Villatte was ordered merely to 'resist weakly' and then retire so that the enemy would be drawn towards the main French force.

Chapter 6. BARROSA'S BLOOD-DRENCHED HILL
1. Oman, *op. cit.*, vol. IV, pp.105–6; Verner, *op. cit.*, p.196.

2. Aspinall–Oglander, *op. cit.*, p.222; G. Glover, *op. cit.*, p.48.
3. Fortescue, *op. cit.*, vol. VIII, p.48.
4. Henegan, *op. cit.*, p.208.
5. Napier, *op. cit.*, vol. III, p.444.
6. O'Neil, *op. cit.*, p.126.
7. Verner, *op. cit.*, p.200.
8. Graham's report on the Battle of Barossa, *Wellington's Despatches*, vol.7, pp.393–8.
9. 'Extracts from the Report of Brigadier-General Dilkes', *Wellington's Supplementary Despatches*, vol.7, p.126.
10. Beamish, *op. cit.*, pp.310–11.
11. D. Chandler, *The Campaigns of Napoleon*, p.1125.
12. Oman, *op. cit.*, vol. IV, pp.108–9; Napier, *op. cit.*, vol. III, p.445.
13. Fortescue, vol. VIII, *op. cit.*, p.50; Henegan, *op. cit.*, p.209.
14. Fortescue, *op. cit.*, vol. VIII, p.50.
15. Sturgis, p.184. Fortescue, *op. cit.*, vol. VIII, p.50, wrote that La Peña was on Barossa when the French attacked and 'lost his head completely; for without losing a moment he gave the word for immediate retreat upon Cadiz.'
16. Sturgis, *op. cit.*, p.185.
17. Verner, *op. cit.*, p.201.
18. Verner, *ibid.*
19. G. Glover, *op. cit.*, p.48. As O'Neil also observed, even if La Peña did not receive the message he must have heard the sound of the French artillery, O'Neil, *op. cit.*, p.132.
20. Delavoye, *op. cit.*, p.468; *Wellington's Despatches*, vol.7, pp.393–8.
21. G. L. Gower, *Private Correspondence*, p.382.
22. Sturgis, *op. cit.*, p.185.
23. Fortescue, *op. cit.*, vol. VIII, p.51.
24. Oman, *op. cit.*, vol. IV, p.110.
25. Beamish, *op. cit.*, pp.311–2; O'Neil, *op. cit.*, p.126.
26. 'Report of Major-General Whittingham, commanding the cavalry', *Wellington's Supplementary Despatches*, vol. 7, pp.130–1.
27. Fortescue, *op. cit.*, vol.VIII, pp.51–2.
28. Sturgis, *op. cit.*, pp.186–7. Fortescue, *op. cit.*, vol.VIII, p.53 disputes the claim made by Blakeney that Graham ordered Browne's battalion to close ranks, citing the fact that Barnard's rifles were allowed to operate in open order and achieved more success that Browne did with his closely formed battalion.
29. Sturgis, *op. cit.*, pp.187–8.
30. O'Neil states that almost half of Brown's detachment fell at the first volley, O'Neil, *op. cit.*, p.133.
31. Sturgis, *op. cit.*, pp.188–9.
32. G. Glover, *op. cit.*, p.48.
33. 'Extract from the Report of Brigadier-General Dilkes', *Wellington's Supplementary Despatches*, vol. 7, pp.126–7.
34. 'Extract from the Report of Lieutenant-Colonel Norcott, commanding 2nd Battalion 95th Regiment', *Wellington's Supplementary Despatches*, vol. 7, pp.128–9.
35. 'Extract from the Report of Brigadier-General Dilkes', *Wellington's Supplementary Despatches*, vol. 7, pp.126–7. Captain Hamilton, Assistant-Quartermaster-General explained

that the Guards advanced, 'gradually bringing their right shoulders forward', *Wellington's Supplementary Despatches*, vol. 7, p.130.

36. Sturgis, *op. cit.*, p.194.
37. Oman, vol. IV, *op. cit.*, pp.114–5.
38. G. Glover, *op. cit.*, p.48; Fortescue, *op. cit.*, vol. VIII, pp.54–5.
39. Fortescue, *op. cit.*, vol. VIII, p.55.
40. Sturgis, *op. cit.*, p.195.
41. G. Glover, *op. cit.*, p.48.
42. O'Neil, *op. cit.*, p.133.
43. *Ibid.*
44. This comes from Sturgis, *op. cit.*, p.195. According to Stanhope, Graham's exact words were, 'Men, cease firing and charge', G. Glover, *op. cit.*, p.49, whereas the Royal Irish Museum website claims that that he shouted, 'Now my lads, there they are. Spare your powder, but give them steel enough', www.royalirishrangers.co.uk.
45. Sturgis, *op. cit.*, p.195.
46. *Ibid*, p.192.
47. Extract from the Royal Engineers Museum website, www.re–museum.co.uk
48. Sturgis, *op. cit.*, p.196.
49. Oman, vol. VIII, *op. cit.*, p.116.
50. Fortescue, *op. cit.*, vol. VIII, p.54; Verner, *op. cit.*, p.202. Dilkes himself gives this as two companies which he had been instructed to send to help Wheatley; extract from the Report of Brigadier-General Dilkes', *Wellington's Supplementary Despatches*, vo. 7, pp.126–7. Oman, *op. cit.*, vol. IV, p. 113, has made sense of this by explaining that Dilkes was asked to send a few companies to cover the guns, but Graham had already set aside two companies of the 47th for the same purpose, which meant that the Coldstreamers were not required for that purpose and so they fell into line in a gap in the front of Wheatley's brigade.
51. Surtees, *op. cit.*, p.106.
52. *Ibid.*
53. Verner, *op. cit.*, pp.204–5.
54. Bunbury, *op. cit.*, vol. I, p.75.
55. Fortescue, vol. VIII, *op. cit.*, p.51.
56. Fortescue, *op. cit.*, vol. VIII, p.57.
57. Bunbury, *op. cit.*, vol. I, p.76.
58. Surtees, *op. cit.*, p.108; Bunbury, *op. cit.*, vol. I, pp.77 and 80–1. According to Bunbury, Bushe's death was 'much lamented' by the ladies at Cadiz!
59. Bunbury, *op. cit.*, vol. I, p.77; Surtees, *op. cit.*, p.109.
60. In recommending his Sergeant of Drivers for promotion to Staff Sergeant, Second Captain Gardiner wrote that 'he did not know what sort of a pen man he is, but his merit is in overcoming the difficulties that occur in the course of active service, M. Laws, 'The Royal Artillery at Barrosa, 1811', p.204.
61. G. Glover, *op. cit.*, p.48.
62. Oman, *op. cit.*, vol. IV, p.119; Fortescue, *op. cit.*, vol. VIII, p.56.
63. Delavoye, *op. cit.*, p.471.
64. Surtees, *op. cit.*, p.107.
65. *Ibid*, p.114.

66. P. Facey, *Diary of a Veteran*, p.20. The 1st and 2nd Battalions of the 8em actually numbered 1,468, see Appendix II.

67. Verner, *op. cit.*, p.207

68. Knox, *op. cit.*, p.34; R. Rait, *Life of Lord Gough*, vol. I, pp.52–3.

69. Baron Lejeune, *Memoirs*, vol. 2, p.67.

70. Oman, *op. cit.*, vol. IV, p.121.

71. 'The Battle of Barossa', *Tales of the Wars*, No.51, Saturday, December 17, 1836.

72. According to Surtees, *Twenty-Five Years in the Rifle Brigade*, p.107, there was some dispute between the 87th and the Guards about which battalion had delivered the charge that resulted in the capture of the Eagle. It is often stated that as Masterson seized the eagle he cried out, 'Bejabers boys, I have the cookoo', and this is repeated by Richard Holmes in *Redcoat*, p.215. However, this is disputed by Richard Docherty of the Royal Irish Fusiliers Regimental Museum, who states that Masterson's native language was Gaelic and whilst he would have had to learn the English drill commands it is unlikely that he would have spoken in English to his comrades. It is to be noted that 'Faugh A Ballagh' is usually translated as 'clear the way', but when shouted is more like 'get out of the way'. Knox, *Diary of a Veteran*, p.31, states that Keogh was killed by a musket ball through the heart.

73. Rait, *op. cit.*, p.53.

74. C. Cadell, *Narrative of the Campaigns of the Twenty-Eight Regiment*, p.96

75. Fortescue, *op. cit.*, vol. VIII, p.60.

76. *Wellington's Supplementary Despatches*, vol.7, p.132.

77. Verner, *op. cit.*, p.208.

78. *Wellington's Supplementary Despatches*, vol.7, p.127.

79. Beamish, *op. cit.*, vol. I, p.313.

80. Cadell, *op. cit.*, pp.96–7.

81. Sturgis, *op. cit.*, p.198

82. Fortescue, *op. cit.*, vol.VIII, p.61.

83. *Wellington's Despatches*, vol.7, pp.393–8.

Chapter 7. 'A GREAT AND GLORIOUS TRIUMPH'

1. Henegan, *op. cit.*, p.215–6.

2. Delavoye, *op. cit.*, pp. 469–70; C. H. Gifford, *History of the Wars Occasioned by the French Revolution*, p.734.

3. 'Extract from the Report of Lieutenant-Colonel the Honourable F. C. Ponsonby, Assistant-Adjutant-General', in *Wellington's Supplementary Despatches*, vol.7, pp.127–8.

4. Sarrazin, *op. cit.*, p.125.

5. M. Spurrier (ed.), 'Letters of a Peninsular War commanding officer; the letters of Lieutenant Colonel, later General, Sir Andrew Barnard, G.C.B', *Journal of the Society for Historical Research*, vol. XLVII, No.191, pp.135–6, quoted in Esdaile, *Peninsular War*, p.337.

6. Vernier, *op. cit.*, pp.209–10.

7. G. Glover, *op. cit.*, p.49.

8. See www.royalirishregiment.co.uk.

9. Anthony Brett-James, *General Graham, Lord Lynedoch*, pp.219–9.

10. Sturgis, *op. cit.*, p.198.

11. Beamish, *op. cit.*, vol. I, pp.313–4.

12. G. Glover, *op. cit.*, p.49.

13. O'Neil, *op. cit.*, p.135.
14. Southey, *History of the Peninsular War*, vol.III (1832 edition), pp.170–1.
15. G. Glover, *op. cit.*, p.50.
16. 'Extract from the Report of Captain the Honourable J. H. Stanhope, A.D.C. to Lieutenant-General Graham', *Wellington's Supplementary Despatches*, vol.7, p.80.
17. Knox, *op. cit.*, pp.34–5; Gough was granted the brevet rank of Lieutenant Colonel. This, according to Rait, *Life of Lord Gough*, p.58, was the first instance in the history of the British Army where a brevet rank was conferred upon an officer for the conduct of a regiment in action.
18. Surtees, *op. cit.*, pp. 108, 111 & 113.
19. M. Laws, 'The Royal Artillery at Barrosa 1811', *Journal of the Royal Artillery*, vol. LXXVIII, p.204; Oman, *op. cit.*, vol. IV, p.125; Cadell, *op. cit.*, p.96; Verner, *op. cit.*, p.211.
20. G. Glover, *op. cit.*, p.49.
21. Napier, *op. cit.*, vol. III, pp.448–9; Verner, *op. cit.*, p.211; Wellington's Despatches to Beresford 25 March 1811, *Wellington's Despatches*, vol.7, p.400; J. Burgoyne, Life and Correspondence of Sir John Burgoyne, vol.I, p.126.
22. Verner, *op. cit.*, p.213.
23. *Ibid.*
24. Delavoye, *op. cit.*, pp.468–9.
25. Napier, *op. cit.*, vol. III, p.451.
26. *Ibid.*
27. Delavoye, *op. cit.*, p.473.
28. Cadell, *op. cit.*, p.105.
29. Delavoye, *op. cit.*, p.486.
30. Delavoye, *op cit.*, p.473; *Wellington's Despatches*, vol.7, p.397.
31. Oman, *op. cit.*, vol. IV, p.126.
32. Fortescue, *op. cit.*, vol. VIII, p.66. This was soon known about in Cadiz from captured French officers, *Wellington's Supplementary Despatches*, vol.7, p.78.
33. Napier, *op. cit.*, vol. III, pp.449–50.
34. R. Southey, *History of the Peninsular War*, vol.III (1832 edition), p.171; Fortescue, *op. cit.*, vol. VIII, p.66.
35. Delavoye, *op. cit.*, pp. 480–1.
36. *Wellington's Supplementary Despatches*, vol.7, p.79.
37. Aspinall-Oglander, *op. cit.*, p.232.
38. Delavoye, *op. cit.*, p. 474.
39. Sturgis, *op. cit.*, pp.199–200.
40. G. Glover, *op. cit.*, p.51.
41. *Wellington's Supplementary Despatches*, vol.7, pp.80 & 208.
42. Delavoye *op. cit.*, pp.474–6; *Wellington's Supplementary Despatches*, vol.7, p.82.
43. Aspinall-Oglander, *op. cit.*, p.227–8.
44. These were Dilkes, Ponsonby, Norcott, Stanhope, Onsloq, Anson, Hamilton, Acheson and Whittingham, see *Wellington's Supplementary Despatches*, vol.7, pp.126–133.
45. *Wellington's Despatches*, vol.7, pp.395–6.
46. Delavoye, *op. cit.*, p.466.
47. Aspinall-Oglander, *op. cit.*, pp.229–30.
48. Aspinall-Oglander, *op. cit.*, p.230.

49. *Ibid.*
50. Oman, *op. cit.*, vol.IV, p.121. It would appear that that the staff of the eagle did not have a flag attached.
51. Aspinall–Oglander, *op. cit.*, pp. 236–7.
52. Aspinall–Oglander, *op. cit.*, pp.235–6.
53. R. Southey, *History of the Peninsular War*, vol.III (1832 edition), pp.175–6; Sarrazin, *op. cit.*, pp.125–6.
54. Oman, *op. cit.*, vol. IV, p.124; Sarrazin, *Ibid.*
55. Lequetal to Victor, 7 March 1811, TNA WO 1/402.
56. *Wellington's Supplementary Despatches*, vol.7, pp.81–2.
57. *Wellington's Supplementary Despatches*, vol.7, p.81.
58. *Wellington's Supplementary Despatches*, vol.7, p.82.
59. Delavoye, *op. cit.*, p.491.
60. Delavoye, *op. cit.*, p.498.
61. Delavoye, *op. cit.*, pp.507–8.
62. Delavoye, *op. cit.*, p.500.
63. Delavoye, *op. cit.*, pp.528–9.
64. *Wellington's Despatches*, vol.6, p.85.
65. A. Fée, *Souvenirs de la Guerre d'Espangne*, quoted in C. Esdaile, *Peninsular Eyewitnesses*, p.133.
66. G. Glover, *op. cit.*, p.56.

Chapter 8. 'THAT TERRIBLE DAY'
1. Oman, *op. cit.*, vol. IV, p.256.
2. These words were included in the surrender document; see Oman, *op cit.*, vol. IV, pp.254–5.
3. Robert Long, *Peninsular Cavalry General*, pp.70–81.
4. Frederick Myatt, *British Sieges of the Peninsular War*, p.28.
5. Napier, *op. cit.*, vol. III, pp.533–4.
6. Memorandum from Berthier, 30 March 1811, quoted in Oman, *op. cit.*, vol.VI, pp.364–5.
7. A. Bryant, *Years of Victory*, p.432.
8. Myatt, *op. cit.*, p.33.
9. Oman, *op. cit.*, vol. IV, pp.375–7.
10. Esdaile, *The Peninsular War*, pp.344–5.
11. Bryant, *op. cit.*, pp.434–5.
12. C. Leslie, *Military Journal of Colonel Leslie of Balquhain*, p.222.
13. Though it was Lowry Cole who made the unauthorised decision to advance, the move was actually suggested by two of his staff officers; see M. Glover and J. Riley, *That Astonishing Infantry*, pp.57–8.
14. Napier, *op. cit.*, vol. III, pp.546–7.
15. Quoted in Bryant, *op. cit.*, p.440.
16. Oman, *op. cit.*, vol. IV, pp.392–5.
17. Bryant, *op. cit.*, pp.440–1.
18. Verner, *op. cit.*, pp.305–7.
19. *Wellington's Supplementary Desptaches*, vol.7, pp.162 & 188.
20. Delavoye, *op. cit.*, p.533.
21. *Wellington's Supplementary Desptaches*, vol.7, pp.139–40.

22. Oman, *op. cit.*, vol. IV, p.441.

23. F. Myatt, *op. cit.*, p.36.

24. *Wellington's Despatches*, vol.7, pp.620–21.

25. R. Parkinson, *The Peninsular War*, p.142.

26. *Wellington's Despatches*, vol.8, pp.41, 56 & 123.

27. *Wellington's Despatches*, vol.8, p.127.

28. Oman, *op. cit.*, vol. IV, pp.475–6.

29. Graham to Liverpool, 27 May 1811, TNA WO 1/252, ff.331–2.

30. Oman, *op. cit.*, vol. IV, pp. 478–9.

31. Henegan, *op. cit.*, 228–9.

32. Alezander Dallas, *Felix Alvarez*, pp.44–6.

33. 'De las bombas que tiran los Gavachos, se hacen las Gaditanas tirabuzones', Oman, *op. cit.*, vol. V, p.108. See also Esdaile, *Peninsular War*, p. 283.

Chapter 9. A CONFUSION OF COMMANDS

1. Bunbury, *op. cit.*, vol. I, p.96.

2. Oman, *op. cit.*, vol. IV, pp.593–4

3. John T. Jones, *Journals of Sieges Carried Out by the Army under the Duke of Wellington in Spain*, p.469.

4. According to Fortescue, *History of the British Army*, vol. VIII, p.326, Mr Stuart sent a counter-mission, armed with richer gifts, to the same ruler, and quickly persuaded him to continue supplying the Allies as before.

5. The force sent from Cadiz, as given in TNA, WO1/252, p.487, was as follows:
   Eight companies, 2nd Battalion 47th Foot, 534 men
   Eight companies, 2nd Battalion 87th Foot, 480
   One company 2nd Battalion 95th Rifles, 70
   Detachment 2nd KGL Hussars, 52 men with 60 horses
   Hughes' Company Royal Artillery, 40 men
   Detachment Royal Artillery Drivers, 40 men with 70 horses
   Total: 1216, with 130 horses.

6. Oman, *op. cit.*, vol. V, p.112; Verner, *op. cit.*, p.313; *Wellington's Despatches*, vol.8, p.356.

7. Bunbury, *op. cit.*, vol. I, pp.101–4.

8. John T. Jones, *An Account of the War in Spain, Portugal and the South of France*, pp.43–4.

9. Jones, *Journals of Sieges*, pp.468–9.

10. Verner, *op. cit.*, pp.313–4.

11. See Appendix.

12. Oman, *op. cit.*, vol. V, pp.114–5.

13. Wellington's words on this were: 'From the accounts which I have received of that place it appears to me quite impossible to defend it, when the enemy shall be equipped to attack it. The utmost that can be done is to hold the island contiguous to Tarifa, for which object Colonel Skerrett's detachment does not appear to be necessary. I do not believe that the enemy will be able to obtain possession of the island, without which the town will be entirely useless to them.' Wellington did not see why British troops should be expected to hold the island, which could easily be defended by the Spaniards. *Wellington's Despatches*, vol.8, p.356.

14. *Wellington's Despatches*, vol.8, p.403.

15. Verner, *op. cit.*, pp.315–6.

16. Verner, *op. cit.*, pp.316–7.
17. Fortescue, *op. cit.*, vol. VIII, pp.330–1.
18. Verner, *op. cit.*, p.317.
19. *Wellington's Despatches*, vol.8, p.561.
20. Verner, *op. cit.*, p.318.
21. Fortescue, *op. cit.*, vol. VIII, p.331.
22. Napier, *op. cit.*, vol. IV, pp.564–5.
23. Bunbury, *op. cit.*, vol. I, pp.121–2.
24. Rait, *Life of Lord Gough*, pp.82–3.
25. Jones, *Journals of Sieges*, p.476.
26. Tarifa Anecdotes, pp.64–6.
27. Bunbury, *op. cit.*, vol. I, p.123; Oman, *op. cit.*, vol. V, p.125.
28. Jones, *Journals of Sieges*, p.476.
29. Bunbury, *op. cit.*, vol. I, p.128.
30. Rait, *op. cit.*, p.84.
31. Bunbury, *op. cit.*, vol. I, p.129.
32. Verner, *op. cit.*, p.321.
33. Oman, *op. cit.*, vol. V, p.127.
34. Fortescue, *op. cit.*, vol. VIII, pp.335–6.
35. *Ibid*.
36. Bunbury, *op. cit.*, vol. I, p.131.
37. This dispute was glossed over at the time to such an extent that Lieutenant Colonel John Jones, normally a most careful historian and one who served in the Peninsula under Wellington, wrote in his history that 'Colonel Skerrett made the most skilful arrangements to meet the increased danger, and showed such confidence that the French, fearing a second repulse, retired.' J. Jones, *An Account of the War in Spain*, vol. II, p.45.
38. Napier, *op. cit.*, vol. IV, p.568.
39. Wellington to Cooke 1 February 1812, in Napier, *op. cit.*, IV, p.566.
40. *Wellington's Despatches*, vol.8, p.561–2.
41. Bunbury, *op. cit.*, vol. I, pp.115–7.

Chapter 10. 'A DAY OF UNEQUALLED JOY'

1. Oman, *op. cit.*, vol. IV, pp.600–5.
2. Napier, *op. cit.*, vol. IV, p.568.
3. *Wellington's Supplementary Despatches*, vol.7, pp.187–194. Wellesley continued to worry about affairs in Cadiz, as he wrote again on the subject towards the end of August, 'There is certainly a strong French party at this place and I am very much afraid that the mercantile people here are in the French interest', *Supplementary Despatch, ibid*, p.207.
4. Alcala Galiano, *Memorias* vol.1, pp.316–7, quoted in C. Esdaile, *The Peninsular War* p.401.
5. See Oman, *op. cit.*, vol. V, p.265.
6. *Wellington's Despatches*, vol.7, p.523.
7. *Wellington's Despatches*, vol.7, p.599.
8. A. Thiers, *History of the Consulate and Empire of France Under Napoleon*, vol. 12, pp.138 & 142. Soult to Joseph, *Correspondence*, ix, pp.45–7.
9. Soult to Joseph, Seville, 12 August, in Joseph's *Correspondence*, ix, pp.67–8, cited in Oman, *op. cit.*, vol. V, p.538.

10. Oman, *op. cit.*, V, p.493; Fortescue, *op. cit.*, vol. VIII, p.69.
11. Jones, *Account of the War in Spain*, p.94.
12. Alezander Dallas, *Felix Alvarez*, pp.62–3.
13. Jones, *Account of the War in Spain*, p.116.
14. Sazzarin, *op. cit.*, p. 209.
15. Quoted in Esdaille, *Peninsular War*, *op. cit.*, p.401.
16. Alezander Dallas, *op. cit.*, pp.63–5.
17. Meredith Hindley, 'The Spanish Ulcer: Napoleon, Britain, and the Siege of Càdiz', *Humanities* magazine, January/February 2010.
18. As far as the Spaniards were concerned, Skerrett was 'the British commander who had so nobly defended the walls of that place,' Alezander Dallas, *op. cit.*, pp.55–6.
19. Sarrazin, *op. cit.*, p.210.
20. *Wellington's Supplementary Despatches*, vol.7, p.421.

Chapter 11. LONG SHADOWS
1. O'Neil, *op. cit.*, p.138.
2. Marquis of Londonderry, *Story of the Peninsular War*; D. Gates, *The British Light Infantry Arm 1790–1815*; M. Windrow & G. Embleton, *Military Dress of the Peninsular War*; M. Glover, *The Napoleonic Wars: An Illustrated History 1792–1815*, to name but a few.
3. Fortescue, *op. cit.*, vol.VIII, p.63.
4. Lejeune, *Memoirs*, vol. 2, p.68.
5. A. Thiers, *op. cit.*, vol.12, pp.220–1.
6. William Glen, 'The Battle Song'; Lord Byron, 'Childe Harold's Pilgrimage'; Robert Southey, 'At Barossa'.
7. Sarrazin, *op. cit.*, p.228.
8. Thiers, *op. cit.*, vol. *op. cit.*, vol.12, p.138.
9. In August 1810, when the French forces in Spain were considered by Wellington to amount to 250,000 men, some 60,000 of these, or almost a quarter of all the French troops in the Peninsular, were in Andalusia; *Wellington's Despatches*, vol.6, pp.605–6.
10. Sarrazin, *op. cit.*, pp.37 & 265. Sarrazin says that the failure to capture Cadiz was because 'Joseph's indolence prevented Marshal Soult's punctuality.'
11. These places were Badajoz, Ciudad Rodrigo, Astorga and of course Cadiz, *Wellington's Despatches*, vol. 7, *Memorandum of Operations in 1810*, p.296.
12. Napier, *op. cit.*, vol. III, pp.121–2.
13. Fortescue, *op. cit.*, vol.VII, p.363.
14. *Ibid*, p.366.
15. James P. Herson Jr., *op. cit.*, Introduction.
16. Sarrazin, *Ibid*; G. Glover, *op. cit.*, p.28.
17. *Wellington's Supplementary Despatches*, vol.6, p.492.
18. *Wellington's Supplementary Despatches*, vol.7, pp.8–9.
19. *Wellington's Supplementary Despatches*, vol.6, p.493.
20. Esdaile, *The Peninsular War*, pp.290–295.
21. Southey, *History of the Peninsular War*, vol. IV, p.396; M. De Rocca, *Memoirs of the Wars of the French in Spain*, pp.305 & 382.
22. *Wellington's Supplementary Despatches*, vol.6, pp.483–4.
23. 'How would it be when the French army of Andalusia would be brought against us?' He

continued. 'Would the Spanish force, which a part of that army keeps shut up in Cadiz, be equal to the whole of it in the field? Not unless, by a miracle, Heaven would add to their numbers!' *Wellington's Despatches*, vol.6, p.404.

24. Oman, *op. cit.*, vol. IV, p.96.

25. Wellington to Henry Wellesley, 20 March 1811, *Wellington's Despatches*, vol.7, p. 382.

26. *Wellington's Despatches*, vol.7, pp.126–7.

27. *Wellington's Despatches*, vol.6, p. 204.

28. J. J. Pelet, *The French Campaign in Portugal*, pp.43 & 331.

29. Esdaile, *Napoleon's Wars*, p.371.

30. *Wellington's Despatches*, vol 6, p.36. He also told Graham shortly after his arrival in Cadiz that 'I must inform you that it is impossible to maintain an army in the Peninsula, and to perform the engagements into which the King has entered with the Portuguese Government, without the assistance of the money procured at Cadiz', *Wellington's Despatches*, vol 6, pp.37–8. See also vol.6, pp.116–7 & 454.

31. Aspinall–Oglander, *op. cit.*, p.205.

32. Cited by Meredith Hindley in 'The Spanish Ulcer: Napoleon, Britain, and the Siege of Càdiz', *Humanities* magazine, January/February 2010

33. Napier, *op. cit.*, vol. III, pp.119–20.

34. *Wellington's Despatches*, vol 5, pp.511–2.

35. *Wellington's Despatches*, vol.5, p.533.

36. *Wellington's Supplementary Despatches*, vol.6, p.493.

37. *Wellington's Despatches*, vol. 5, pp. 522–3.

38. *Wellington's Despatches*, vol.6, pp.157–8.

39. *Wellington's Despatches*, vol 6, p.288.

40. Oman, *op. cit.*, vol. V, p.545.

41. Fortescue, *op. cit.*, vol. VIII, p.69.

42. Cited by Meredith Hindley in 'The Spanish Ulcer: Napoleon, Britain, and the Siege of Càdiz', *Humanities* magazine, January/February 2010.

43. Jan Read, *op. cit*, pp.227–31.

44. Jan Read, *op. cit.*, p.229.

45. Jones, *An Account of the War in Spain*, pp.375–6.

46. Walton, *The Revolutions of Spain*, vol. I, p.201.

47. *Wellington's Despatches*, vol. 6, pp.559–60.

48. Jan Read, *op. cit.*, p.230.

Bibliography

PRIMARY SOURCES

The National Archive, Kew
WO 1/252, *War Department In-Letters and Papers: Graham and Cook*
WO 1/255, *Commander-in-Chief: Dispatches from Commanders at Lisbon, Gibraltar, Corunna, Cadiz, Isla de Leon 1800–12.*
WO 1/402, *War Department In-Letters and Papers: Intelligence from Cadiz on affairs in Southern Spain, 1811.*
WO 6/44, *Cadiz 1810–1814: Out-Letters*
WO 28/321, *Entry Book of Orders, Spain, 10 March 1811 to 12 January 1812.*
WO 28/339, *Journal of the Proceedings of the British Army serving at Cadiz and the I. de Leon.*
WO 28/340, *Journal of the Cadiz Force.*

The National Army Museum
William Stewart, *Cumloden Papers*, Edinburgh, 1871.

Published books

Bunbury, T., *Reminiscences of a veteran: being personal and military adventures in Portugal, Spain, France, Malta, New South Wales, Norfolk Island, New Zealand, Andaman Islands, and India* (Charles Skeet, London, 1861).
Burgoyne, J., *Life and Correspondence of Field Marshal Sir John Burgoyne*. Edited by George Wrottesley (Bentley, London, 1873).
Dallas, A. R. C. *Felix Alvarez: or Manners in Spain containing Descriptive Accounts of some of the Prominent Events of The Late Peninsular War* (Baldwin, Cradock and Joy, London, 1818).
Delavoye, A. M., *Life of Thomas Graham, Lord Lynedoch*, (Marchant Singer, London, 1880).
De Rocca, M., *Memoirs of the War of the French in Spain*. Translated by Maria Graham (John Murray, London, 1815).
Donaldson, J., *Recollections of the Eventful Life of a Soldier: including. The War in the Peninsula and Scenes and Sketches in Ireland by Joseph Donaldson, Sergeant in the Ninety-Fourth Scots Brigade* (Spellmount, Staplehurst, 2000).
Glover, G. (ed.), *The Diary of a Veteran: The Diary of Sergeant Peter Facey, 28th (North Gloucester) Regiment of Foot 1803–1819* (Ken Trotman, Godmanchester, 2007).
Glover, G. (ed.), *Eyewitness to the Peninsular War and the Battle of Waterloo: The Letters and Journals of Lieutenant Colonel The Honourable James Stanhope, 1803 to 1825, Recording his Service with Sir John Moore, Sir Thomas Graham and the Duke of Wellligton* (Pen & Sword, Barnsley, 2010).
Gower, G. L., *Private Correspondence 1781 to 1821*. Edited by C. Granville (John Murray, London, 1916).
Henegan, R. D., *Seven Years' Campaigning in the Peninsula and the Netherlands from 1808 to 1815* (Henry Colburn, London, 1846).
Jones, J. T., *Journals of Sieges Carried on by the Army Under the Duke of Wellington, in Spain,*

Between the Years 1811 and 1814, Volume II (T. Egerton, London, 1827).

Knox, W., *At Barrosa with the 87th: The Diary of Lieutenant Wright Knox* (Napoleonic Archive, Darlington).

Lejeune, Baron, *Memoirs of Baron Lejeune, Aide-de-Camp to Marshals Berthier, Davout, and Oudinot*. Translated by Mrs. A. Bell. (Longmans, Green, & Co., London, 1897).

McGuffie, T. H. (ed.), *Peninsular Cavalry General (1811-13): The Correspondence of Lieutenant-General Robert Ballard Long* (George Harrap, London, 1951).

North, J. (ed.), *In the Legions of Napoleon: The Memoirs of a Polish Officer in Spain and Russia, 1808–1813* (Stackpole Books, London, 1999).

O'Neil, C., *The Military Adventures of Charles O'Neil* (Spellmount, Staplehurst, 1997).

Pelet, J.J., *The French Campaign in Portugal 1810-1811*. Translated and edited by D.D. Horward (University of Minnesota Press, Minneapolis, 1973).

Sarrazin, J., *History of the War in Spain and Portugal from 1807 to 1814* (Edward Searle, Philadelphia, 1815).

Sturgis, J., *A Boy in the Peninsular War: The Autobiography of Robert Blakeney Subaltern in the 28th Regiment* (John Murray, London, 1899).

Wellesley, F. A. (ed.), *The Diary and Correspondence of Henry Wellesley First Lord Cowley, 1790-1846* (Hutchinson, London, 1930).

Wellington, A., *The Dispatches of Field Marshal the Duke of Wellington, during His Various Campaigns etc.* Edited by J. Gurwood (John Murray, London 1837–39).

_____ *Supplementary Despatches, Correspondence and Memoranda of Field Marshal Arthur, Duke of Wellington*. Edited by his son (John Murray, London 1857–72).

SECONDARY SOURCES

Published books

Aspinall-Oglander, C., *Freshly Remembered – the Story of Thomas Graham, Lord Lyndoch* (Hogarth Press, London, 1956).

Atkinson, C. T., *Regimental History: The Royal Hampshire Regiment, vol.1, 1702–1914* (The University Press, Glasgow).

Beamish, Ludlow N., *History of the King's German Legion* (Buckland and Brown, London, 1832).

Brett-James, A., *General Graham, Lord Lynedoch* (MacMillan, London, 1959).

Browne, J. A., *England's Artillerymen: An Historical Narrative of the Services of the Royal Artillery* (Hall, Smart, and Allen, London, 1865).

Bryant, A., *Years of Victory, 1802–1812* (Collins, London, 1951).

Cadell, C., *Narrative of the Campaigns of the 28th Regt. From 1802 to 1832* (Whittaker & Co., London, 1835).

Chandler, D., *The Campaigns of Napoleon* (Macmillan, New York, 1966).

Clowes, W., *Leigh's New Picture of London* (Samuel Leigh, London, 1819).

Dallas, Alexander R. C., *Felix Alvarez; or Manners in Spain containing Descriptive Accounts of Some of the Prominent Events of the Peninsular War* (Baldwin, Cradock, & Joy, London, 1818).

Daniell, D. S., *Cap of Honour: The Story of the Gloucester Regiment (the 28th/61st Foot) 1694–1950* (George G. Harrap & Co. Ltd., London, 1951).

Esdaile, C., *The Peninsular War: A New History* (Allen Lane, London, 2002).

Esdaile, C., *Napoleon's Wars, An International History, 1803–1815* (Allen Lane, London, 2007).

BIBLIOGRAPHY

Esdaile, C., *Peninsular Eyewitnesses: The Experience of War in Spain and Portugal 1808–1813* (Pen & Sword Books, Barnsley, 2008).

Fletcher, I., *Bloody Albuera: The 1811 Campaign in the Peninsular* (Crowood Press, Ramsbury, 2000.

Fortescue, J., *A History of the British Army*, Vols. VII & VIII (Macmillan, London, 1935).

Gifford, C. H., *History of the Wars Occasioned by the French Revolution* (W. Lewis, London, 1817).

Glover, M. and J. Riley, J., *That Astonishing Infantry: The History of The Royal Welch Fusiliers, 1689–2006* (Pen & Sword Military, Barnsley, 2008).

Grehan, J., *The Lines of Torres Vedras: The Cornerstone of Wellington's Strategy in the Peninsular War 1809–1812.* (Spellmount, Staplehurst, 2000).

Grehan, J., *Britain's German Allies of the Napoleonic Wars* (Partizan Press, Nottingham, 2010).

Heathcote, T. A., *Wellington's Peninsular War Generals & Their Battles, A Biographical and Historical Dictionary* (Pen and Sword, Barnsley, 2010).

Holmes, R., *Redcoat: The British Soldier in the Age of the Horse and Musket* (HarperCollins, London, 2001).

Jones, John T., *An Account of the War in Spain, Portugal and the South of France from 1808 to 1814 inclusive*, vol. II (T. Egerton, London, 1821).

Jones, John T., *Journals of Sieges Carried Out by the Army under the Duke of Wellington in Spain Between the Years 1811 and 1814*, vol. II, (T. Egerton, London, 1827).

Lachouque, H. *Napoleon's War in Spain: The French Peninsular Campaigns, 1807–1814.* Translated by J. Tranie & J. Carmigniani (Arms and Armour Press, London, 1982).

Leslie, C., *Military Journal of Colonel Leslie of Balquhain: whilst serving with the 29th Regt. in the Peninsula, and the 60th Rifles in Canada, 1807–1832* (Aberdeen University Press, Aberdeen, 1887).

Leslie, J. H., *The Services of the Royal Regiment of Artillery in the Peninsular War 1808 to 1810* (R.A. Institute, Woolwich, 1905).

Muir, R., Muir, H., Burnham, R., and McGuigan, R., *Inside Wellington's Peninsular Army 1808–1814* (Pen & Sword, Barnsley, 2006).

Myatt, F., *British Sieges of the Peninsular War* (Spellmount, Speldhurst, 1987).

Napier, W. F. P. *History of the War in the Peninsula and the South of France from the Year 1807 to the Year 1814* (six volumes, London, 1828–45, reprinted by Constable, London 1992–3).

Oman, C., *A History of the Peninsular War* (seven volumes, Oxford 1902–30, reprinted by Greenhill Books, London, 1995–6).

Parkinson, R., *The Peninsular War* (Hart-Davis MacGibbon, London, 1973).

Rait, R. S., *The Life and Campaigns of Hugh Viscount Gough, Field Marshal*, vol.1 (Constable, London, 1903).

Rawson, Andrew, *The Peninsular War, A Battlefield Guide* (Pen & Sword, Barnsley, 2009).

Southey, R., *History of the Peninsular War* (John Murray, London, 1928).

Surtees, W., *Twenty Five Years in the Rifle Brigade* (Blackwood, London, 1833).

Thiers, M. A., *History of the Consulate and the Empire of France under Napoleon* (Willis and Sotheran, London, 1856).

Thornton, C., *Annals of the Peninsular Campaigns* (Carey & Lea, London, 1831).

Walton, W., *The Revolutions of Spain from 1808 to the End of 1836* (Richard Bentley, London, 1837).

Verner, W., *History and Campaigns of the Rifle Brigade, Part II, 1809–1813* (John Bale, Sons & Danielsson, London, 1919).

Magazine and Journal articles
Bendall, S., 'The French Siege of Cadiz in the Peninsular War', *Journal of the Society for Army Historical Research*, No.331, 2004.
Crawley, W., 'French and English Influences in the Cortes of Cadiz, 1810–1814', *Cambridge Historical Journal*, vol.6, No.2 (1939).
Cusick, R., 'The Siege of Tarifa – Dec. 1811 – Jan. 1812', *First Empire*, January 2008.
_____. 'The Battle of Barossa', *First Empire* 102 & 103 September-December 2008.
Meredith H., 'The Spanish Ulcer: Napoleon, Britain, and the Siege of Càdiz', *Humanities* magazine, volume 31, Number 1, January/February 2010.
Laws, M. E. S., 'The Royal Artillery at Barrosa 1811', *The Journal of the Royal Artillery*, Vol. LXXVIII, No.3, 1951.
Spurrier, M. C. (ed.), 'Letters of a Peninsular War Commanding Officer: The letters of Lieutenant-Colonel, later General, Sir Andrew Barnard, G.C.B.', *Journal of the Society for Army Historical Research*, Vol. 47, 1968, pp.131–148.
'The Battle of Barossa', *Tales of the Wars, or, Naval and Military Chronicle*, No.51, December 17, 1836.

MA Thesis
James P. Herson Jr., *'For the Cause' Cadiz and the Peninsular War. Military and Siege Operations From 1808 to 1812*, Department of History, Florida State University, College of Arts and Science, 1992.

Internet sources
R. Herr, 'An Historical Essay on Modern Spain: The French Explosion and the Birth of Political Controversy', *The Library of Iberian Resources Online* libro.uca.edu/herr/ms04.htm. Retrieved 19 July 2012.
L.S. Muzás, [translated by C. Miley], *Trophies Taken by the British from the Napoleonic Army During the War of Spanish Independence (Peninsular War) 1808–1814*, www.napoleonic-series.org. Retrieved 8 June 2012.

Index

INDEX